The Group Theatre: Passion, Politics, and Performance in the Depression Era
by Helen Chinoy and edited by Don B. Wilmeth and Milly S. Barranger
Cultivating National Identity through Performance: American Pleasure Gardens and Entertainment by Naomi J. Stubbs
Entertaining Children: The Participation of Youth in the Entertainment Industry edited by Gillian Arrighi and Victor Emeljanow
America's First Regional Theatre: The Cleveland Play House and Its Search for a Home by Jeffrey Ullom
Class Divisions on the Broadway Stage: The Staging and Taming of the I.W.W. by Michael Schwartz

PALGRAVE STUDIES IN THEATRE AND PERFORMANCE HISTORY is a series devoted to the best of theatre/performance scholarship currently available, accessible, and free of jargon. It strives to include a wide range of topics, from the more traditional to those performance forms that in recent years have helped broaden the understanding of what theatre as a category might include (from variety forms as diverse as the circus and burlesque to street buskers, stage magic, and musical theatre, among many others). Although historical, critical, or analytical studies are of special interest, more theoretical projects, if not the dominant thrust of a study, but utilized as important underpinning or as a historiographical or analytical method of exploration, are also of interest. Textual studies of drama or other types of less-traditional performance texts are also germane to the series if placed in their cultural, historical, social, or political and economic context. There is no geographical focus for this series and works of excellence of a diverse and international nature, including comparative studies, are sought.

The editor of the series is Don B. Wilmeth (Emeritus, Brown University), PhD, University of Illinois, who brings to the series over a dozen years as editor of a book series on American theatre and drama, in addition to his own extensive experience as an editor of books and journals. He is the author of several award-winning books and has received numerous career achievement awards, including one for sustained excellence in editing from the Association for Theatre in Higher Education.

Also in the series:

Undressed for Success by Brenda Foley
Theatre, Performance, and the Historical Avant-garde by Günter Berghaus
Theatre, Politics, and Markets in Fin-de-Siècle Paris by Sally Charnow
Ghosts of Theatre and Cinema in the Brain by Mark Pizzato
Moscow Theatres for Young People: A Cultural History of Ideological Coercion and Artistic Innovation, 1917–2000 by Manon van de Water
Absence and Memory in Colonial American Theatre by Odai Johnson
Vaudeville Wars: How the Keith-Albee and Orpheum Circuits Controlled the Big-Time and Its Performers by Arthur Frank Wertheim
Performance and Femininity in Eighteenth-Century German Women's Writing by Wendy Arons
Operatic China: Staging Chinese Identity across the Pacific by Daphne P. Lei
Transatlantic Stage Stars in Vaudeville and Variety: Celebrity Turns by Leigh Woods
Interrogating America through Theatre and Performance edited by William W. Demastes and Iris Smith Fischer
Plays in American Periodicals, 1890–1918 by Susan Harris Smith
Representation and Identity from Versailles to the Present: The Performing Subject by Alan Sikes
Directors and the New Musical Drama: British and American Musical Theatre in the 1980s and 90s by Miranda Lundskaer-Nielsen
Beyond the Golden Door: Jewish-American Drama and Jewish-American Experience by Julius Novick
American Puppet Modernism: Essays on the Material World in Performance by John Bell

On the Uses of the Fantastic in Modern Theatre: Cocteau, Oedipus, and the Monster
    by Irene Eynat-Confino
Staging Stigma: A Critical Examination of the American Freak Show
    by Michael M. Chemers, foreword by Jim Ferris
Performing Magic on the Western Stage: From the Eighteenth-Century to the Present
    edited by Francesca Coppa, Larry Hass, and James Peck, foreword by Eugene Burger
Memory in Play: From Aeschylus to Sam Shepard by Attilio Favorini
Danjūrō's Girls: Women on the Kabuki Stage by Loren Edelson
Mendel's Theatre: Heredity, Eugenics, and Early Twentieth-Century American Drama
    by Tamsen Wolff
Theatre and Religion on Krishna's Stage: Performing in Vrindavan by David V. Mason
Rogue Performances: Staging the Underclasses in Early American Theatre Culture
    by Peter P. Reed
*Broadway and Corporate Capitalism: The Rise of the Professional-Managerial Class,
    1900–1920* by Michael Schwartz
Lady Macbeth in America: From the Stage to the White House by Gay Smith
Performing Bodies in Pain: Medieval and Post-Modern Martyrs, Mystics, and Artists
    by Marla Carlson
*Early-Twentieth-Century Frontier Dramas on Broadway: Situating the Western
    Experience in Performing Arts* by Richard Wattenberg
Staging the People: Community and Identity in the Federal Theatre Project
    by Elizabeth A. Osborne
Russian Culture and Theatrical Performance in America, 1891–1933
    by Valleri J. Hohman
Baggy Pants Comedy: Burlesque and the Oral Tradition by Andrew Davis
Transposing Broadway: Jews, Assimilation, and the American Musical
    by Stuart J. Hecht
*The Drama of Marriage: Gay Playwrights/Straight Unions from Oscar Wilde to the
    Present* by John M. Clum
*Mei Lanfang and the Twentieth-Century International Stage: Chinese Theatre Placed
    and Displaced* by Min Tian
Hijikata Tatsumi and Butoh: Dancing in a Pool of Gray Grits by Bruce Baird
Staging Holocaust Resistance by Gene A. Plunka
Acts of Manhood: The Performance of Masculinity on the American Stage, 1828–1865
    by Karl M. Kippola
Loss and Cultural Remains in Performance: The Ghosts of the Franklin Expedition
    by Heather Davis-Fisch
Uncle Tom's Cabin *on the American Stage and Screen* by John W. Frick
Theatre, Youth, and Culture: A Critical and Historical Exploration
    by Manon van de Water
Stage Designers in Early Twentieth-Century America: Artists, Activists, Cultural Critics
    by Christin Essin
Audrey Wood and the Playwrights by Milly S. Barranger
Performing Hybridity in Colonial-Modern China by Siyuan Liu
A Sustainable Theatre: Jasper Deeter at Hedgerow by Barry B. Witham

Class Divisions on the Broadway Stage

The Staging and Taming of the I.W.W.

Michael Schwartz

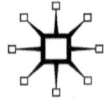

CLASS DIVISIONS ON THE BROADWAY STAGE
Copyright © Michael Schwartz, 2014.
Softcover reprint of the hardcover 1st edition 2014 978-1-137-35304-7
All rights reserved.

First published in 2014 by
PALGRAVE MACMILLAN®
in the United States—a division of St. Martin's Press LLC,
175 Fifth Avenue, New York, NY 10010.

Where this book is distributed in the UK, Europe and the rest of the world, this is by Palgrave Macmillan, a division of Macmillan Publishers Limited, registered in England, company number 785998, of Houndmills, Basingstoke, Hampshire RG21 6XS.

Palgrave Macmillan is the global academic imprint of the above companies and has companies and representatives throughout the world.

Palgrave® and Macmillan® are registered trademarks in the United States, the United Kingdom, Europe and other countries.

ISBN 978-1-349-46950-5   ISBN 978-1-137-35305-4 (eBook)
DOI 10.1057/9781137353054

Library of Congress Cataloging-in-Publication Data

Schwartz, Michael, 1963 October 18–
    Class divisions on the Broadway stage : the staging and taming of the I.W.W. / by Michael Schwartz.
       pages cm—(Palgrave studies in theatre and performance history)
    Includes bibliographical references and index.

    1. American drama—20th century—History and criticism.
 2. Industrial Workers of the World—In literature. 3. Theater and society—New York (State)—New York—History—20th century.
 4. Class consciousness—New York (State)—New York—History—20th century. 5. Labor movement in literature. 6. Class consciousness in literature. I. Title.

PS338.I58S37 2014
812'.5093553—dc23   2013050447

A catalogue record of the book is available from the British Library.

Design by Newgen Knowledge Works (P) Ltd., Chennai, India.

First edition: July 2014
10 9 8 7 6 5 4 3 2 1

For Kathy

Contents

Acknowledgments   xi

1. To Stop the World: The Most Stupendous Impossibles   1
2. Where Do I Get Off? The Wobblies I.W.W. Spurn *The Hairy Ape*   23
3. No Kick Coming: The Romantic Wobbly of Sidney Howard's *They Knew What They Wanted*   43
4. Jazzing the Wobblies: John Howard Lawson's *Processional*   59
5. Dead Hand of the Dead: Anderson and Hickerson's *Gods of the Lightning*   75
6. "We Even Sing 'em in Jap and Chink": Upton Sinclair's Workers' Theatre Contribution   93
7. You I-Won't-Work Harp: I.W.W. Elegy in *The Iceman Cometh*   109
8. Postscript: Not Time Yet   127

Notes   143
Works Cited   167
Index   185

Acknowledgments

The following were instrumental in getting this project together: Carol Connell at the Stapleton Library of Indiana University of Pennsylvania (IUP); Steven A. Schwartzman Building of the New York Public Library (the one with the lions out front); McFarland & Company, Inc. for their generous and timely cooperation; and Dana Popovic, who let us crash in her conveniently located vacant coop. I am particularly grateful to the Department of Theater and Dance at IUP for their understanding and support while I burrowed deep in my office and responded to pleasantries only with the occasional grunt. The American Society for Theatre Research focus group on Post-Union, Post-Class—Barry Witham, Mary McAvoy, Jeff LaRocque, Bahar Karlida, and Trish Everett—was instrumental in providing collegial and insightful feedback. At Palgrave, deepest appreciation goes to Don Wilmeth for his great support and guidance, to the remarkably patient Robyn Curtis, and to Erica Buchman, whose emails never fail to instill in me the fear of a wrathful Creator. My greatest thanks goes to my greatest asset, my wife, Kathleen Kerns.

1. To Stop the World: The Most Stupendous Impossibles ❧

James Jones, writing through the character of James Malloy in *From Here to Eternity*, might well be addressing the general reader of this study:

> You don't remember the Wobblies. You were too young... There has never been anything like them, before or since. They called themselves materialist-economists, but what they really were was a religion. They were workstiffs and bindlebums like you and me, but they were welded together by a vision we dont [sic] possess. It was their vision that made them great. And it was their belief in it that made them powerful. And sing! you never heard anybody sing the way those guys sang! Nobody sings like they did unless its [sic] for a religion. (Jones 640)

Novelist Jones has his character begin an important speech with "You don't remember the Wobblies." The character is speaking in 1941, and he is not asking if the listener remembers the workers who made up the Industrial Workers of the World (I.W.W.), an organization formed some 36 years previously—he is assuming that the Wobblies, as the I.W.W. were popularly called, are indeed forgotten. And by 1941, to a large degree, he was right. Times, fears, labor conflicts, and unions had all undergone considerable shifts since the days the Wobblies were most enterprising and active.

In fact, a researcher can find many examples of putting the Wobblies in the past tense sooner than James Jones's former radical character does. For example, Susan Duffy, in her study *American Labor on Stage*, analyzes a 1931 Provincetown Playhouse production (one that was not performed in New York) of the play *Strike!*, by Mary Heaton Vorse and William Dorsey Blake, concerning a strike in the south. A character named Roger offers a comparison between Wobblies and contemporary union organizers: "In circumstances like these the Wobblies were hell-raisers. We don't seem to have any cussing hell-raisers in the labor movement any more. There isn't a hard loined son of a gun among them all" (qtd. in Duffy 68).[1] Wobblies, even by the early 1930s, for many both within and outside of the working class, were cussing, hard-loined sons of gun from another era—a Wobbly was someone one's parents and grandparents remembered, most likely with a faint sense of amusement: "Those Wobblies. I remember. Always singing. Mostly regular fellows, but always mad about something or other."[2]

At one time, however, the I.W.W. loomed large in the public consciousness, even if the public was not entirely conscious of what the I.W.W. was and what it stood for—"public imagination" might be a better description. The I.W.W. was, in many ways, a highly theatrical, highly colorful (and, as Jones points out, highly musical) organization.[3] In some ways, perhaps, their stories, songs, and overall flair for entertainment were a natural fit for the world of Broadway, or so it would appear. Rather, more accurately, the Wobblies were a natural fit for theatre, but perhaps not commercial theatre.[4] In a real sense, the strongly anticapitalist ideals and agenda of the I.W.W. were dragged, kicking and screaming, onto the business-minded Broadway stage. These areas of agreement and tension will be the primary focus of this study. Just as there has never been anything like the Wobblies before or since, there has never been anything like the "Wobblies on Broadway" before or since. As mismatched as the Wobblies and Broadway might well have been, the theatrical and artistic results provide an interesting and revealing way to look at American class, labor, and theatre history.

This monograph is not a history of the I.W.W., even a brief one, although it does draw from I.W.W. history. Nor is this study meant specifically to advocate Wobbly causes—the reader is welcome to make the determination for him or herself whether or not our current century would be an opportune time for a Wobbly resurgence. This study does not also intend to argue for the martyrdom of certain key Wobbly figures, although the extent to which such figures became "folk heroes" is a significant point. What this study is meant to accomplish is to provide an examination of how the I.W.W. was staged on Broadway through the relatively small number of plays where such staging took place, and to place these stagings within the context of labor and class development that, in many ways, "directed" these productions.

Appropriately for a theatre study, this work is primarily concerned with stories and storytelling. The Industrial Workers of the World, popularly known as "Wobblies," were the subjects and creators of a considerable body of stories both positive and negative, heroic and villainous, constructive and destructive. These stories, even the most inflammatory and the most hagiographic, were based, at least to some degree, on facts. While it is certainly true, as Paul Brissenden noted in his landmark dissertation-turned-book *The I.W.W.: A Study in American Syndicalism*, that "even what the Wobblies say about themselves must be taken with a certain amount of salt" (9), it is also true that in the case of the I.W.W., the truth of the mythmaking and legend-building brings as much to bear on this study as the "cold, hard facts" do. Further, to get a sense of what the "Wobblies on Broadway" meant in terms of class distinctions and class movement, we need to get at the truth of perception—how did Broadway playwrights present their Wobbly characters, and how did audiences of the time see them? To go further, what did these plays ask of their audiences? Understanding? Sympathy? Support? These levels and layers of truth—sometimes complementary, and sometimes contradictory—form the often fluid foundation of the staging of the I.W.W. on Broadway.

The basic story, or stories, of the I.W.W. were well established by the time a Broadway play put a Wobbly onstage for the scrutiny of an audience in the 1920s. Since their cause and identification were radical, "they were attacked with all the weapons the system could put together: the newspapers, the courts, the police, the army, mob violence," as sympathetic historian Howard Zinn notes (332). The stories, songs, myths, and folklore that came from the I.W.W. themselves, their supporters, and their detractors, became a greater part of the popular culture than its relatively small membership would indicate.[5]

The Wobbly agenda was simple and direct, rooted in a firm belief in solidarity and sheer numbers in a time of terrible labor conditions. As organizer Joseph Ettor put it: "If the workers of the world want to win, all they have to do is recognize their own solidarity. They have nothing to do but fold their arms and the world will stop" (qtd. in Zinn 331). The Wobblies, with the force of free speech, strikes, and other forms of what they referred to as "direct action," as well as with songs, skits, satire, and legend-building, set out to stop the world. While the obvious observation that the industrial world most certainly did not stop would indicate failure on the part of the Wobblies, the notions of "success" and "failure" when approaching this subject are not as clear as one might imagine. Where Wobblies did succeed was not necessarily on the Broadway stage, but on the international stage in terms of projecting their character to a wide audience. On the other hand, however, it can fairly be said that how audiences of all kinds received the character of the Wobbly was fraught with distortions and exaggerations. As Brissenden pointed out, writing in 1918, "though nowadays well aware of the existence of the I.W.W., the public still knows little about the organization and its members. Moreover, a great deal of what it does know is false. For thirteen years, the I.W.W. has been consistently misrepresented—not to say vilified—to the American people" (Brissenden 8). The Broadway audiences who encountered stage Wobblies would bring a great deal of this wrong information and misinformation to their reading of the plays featured in this study.

In the extremely colorful case of the I.W.W., history, legend, and fearmongering merge in ways that create the popular picture of the "Wobbly." The way the Wobblies saw themselves and the way they were portrayed by the mainstream press play a large role in how audiences read the idea of I.W.W. Indeed, a good part of the I.W.W.'s self-promoting and self-mythologizing was theatre-based; many Wobbly leaders were skilled orators who often used theatres to deliver their inspirational speeches. Mother Jones, for instance, took to a packed theatre in Pittsburgh (a city known in Wobbly lingo as "The Big Smoke") in May of 1913 to promise on behalf of the striking miners: "I'm going back to West Virginia. If I can't go on a train, I'll walk in" ("Mother Jones Is Defiant" 2).

Besides speaking in packed theatres, the Wobblies also used performance techniques to spread their message in a way that was meant to educate the "scissor bills" and the "Mr. Blocks" (Wobbly names for workers who unthinkingly did whatever the bosses told them to do) to the way to create the "One Big Union" that was meant to break the back of the capitalists. The evidence of this performance is abundant, including the *Little Red Songbook*—full of songs meant to spread the word, often featuring parody lyrics of already familiar songs, to encourage sing-alongs. As the I.W.W. website notes—interestingly, without precision: "Since the early 1910s, the IWW has published at least 38 editions of this famous collection of labor hymns and anthems, and yes, always with a bright red cover!" ("IWW Cultural Icons"). Creation of the songbook is credited to Wobblies from Spokane, Washington, then in the midst of one of many free-speech fights, who put together what was originally known as *Songs of the Workers, on the Road, in the Jungles, and in the Shops: Songs to Fan the Flames of Discontent* ("Industrial Workers of the World Photograph Collection"). While the Wobblies, as will be noted, directly eschewed violence, their rhetoric, rife with fiery and revolutionary imagery, was often taken literally by fearful middle- and upper-class participants in the world of corporate capitalism, and American corporate capitalism in particular.[6] Worth noting also is the fact that Wobblies did get a genuine kick out of flame-fanning, and getting into what they colorfully referred to as "scraps."

The creation and implementation of songs, along with skits, poems, and monologues, even served the Wobblies in prison. To take one example, the Wobbly prisoners put together an evening of entertainment on 2 December 1917, at the Cook County Jail in Chicago. The program, scrawled in pencil, included skits, chorus numbers, stories, readings, and monologues "given by class war prisoners in the Cook Co. Jail" (Kornbluh *Rebel Voices* 330). Entertainment and performance were a large part of Wobbly persuasive strategy—simultaneously making fun of the (presumably doomed) capitalist class while proving that the Wobblies were so hardy that even in confinement, they were never far from singing another song and cracking another joke at the expense of the employing class. The folk songs and folk singing combined to create folk heroes and heroines.

The making of folk heroes and legends, the belief in a greater cause with what could be taken to be religious fervor (as James Jones emphasizes in his novel), and the mocking of organized religion itself, perhaps, best come together in a Joe Hill song, "The Preacher and the Slave," which first appeared in the third edition of the *Songbook* (Kornbluh *Rebel Voices*132). Joe Hill himself, a tireless organizer, songwriter, and leader (and, it might be added, canny self-promoter), became the key Wobbly folk hero and martyr, following his execution in 1915, notoriously for a crime where evidence seemed severely lacking.[7] The song, sung to the tune of the hymn "In the Sweet By and By," became central to Wobbly identity, and Hill is credited for contributing a key expression to the American vernacular: "pie in the sky," the implication that life on earth is to be accepted without thinking, while one is meant to patiently await one's reward (pie) in heaven (in the sky).[8] Both Maxwell Anderson (with Harold Hickerson) and Upton Sinclair employ the song in their plays at appropriate dramatic moments. Hill's memorial service in Chicago attracted some nine thousand people—according to a special report to the *New York Times*, roughly three thousand managed to get inside, while six thousand more also tried to enter. The reporter noted, with no particular desire to disguise contempt, that "Anarchists, Nihilists, some Socialists, 'bums' and hoboes generally, of whom less than 10 per cent were American, assembled for the ceremony in the West

Side Auditorium" ("Hillstrom is Cremated" 7).[9] The attitude of the reporter gives us considerable information on the regard (or lack thereof) for the Wobblies and those who supported them, which will be important to consider when we look at the Wobblies onstage.

THE FIRST WOBBLIES ON BROADWAY: THE PATERSON SILK STRIKE PAGEANT

Strictly speaking, if we want to begin with the Wobblies on Broadway, we learn that they actually presented themselves on the Big Stem first. The show they presented had a venue no less prestigious than Madison Square Garden—the famous (or infamous) Paterson Strike Pageant of 7 June 1913. The strike itself had begun in the industrial New Jersey city of Paterson in February of that year. The workers lobbied for, among other rights, an eight-hour work day, a more reasonable number of looms for each operator, and fairer wage scales. As I.W.W. historian Joyce Kornbluh notes, "The strike became industry-wide on February 25 when several thousand workers left their looms and held a mass meeting, addressed by I.W.W. organizers Elizabeth Gurley Flynn, Carlo Tresca, and Patrick Quinlan. Within the week, 25,000 workers were on strike, virtually all the silk workers in Paterson. Close to 300 silk mills in Paterson shut down" (Kornbluh *Rebel Voices* 198). The strike proved long-lasting and costly for the Wobblies and their members, so a novel money-raising scheme came into being.

The strike needed money and publicity, and John Reed, who would later write the landmark firsthand account of the Russian Revolution *Ten Days That Shook the World*, conceived a pageant in six scenes, training workers to recreate scenes from the strike. In this way, the revolutionary ideal of the Wobblies was staged with the direct simplicity of one of the oldest of theatrical devices.[10] Despite the best efforts and support of Reed's friends and the well-to-do divorcee Mabel Dodge, the pageant production team could only rent Madison Square garden for one night. Some 15 thousand persons came to the event, many at reduced prices, and many others free with the presentation of their I.W.W. cards. (The decision to be lenient regarding admission would prove costly to the Wobblies later.) In utilizing the format of the theatrical pageant, the workers were able to present scenes that included a reenactment of Valentino Modestino's funeral (an innocent bystander shot by detectives firing on the strikers), revolutionary songs, parades, and strike meetings (Kornbluh *Rebel Voices* 201–202).

Fascinated newspaper reviewers were often impressed with the conveying of emotional weight and message, even if they were at odds with the I.W.W. agenda. Certainly the *New York Times* reporter was impressed with the sheer scale of the enterprise: "It is doubtful if Madison Square Garden, even at the close of the bitterest political campaigns, ever held a larger audience than that which packed that great auditorium last night... 1,029 Paterson strikers of many nationalities and ages played the leading as well as all of the minor parts" ("Paterson Strikers Now become Actors" 7). Progressive writer Randolph Bourne, who would die five years later in the flu epidemic following the Great War, wrote of the pageant, "Crude and rather terrifying," but that it was also "something genuinely and excitingly new" (Blake, "A New Social Art").

Nevertheless, the agenda and content did not go unnoticed, to put the matter mildly, and the criticism and fear of the I.W.W. message was an important element of the public perception of the union. A particularly pointed *New York Times* editorial blasted the I.W.W. and its motives for presenting the pageant: "Under the direction of a destructive organization opposed in spirit and antagonistic in action to all the forces which have upbuilded this republic, a series of pictures in action were shown with the design of stimulating mad passion against law and order and promulgating a gospel of discontent.... Their aim is not to upbuild industry but to destroy the law" ("Two Pageants—A Contrast" 8).[11]

The pageant itself wound up a financial failure, as did, eventually, the strike itself. Through a combination of misunderstandings, anti–I.W.W. malice, and perhaps a fair dose of *schadenfreude*, the press circulated rumors of willful misappropriation and theft to account for the lack of funds.[12] In a fairly even-handed account, "Deficit of $1,996 from Strike Show," the *New York Times* reported that lawyer Jessie Ashley saw any accusations of dishonesty as "outrageous" ("Deficit" 18). What seems more likely was a result of naïve underestimates of costs and unreasonable expectations on return—or, as Anne Huber Tripp perceptively writes, the consequences of the event "turn[ing] from a fund-raiser to an artistic spectacular" (Tripp 151). But the idea of strikes and Wobblies creating drama that could engage an audience was not lost on the theatrical world. George "Cram" Cook and Susan Glaspell, who would soon set up shop in Provincetown, were both greatly impressed by the potential of the pageant and its possibilities to create a true theatrical community with a purpose.[13] The Provincetown Players, of course, would present the first plays of Eugene O'Neill, and would also later provide a home for the New Playwrights Theater's production of *Singing Jailbirds*. They would also produce a distinctively Wobbly play early in their tenure before they moved to downtown New York. The I.W.W. had brought their own form of theatre to Broadway, if for only the one performance, and legitimate theatre was about to answer in kind.

EARLY PROVINCETOWN: CONTEMPORARIES

The first season of the Provincetown Players (the summer of 1915) attracted a playwright who would gain greater fame as a short-story writer. His name was Wilbur Daniel Steele, and the case of I.W.W. leader Frank Tannenbaum sufficiently fueled his indignation to create "Contemporaries."[14] Tannenbaum, as a criminologist, would later theorize the "dramatization of evil...the making of a criminal and the lure of criminal behavior" (Townsend, "Frank Tannenbaum: Dramatization of Evil"). As a young man, however, Tannenbaum achieved notoriety by leading a large group of homeless men into a church, and subsequently serving six months in prison for inciting a riot, despite a lack of report of any sort of disorderly conduct. Comparisons to Jesus helping the poor surfaced in the workers' press, and Steele, accordingly, wrote a timely allegory that seemed to be about Tannenbaum, but a last-minute twist reveals the story actually takes place in New Testament-era Jerusalem.[15] While the play did not travel to New York, the production revealed a company keenly interested in contemporary issues, including issues of labor and class struggle, and the possibility of building an audience.

THE SIX "BROADWAY WOBBLY" PLAYS (PLUS ONE)

This study examines six plays that involve the I.W.W.—that is, at some point a character identifies himself or is identified as a "Wobbly." The plays under study were first produced in the 1920s, with the exception of Eugene O'Neill's *The Iceman Cometh*. In chronological order, the "Wobbly" plays interrogated in this book are O'Neill's *The Hairy Ape* (1922), Sidney Howard's *They Knew What They Wanted* (1924), John Howard Lawson's *Processional* (1925), Maxwell Anderson and Harold Hickerson's *Gods of the Lightning* (1928), Upton Sinclair's *Singing Jailbirds* (copyright 1924 by Sinclair, first produced 1928), and O'Neil's *Iceman* (1946). The first five plays were performed shortly after the I.W.W.'s most active period and following a series of devastating setbacks for the organization. Nevertheless, the Wobblies were still very much a current presence in the news and in the public imagination throughout the 1920s, and this presence plays a direct role regarding how the Wobblies were staged in this first group. The final "Wobbly play" under consideration, *The Iceman Cometh*, followed World War II when, as we have noted and will examine further, the idea of the Wobbly was for many an already distant memory despite the persistence of the Wobblies themselves. After the examination of *Iceman*, there will follow a look at one more recent play, or more accurately a portion of a larger play, *The Kentucky Cycle*, that also enters Wobbly territory, which will serve as a portion of this study's postscript.

As is most likely appropriate for a series of plays about Wobblies (or, at least, involving Wobblies), the plays all share a certain sense of engagement with social struggle, and a particular liveliness long associated with the Wobbly agenda. The onstage Wobblies tend to be impulsive, articulate, and in many cases, musically inclined—or, at least, they tend to sing. The other element the plays have in common is one that this study returns to and explores quite frequently throughout, because much of the tone of this particular element would appear to be something of a product of the 1920s atmosphere. This element consists of a sense of fatalism and pessimism about the world—a sense that despite the idealism, fire, and vigor of the Wobblies, their efforts to stop the world are doomed before they start. The world is not going to change, the plays and their characters say throughout this work; human nature is human nature, which is fundamentally greedy and corrupt. This balance between capturing Wobbly passion and (often regretfully) accepting the world as it is provides a good deal of the tension in the plays of the period.

This study takes into account four interrelated factors as it proceeds chronologically through the 1920s and negotiates the jump to just after World War II. The first factor concerns the factual Wobbly activities occurring during the production of these plays—strikes, protests, and the often voluble coverage of these activities. Along with the activities of protest, the study considers how the Wobblies created their own legend(s) during this time through songs, skits, and extensive mythmaking. The famous line from John Ford's western *The Man Who Shot Liberty Valence* is particularly pertinent in this case: "When the legend becomes fact, print the legend." To appreciate Wobbly identity, one must often begin by remembering that, in many cases, the legend is indeed the fact.

Another important consideration, as noted, will be the perception of Wobblies from the point of view of the plays' audiences—in other words, how did Broadway audiences see and hear "Wobblies"? The study will seek to define "Broadway audiences" and identify their class concerns, which in turn will provide important clues as to how they would have felt about "Wobbly" characters onstage. This distinction will be particularly important regarding Sinclair's play, and, to a large extent, Anderson's contribution, which courted a different audience in terms of sympathetic point of view; these two plays spoke to and sought a "workers'" audience. "Now, the character of the I.W.W. and its reputation are two entirely different things," warns a Wobbly informational pamphlet from the late 1920s, roughly the time of the productions of *Gods of the Lightning* and *Singing Jailbirds*. ("The I.W.W.: What It Is and What It is Not"). Nevertheless, Wobbly character and reputation are important elements of the plays that sought to stage the Wobblies on Broadway, even if the boundaries between character and reputation often remain determinedly fuzzy. To examine how the audiences "read" the Wobblies on Broadway, it will be necessary to explore what Marco de Marinis refers to as the dramaturgy of the spectator—looking at the audience in terms of a "target" for the production, as well as in terms of the operative actions the audience performs in their role as audience, for example, "perception, interpretation, aesthetic appreciation, memorization, emotive and intellectual response" (de Marinis 100–101). How audiences perceived, interpreted, appreciated, and responded to the Broadway Wobblies will be of particular interest in this study.

This book also explores the playwrights' perceptions of the Wobblies. In examining all the I.W.W. characters in the plays under study, one finds heroes, dreamers, fools, and hard-line anarchists—indeed, O'Neill's *Iceman* provides something of a mini-history of how and where the various schools of anarchist thought both formed and diverged from the Wobbly agenda. How and why the playwrights echo and implement Wobbly songs and credos will serve as a topic of discussion, as well the writers' other experiences and writings about the I.W.W.

Finally, the study investigates the "performances" of the Wobblies on Broadway—how did they look and sound? How the Wobbly characters dressed, their size and physicality, as well as their overall attitudes, all add to the overall picture the study attempts to paint of the Broadway stage Wobbly. George Abbott, for example, who essayed the lead role in *Processional*, was a tall, physically imposing man, especially compared to the rest of the cast. On the other hand, as we discuss further, whether or not Abbott was truly playing a Wobbly poses another series of questions. Other actors who took on the role of the Wobbly provide different embodiments with varying degrees of danger, sex, and ordinariness, and all these factors registered, consciously or not, with their Broadway audiences.

Applying a theoretical lens on the stage Wobblies requires taking into account how culture is played and enacted in a time when the elements of modern American capitalist society wrought great changes in the country and indeed the world. The theories and insights of Theodor Adorno will prove useful in getting at the subversive cultural strategies of the Wobblies, as well as how Broadway, in turn, used, echoed, and sometimes "sub-subverted" the Wobbly agenda. Inasmuch as staging Wobblies directly relates to the idea of the oppressed in society—in this case, the workers—the relation of culture to the oppressed serves as a major theme in this study as well. Adorno felt that "art" must be completely removed from the marketplace in order to be truly progressive (Gartman 43). One of the tensions and possible contradictions this study examines is the tension between the attempt to create popular Broadway art that is completely dependent upon the marketplace through the use of Wobbly (progressive) characters and themes. This tension will also serve as an entry into the kind of class transgression that the plays and their manner of production represent as audiences watched with varying degrees of appreciation, interest, and curiosity.

WOBBLY OVERVIEW

To begin, we should provide a brief overview of the I.W.W., as well as an overview of responses to and interpretations of their activities up to the point of the performance of the first play under study. The reader will be introduced to a group which saw the I.W.W. as their religion, local jails as their address, and "worker" as their identification. While the "gospel" of the I.W.W. would seem, at first glance, to be at considerable odds with the world of Broadway, in some ways these stories fit the Big Stem strangely well. The I.W.W. thrived on cheer and sentiment at least as much as Broadway did, although the objects of such cheer and sentiment for these two naturally antagonistic entities were vastly different.

Fred Thompson's fiftieth anniversary compilation, *The I.W.W.: Its First Fifty Years*, explains the I.W.W.'s origins this way:

> There was too much "organized scabbery" of one union on another, too much jurisdictional squabbling, too much autocracy, and too much hobnobbing between prosperous labor leaders and the millionaires in the National Civic Federation. There was too little solidarity, too little straight labor education, and consequently too little vision of what could be won, and too little will to win it. (Thompson 1955 5)

In June 1905, the Industrial Union Congress launched the I.W.W. with a preamble stating their agenda and their worldview—a worldview that might well seem familiar in light of recent activist events: "The working class and the employing class have nothing in common. There can be no peace so long as hunger and want are found among millions of working people and the few, who make up the employing class, have all the good things of life."[16] From the opening sentence, the concept of disrupting the peace, or the denial of any kind of peace, formed the seeds of the suspicion, which quickly grew to a conviction that the Wobblies were a group that threatened violence.

Commentary on the I.W.W. fed into the inherent drama of the Wobblies early on. American Federation of Labor founder and president Samuel Gompers witnessed at least some part of the first meeting, and dismissively declared: "As time goes on the active participants in the labor movement of the future, students, thinkers, historians, will record the Chicago meeting as the most vapid and ridiculous in the annals of those who presume to speak in the name of labor, and the participants in the gathering as the most stupendous impossibles the world has yet seen" (qtd. in Brissenden 106). John

Graham Brooks's 1913 examination of the Wobblies in *American Syndicalism* emphasizes the "alien" nature of I.W.W. thought in the kind of purple prose that was typical of the period:

> Like the sound of a bell in the night, the "Industrial Workers of the World" strike an alarm note that seems as new and strange to us as if some unknown enemy were at the gate. Both the purpose and the weapons used are alien and uncanny to our thought. We are just becoming half wonted to Socialism, but the defiant, riotous ways of this American Syndicalism are past understanding. (73)

One of the unstated, though implied, goals of the Broadway productions was to bring these "unknown enemies" into the spotlight and reveal that the enemy was perhaps not so different from many members of its audience. This revelation was not always welcome for the audience members.

Brooks provides a partial scenario for the origins of the I.W.W., particularly drawing upon his reports of the 1903 Western Federation of Miners strike in Colorado. As Brooks noted: "In the murky terrors of that miners' strike, the vehement and practical thing called I.W.W. had its birth. Grimy and hot, it rose there as from a sulphurous pit." Brooks's source was "one of the more daring leaders in that strike," who claimed "the I.W.W. was hammered out in the fires of that conflict" (75). While Brooks's words reflect "his era's hostility toward the Wobblies" (Conlin 316), the chronology and details of I.W.W. origin given are largely accurate. [17]

Potential Wobbly play audiences could, and most likely often did, acquaint themselves with many of the dire, and not infrequently hysterical, warnings about Wobblies. Charles Willis Thompson, in his *Times* article "The New Socialism That Threatens the Social System: The New Socialism That Threatens Society," sets down for the reader the considerable danger of the I.W.W. in plain terms: "The I.W.W., the full name of which is the Industrial Workers of the World, is an association which ought not to be overlooked or slighted. It is the business of every American citizen to acquaint himself fully with what it aims at and what it stands for. For the

I.W.W. is the most serious menace the present system of society has ever been called upon to face" (Thompson SM1). And William Howard Taft, for his part, addressing Yale in 1913 just after his term as president, blasted the I.W.W. for "their impudent, lawless, selfish, and unjust demands that are based on the proposal that society owes them a living, whether they make effort and labor or not" ("Taft Blames I.W.W." 4). Wherever one stood on the Wobbly question, the fact remained that drama followed their activities across the country. That some of that drama should wind up on Broadway, if for a limited amount of time, was perhaps inevitable.[18]

Nevertheless, even in the Wobblies' most productive and arguably notorious years, some observers noted the distinctions between the Wobbly of the popular imagination and the actual dimensions of the union itself. As R. F. Hoxie wrote in "The Truth About the I.W.W." in 1913, "the I.W.W., instead of being the grim, brooding power which it is pictured in popular imagination, is a body utterly incapable of strong, efficient, united action and the attainment of results of a permanent character, a body capable of local and spasmodic effort only" (Hoxie 789). In terms of longevity, Hoxie certainly had a point, but the question that remains is an intriguing one: how did such a supposedly weak, inefficient, and "spasmodic" group loom so large in the popular mind? And how was this power utilized and appropriated by theatre artists?

The First Wobblies

To return to the beginning, the June 1905 convention in Chicago that made the I.W.W. official has been written about extensively. As Howard Zinn reports: "One morning in June 1905, there met in a hall in Chicago a convention of two hundred socialists, anarchists, and radical trade unionists from all over the United States. They were forming the I.W.W.—the Industrial Workers of the World" (Zinn 329). The plan was to create an organization that would help overthrow capitalism in the United States. Joyce Kornbluh notes that the union was "based on the principles of Marxist class conflict and the indigenous American philosophy of industrial unionism...the I.W.W. sought to recruit unskilled and exploited immigrants, non-whites, women, and migrant workers who were excluded from craft unions of skilled workers organized by the [American Federation of Labor] AFL" (Kornbluh "Short History"). Of note here and later in our study is the I.W.W.'s strategy of inclusion and their insistence that their platform was unionist. The I.W.W. would build up a long history of association with various kinds of anarchism, particularly syndicalism and anarcho-syndicalism, and this association was largely due to their inclusiveness, as well as to their shared goals of putting an end to the current economic system.

The relationship between Wobblies and syndicalists was complicated, and such complications were as much a result of the Wobbly platform as were the generalizations spread by the press and by popular imagination. Brissenden, while subtitling his examination of the Wobblies "A Study of American Syndicalism," points out that "the I.W.W. had had no direct contact with French syndicalism previous to 1908. Moreover, its relations with the French movement have not at any time been as close or as definite as generally imagined. The I.W.W. *organization* is an indigenous American product, if there ever was such a thing" (Brissenden 278, emphasis in original). While I.W.W. leaders read syndicalist literature, made direct contact with some syndicalist spokesmen, and appropriated the syndicalist tactics of direct action, the Wobblies did not care to identify themselves as syndicalists. According to the general bylaws, "the I.W.W. refuses all alliances, direct or indirect, with any political parties or anti-political sects..." As the website explains, while syndicalists and anarcho-syndicalists were (and are) welcome in the I.W.W. (as workers, since all workers are welcome), the I.W.W. is neither expressly political or expressly antipolitical—leading to some understandable confusion on how to classify the Wobblies (iww.org). A distrust of movements that have anything to do with politics was part of the I.W.W. platform from its early days, an idea perhaps most succinctly summed up by Vincent St. John in 1924: "It will never be necessary for the I.

W. W. to endorse any political party, whether we will gain support or not by so doing. Neither will the I. W. W. carry on propaganda against political action. To do so would be as useless as to carry on a campaign for it" ("The I.W.W. and Political Parties"). Ideally, for the Wobblies (again in St. John's words), "knowledge and organization" were the two key principles for the workers to keep in mind—all other political or antipolitical ideas merely got in the way.

With regard to the distinctions, relationships, and differences between these different kinds of radicals—in particular, anarchists, socialists, and syndicalists—it is important to keep in mind that a great deal of the general public, including the general public who frequented the theatres of Broadway, were either ignorant or indifferent to such distinctions. A key example of this kind of confusion centers around the use and meaning of the term "sabotage."

For the Wobblies, "sabotage" was not a physically violent act, but a form of "direct action at the point of production." As the I.W.W. website explains, "One specific form of direct action (by no means the *only* such form) is Collective Withdrawal of Efficiency, sometimes better known by the unfortunate and controversial term **Sabotage**" ("Direct Action and Sabotage," emphasis and bold in original). The perpetration of sabotage meant a slowdown of work, decreasing the quality of work, and generally performing in an inefficient manner. The importance of efficiency in the early twentieth century in the world of corporate capitalism can hardly be overstated. Efficiency experts, led by the demonstrations, talks, and writings of Frederick Winslow Taylor,[19] led the gospel of efficient business and efficient use of otherwise recalcitrant employees. The Wobblies, probably correctly, asserted that a blow to efficiency was one of the strongest weapons of the workers.

Nevertheless, the violent connotations of the term "sabotage" were neither lost on the general public nor on the socialists who might otherwise have supported Wobbly causes. This rift over the meaning of sabotage came to a head in the 1912 convention of the Socialist Party, when it was decided to rescind and deny membership to anyone who advocated any sort of "crime, sabotage, or other means of violence"

(National Constitution of the Socialist Party, Article II, Section 6, p. 2, Chicago 1914, qtd. in Kornbluh *Rebel Voices* 37).

The I.W.W. platform did not change, and indeed has not essentially changed since the preamble to their constitution was revised in 1908. The Wobblies were particularly active from their beginnings until the dawn of the Great War, a period rife with "rising prices, stationary or declining wages, a series of depressions, and widespread unemployment," as Kornbluh outlines:

> The IWW became a militant expression of class war in the United States, directing or taking part in at least 150 strikes in the pre-World War I period. Among the most significant of these were the Goldfield, Nevada, miners' strike (1906–07), the Lawrence, Massachusetts, textile workers' strike (1912), the lumber workers' strikes in Louisiana and Arkansas (1912–13), the Paterson, New Jersey, silk workers' strike (1913), and the Mesabi Range ironworkers' strike (1916). (Kornbluh "Short History")

The Wobblies scored early successes in the first two decades of the twentieth century through "direct action"—"strikes, free speech fights, boycotts, and demonstrations" (Kornbluh *Rebel Voices* 35). The idea of direct action won out over "working-class political action" largely due, once again, to the inclusiveness of the I.W.W.—women, aliens, and Negroes who were not allowed to vote had no political power, so political action was not a viable choice (35). Strikes in the Pressed Steel Car Company of McKees Rocks, Pennsylvania (1909), the Lawrence textile strike of 1912, and free speech fights, placed the Wobblies in bold print in newspapers across the nation, often painted as "Wobbly menace." The overheated rhetoric of national newspapers, as well as New York newspapers, was highly influential in shaping the Broadway audience's picture of the Wobbly.

The Red Scares of the Great War and dissension in the I.W.W. regarding the rise of communism were the two biggest crippling elements in the Wobbly success as the 1910s drew to a close. Indeed, history often ends its look at the I.W.W. in the early 1920s, that is, the time that audiences first saw them on Broadway.[20] Reports of the death of the I.W.W. were greatly exaggerated, however, both in terms of ongoing "real world" activity and in terms of the public imagination. By the time Eugene O'Neill gave Broadway audiences its first close-up examination of a Wobbly secretary and an onstage union local, the Wobblies were, by no means, past their prime as a force for free speech, and they persisted as a colorful presence in the public imagination. How the Wobblies loomed in the public fancy was a key factor in how the play was discussed and received at the time of its premiere.

On Violence

Part of the suspicion, distrust, and outright panic regarding the Wobblies and their agenda was rooted in a belief that the I.W.W. was a violent organization, one that advocated explosions and violence, and one that would fight the war against capitalism with blood. As noted earlier, considerable suspicion regarding the violence of the Wobblies was a fundamental misunderstanding of their use of sabotage. As Melvyn Dubofsky writes: "In most cases the IWW hoped to gain its ends through nonviolent measures, through what it described as 'Force of education, force of organization, force of a growing class-consciousness and force of working class aspirations for freedom.' One forceful method explicitly advocated by the Wobblies—indeed, the tactic with which they are most indelibly associated—was sabotage" (Dubofsky 162).

A good deal of the charges leveled against the Wobblies for violence had to do with their fighting back, as Howard Zinn recounts:

> Despite a reputation given them by the press, they did not believe in initiating violence, but did fight back when attacked. In McKees Rocks, Pennsylvania, they led a strike of six thousand workers in 1909 against an affiliate of the U.S. Steel Company, defied the state troopers, and battled with them. They promised to take a trooper's life for every worker killed (in one gun battle four strikers and three troopers were killed), and managed to keep picketing the factories until the strike was won (Zinn 331).

In fact, the Wobblies emphasized nonviolent tactics and strategies quite early in their history. For example, in the 11 May 1907, edition of the *Industrial Union Bulletin*, the writers insist unequivocally that violence "has no place in the foundation or the superstructure of this organization" (qtd. in Conlin 319). We find repeated exhortations from I.W.W. leadership to let owners and authorities be responsible for any and all bloodshed; as Conlin cogently points out, "[Big Bill] Haywood and some other Wobblies had an inarticulated conception of the now-familiar idea that nonviolence often frustrated the adversary into the use of violence, and the public's comparison of peaceful workers with violent employers would channel the tide of public opinion to the workers' cause" (Conlin 320). There are cases that supported this idea; and, as we shall see, there were circumstances that led public opinion to believe that the Wobblies were "a conspiracy of desperate villains" (Conlin 316). The question of violence and the perception of the I.W.W. as a violent organization is a major element of the response to the plays discussed in this study.

A LOOK AT THE BROADWAY AUDIENCE

If a Wobbly play becoming a Broadway success is something of a paradox, if not an outright contradiction in terms, the idea of a "working class" play presented for the "employing class" would appear to be a distinct mismatch of message and audience. Indeed, an audience looking for entertainment on the Big Stem in the 1920s would have more in common with the employing class, and those who would support the employing class—in monetary terms, those who could, at least fairly regularly, afford the top ticket prices of the time, peaking at $6.00 per ticket in the mid-1920s (these prices would drop with the Depression, holding steady at $4.00 for several years).[21] Playgoers for the plays under study would largely have been the employing class and the Professional-Managerial Class (PMC)—two classes whose existence depended upon keeping American corporate capitalism running as smoothly as possible. In defining the "Professional-Managerial Class," we rely largely on the definition set forth by John and Barbara Ehrenreich: "Salaried mental workers who do not own the means of production and whose major function in the social division of labor may be described broadly as the reproduction of capitalist culture and capitalist class relations" (Ehrenreich and Ehrenreich 18).[22] While the definition is undeniably loaded, we are, in tackling the Wobblies and Broadway, dealing with equally loaded ideologies.

The newspapers that the audiences read are significant as well. Playgoers, increasingly embodying the cliche of the businessman in a hurry, whether on subways, commuter rails, or in limousines, craved theatre criticism that got to the point early. The *New York Times* emerged as the newspaper for that brand of businessman, with the other dailies increasingly having to acknowledge their interests (Norton 329–330). The employing class read the papers that catered to them, and those who strove to rise in the ranks, including the PMC, read the papers their harried bosses read. It was also these newspapers that gave the audiences their chief news of the Wobblies and other radicals. And since the Wobblies were relentlessly determined to sabotage the business of business, it might truthfully be said that the newspapers, and their readers, literally saw "red." Thus the audiences' view of the "Wobblies on Broadway" was indelibly colored. The Wobbly message, therefore, throughout the plays that present the I.W.W. as characters, was blunted by the point of view of the audiences, critics, and, to a large degree, the playwrights. Part of the labor struggle that emerged as these plays were presented was the tension between the Wobbly message and overall message of Broadway. To a large degree, much of the Broadway audience and critics did not take these labor conflicts, or the desires of the workers, with anything resembling a respectful degree of seriousness, although there were notable exceptions along the way.

With these episodes and bits of background (or backstage) information at hand, we are ready to open the curtain on the Wobblies on Broadway. The first visit will be to an I.W.W. local that turns out to be a significant stop on the journey of fatal self-realization taken by a "hairy ape." Audience members who also visited this particular I.W.W. local were also in for something of a surprise.

2. Where Do I Get Off? The Wobblies I.W.W. Spurn *The Hairy Ape*

On Easter Sunday 1914, visitors flocked New York's Fifth Avenue for the annual Easter Parade, a colorful and ostentatious display of spring fashion that had been going strong for some 40 years. The *New York Times* coverage at the time tells readers that many people were blocking traffic in an attempt to "appear in moving pictures." The story also notes that the I.W.W. had threatened to crash the parade: "The I.W.W. leaders who had threatened to mix into the Fifth Avenue parade a few hundred followers selected with the idea of making by their appearance the strongest contrast with the rest of the brilliant spectacle failed to carry out their plan" ("Fifth Avenue Gay with Easter Host"). Had the plan been carried out, the sight would certainly have been an interesting one—the upper class, in its conscientious display of finery for purposes of simultaneously generating entertainment and admiration, forced to bump up against and rub shoulders with the decidedly shabbier working class (who, rumor had it, were going to "shabby up" even further to make their point). The contrast of bodily types, carriages, and postures would have delighted Pierre Bourdieu in his gathering of material regarding the "habitus," that is, roughly speaking, the physical embodiments and characteristics of particular social conditions (Bourdieu 29). The spectacle that was not to be would probably have fascinated Adorno as well—in a sense, the Wobblies wanted to stage a performance of ugliness that was meant to reveal the ugliness of the divide of social positions, thus disrupting a celebration of the society that created such divides in the first place.¹ At any rate, while it is true that a threat without follow-through from eight years earlier might simply be a coincidence, the idea of contrasting interlopers on Fifth Avenue might have appealed to Eugene O'Neill as he put together his series of scenes that became *The Hairy Ape*. The story is also of some interest as one of many examples of the I.W.W. imprinting upon the national consciousness, even to the point of threatening parades and religious celebrations.

By 1922, when *The Hairy Ape* opened, first downtown at the Provincetown Playhouse and later uptown—that is, on Broadway—at the Plymouth Theater, a great deal had happened to the Industrial Workers of the World as an organization and as a potential force for change. As is well known, one of the biggest events to eventually weaken the Wobblies was the recent Great War.² On principle, the Wobblies had opposed war since roughly 1914, but I.W.W. management was hard-pressed to determine an official Wobbly stance on conscription. The basic argument, as Joyce Kornbluh points out, was that the I.W.W. could be shut down if they opposed the draft, whereas the convincing counterargument was that the I.W.W. was pretty much doomed to be "run out of business" anyway. As it turned out, the I.W.W. Executive Board did try to compromise, encouraging members to go ahead and register, but to do so noting that they were I.W.W. members who were "opposed to war" (Kornbluh *Rebel Voices* 317).

Such compromises might have been sensible, but they did not much protect the I.W.W. either from charges of sedition or from the popular mindset. By September 1917, the government had enough on the Wobblies to bring them to court—officially, the charge was that the I.W.W. was "a vicious, treasonable, and criminal conspiracy which opposed by force the execution of the laws of the United States and obstructed the prosecution of the war" (The United States of America v. William D. Haywood, et al., qtd. in Kornbluh *Rebel Voices* 318). With the charges of wartime conspiracy and sedition, the Wobblies had been formally charged with yelling "fire" in a crowded theatre (White 651), a point to which this study will return in the chapter on Sinclair's *Singing Jailbirds*. The trial was duly noted by the press, and when the *New York Times* claimed in a sub-headline that "Fate of Syndicalist Movement in America Hangs on Outcome," the writer was not far wrong by any means ("I.W.W. Trial Starts Today"). As Brissenden succinctly commented in the preface to his study on the I.W.W., written as the trial was in progress:

> Just now the Industrial Workers of the World, as represented by more than one hundred of its members and officials, is on trial for its life in Chicago. The indictment charges the defendants with conspiring to hinder and discourage enlistment and in general to obstruct the progress of the war with Germany. The specific number of crimes alleged to have been intended runs up to more than seventeen thousand. (Brissenden 7)

The I.W.W. defendants were found guilty as charged. Harrison George, one of the defendants, ended his account in a lively and defiant fashion, with "the boys" clapping their defeated lawyer on the back with cries of "You did your best. It was sure some scrap, anyhow!" George then leaves the reader with the image of the Wobblies being returned to prison singing I.W.W. songs "with the spirit which cannot die" (George 207–208). This chapter of the Wobblies' history, however, was not to end with so much song and good spirits. By the time *The Hairy Ape* opened, key I.W.W. leader and orator Big Bill Haywood had jumped bail in 1921 and fled to Russia, where he would die seven years later, ill and disappointed, not having furthered the cause against world capitalism (Kornbluh *Rebel Voices* 324). Whether Haywood's flight was a fatal blow to the Wobblies has been the subject of some disagreement, as Philip Foner acknowledges in his *History of the Labor Movement in the United States: Postwar Struggles 1918–1920*. While some labor historians note that the Wobblies, after an initial period of anger and disappointment, pretty much set out to let him go and move on, others felt just as strongly that Haywood's departure left the I.W.W. without strong leadership (Foner 228). The loss of the trial and much of its leadership, at any rate, was a serious blow to the Wobblies, one from which they arguably never fully recovered.

Also fueling the wartime and postwar anti-Wobbly sentiment was the Red Scare and what became known as the Palmer Raids, which lasted during the same period from the end of the Great War into the early 1920s. The period of the Red Scare began, appropriately enough, with a literal as well as figurative explosion. In the summer of 1919, a bomb exploded in front of the home of President Wilson's attorney general, A. Mitchell Palmer. Palmer struck back with great force against non-citizen immigrants in general, and Communists in particular. In Palmer's statement "The Case Against the Reds," originally printed in the 1920 edition of *Forum*, he proclaimed the US government to be in jeopardy, and that

> like a prairie-fire, the blaze of revolution was sweeping over every American institution of law and order a year ago. It was eating its way into the homes of the American workmen, its sharp tongues of revolutionary heat were licking the altars of the churches, leaping into the belfry of the school bell, crawling into the sacred corners of American homes, seeking to replace marriage vows with libertine laws, burning up the foundations of society. (Palmer "Case Against the Reds")

In December 1919, Palmer and his men soon rounded up some 249 Russian aliens and sent them back to what was by that time Soviet Russia. The next month, Howard Zinn writes, "four thousand persons were rounded up all over the country, held in seclusion for long periods of time, brought into secret hearings, and ordered deported" (Zinn 375). As we will see throughout the study of this period, the conflation between "Reds" and Wobblies—most of whom were ideologically opposed to Communism—would hurt the Wobbly cause during a time of great fear of the Communist agenda.[3] These elements, part news and part fear, held great sway over the popular imagination by the time O'Neill put a reasonable, plain-speaking, and not the least bit explosive Wobbly onstage in his *Hairy Ape*.

The mainstream press contributed mightily to this fearful interpretation of the I.W.W. "story." A few examples are in order—examples, worth remembering, that most theatergoers would conceivably have read in their newspapers of choice. In a 1919 *New York Times* article titled "What's Wrong with Labor?", the anonymous author opens: "It is generally believed that industrial revolution, if it ever should reach the point of real menace in this country, would come through the radical I.W.W." ("What's Wrong"). A 1920 account of a railroad strike adopts a similarly grim tone: "From the first the chiefs of the Railroad Brotherhoods and the Railroad Managers have been convinced that the railroad strike, now sagging to an inglorious end, was instigated and directed by the I.W.W., with what even more sinister allies behind it can only be conjectured" ("The I.W.W. Strike"). The almost throwaway clause with the adjective "sinister" tells most of the story, a story Broadway audiences would likely have taken as fact.

In April of 1920, reporter Helen Bullitt Lowry more fully delineated the subversive (and sinister?) motives of the Wobblies, noting that the I.W.W. not only wanted to cause strikes, but that they took great pleasure in failed strikes—after all, a successfully settled strike satisfies the workers, but the *dis*satisfied workers are the ones who will bring about "the Revolution." As Lowry elaborates:

> The orderly element of the population, of course, counts upon every class's getting their just desserts in the long run, through the ballot box and the proper enforcement of law and the reforms that come about through education. The orderly element takes no stock in I.W.W. theories or hopes, but must be interested in them from time to time when I.W.W. disturbers manage to hurt business through organized campaigns among the ignorant. (Lowry XX1).

There is at least a grain of truth in Lowry's assessment, or misassessment, depending upon one's point of view. As Bob Black notes in his essay "Beautiful Losers: The Historiography of the Industrial Workers of the World" with regard to strikes and striking: "Strikes and the improvements they sometimes brought were good in themselves but even better as rehearsals for social revolution.... as rehearsals for the strike to end all strikes, the general strike" (Black "Institutional History"). The opinion, therefore, that the strikes engineered by the I.W.W. were meant as a warm-up for "the Revolution" was not entirely off the mark. Certainly, this pervasive sense pervaded the climate of the early 1920s for many, including Broadway audiences—audiences who were often readers of the *New York Times* and would have been familiar with articles like Lowry's. The "uptown" attitude with regard to labor struggles, it seems fair to say, was pretty clearly antiradical. Nevertheless, the I.W.W. themselves may have been down but they were not yet out.

In a roughly contemporaneous I.W.W. pamphlet, "The Immediate Demands of the I.W.W.," the Wobblies set out to keep its readers focused on its success as well as the work ahead, with prose occasionally as purple as that of its worst detractors:

> Those who are old enough to remember the working and living conditions of, for instance, the migratory workers in the opening years of this century and earlier, before the I. W. W. was born, in the construction or the lumber camps, in the wheatfields or in the hopfields, will still shudder at the thought of them and bend their heads in sorrow at the recollection of all the ghastly misery they and their fellow workers had to pass through. To take a job of that kind in those days was to take a plunge into hell itself, and hope there seemed to be none. To become a migratory worker was like saying goodbye to life forever.
>
> It was then that **the I. W. W. came as a real savior**, a child whose father was gruesome economic necessity and whose mother was the rising tide of working class education. Its message of salvation through industrial organization and solidarity carried the force of divine revelation. The already doomed outcast straightened up his back and could see the blue sky of hope once more. ("The Immediate Demands," bold in original)

There were other notable forces at work in American culture that somewhat prepared Broadway audiences for a hairy ape seriocomically influenced by anti-Wobbly propaganda. One somewhat paradoxical force was what could be considered a growing tolerance, and in some cases even a romanticizing of socialism. As Warren Susman notes in *Culture as History*, Americans were increasingly accepting of income tax, "socialized education," and "other transformations of governmental roles previously held to be socialistic attacks on private property and even the gradual but grudging respect to the workers' rights to organizing and bargaining collectively" (Susman 79). In some cases, the attitude toward socialism extended to accepting such attitudes in American heroes, as James Gilbert sums up: "A characteristic American social type was now depicted as a social revolutionary, but he could now be seen as the creator of a new sort of culture contained in songbooks and IWW newspapers and as a prophet in his own life, a man on the fringe of society, yet capable of seeing clearly to its center" (Gilbert 14, qtd. in Susman 78). While the Wobblies on Broadway tend perhaps to fall short of this ideal that was more prevalent in literature than on stage (the work of Jack London, for example), the attitude that was beginning to seep through old barriers was also, if tentatively, finding its way onto the Broadway stage. Literally and figuratively, the stage was set for downtown and uptown audiences to see how Wobblies would handle a "hairy ape." And with this production, critics, audiences, and O'Neill would have to deal with how the anticommercial Wobblies might or might not fit in the world of commercial theatre and story-telling.

Eugene O'Neill's *The Hairy Ape* is unique among the plays discussed in this study. It not only got to the subject of Wobblies early in terms of Broadway, but actually put the physical I.W.W. office itself onstage, or at least one chapter—Local No. 57, according to the stage directions (O'Neill *Hairy Ape* 20). Notably, a number of critics at the time disappointedly felt that O'Neill had stooped to writing I.W.W. tracts and propaganda. Such an opinion, when examined in the context of what O'Neill actually wrote, proves illuminating in terms of the power of mentioning the I.W.W. in a way that approached objectivity—that is, any terms describing the I.W.W. as less than demonizing read to the critics as "radical." The abortive relationship between Yank and the Wobblies should be examined with regard to O'Neill's relationship with the Wobblies, as well as how *The Hairy Ape*'s 1922 audiences might have responded to them.

It is difficult to overestimate Eugene O'Neill's influence on modern American theatre, and modern American theatre audiences, in the 1920s. As O'Neill was positioned (and positioned himself) as the serious modern American playwright par excellence, he played with techniques both realistic and antirealistic, and gave his audiences language and characters that were thrilling and shocking. O'Neill was savvy about his audiences, having developed a reputation as a "Greenwich Village" playwright, and thus associated with downtown, intellectual, and possibly radical art, as well as growing and augmenting his reputation as an American playwright for the world to reckon with—he had, by the time *Hairy Ape* opened, already won Pulitzer Prizes for *Beyond the Horizon* and *Anna Christie*. The Provincetown Playhouse was further able to gain from O'Neill's appeal with audiences that were commercial and curious as well as the ones that were more at home in the Village. The early 1920s were an ideal time for Village regulars to "perform" the Village for the curious tourist, and O'Neill and his work had become a prime attraction.[4] And, as O'Neill biographers, Arthur and Barbara Gelb, point out, "Greenwich Village was a good place for a drunken spree" (Gelb and Gelb 282). The combination of atmosphere and cultural capital that O'Neill had generated most likely proved irresistible to a particular breed of "uptown" tourist.

The "lowdown" appeal of *The Hairy Ape* is borne out by at least one witness. Frederick James Smith, writing as the New York correspondent for the *Los Angeles Times*, breezily noted: "It is interesting to watch the odd audience which jams the tiny remodeled barn—half uptown smartness, and half downtown Bohemianism.... The lavishly dressed matron who sat beside me remarked between shudders that the play was 'noisy but cute.'" Smith also reported that *The Hairy Ape* "was turned down by every one of the commercial managers. They were plainly afraid of what O'Neill said about our smug social system" (Smith "Hopkins Skids" III35).

The seeds of what Wobblies had to say about "our smug social system" vying with and finding space in a Broadway theatre that in many ways epitomized that smug system were planted early. Also notable is the attitude of many audience representatives—"noisy but cute" does not necessarily indicate engaging the material on a serious level. While some audience members no doubt were considering both the plight of the worker and the plight of mankind, there was a sense among many audience members that whatever the class or labor wars were, they did not particularly reach the uptown world.

While the play gave the I.W.W. representatives a chance to speak reasonably about themselves and their organization, O'Neill did not appreciate the focus of critics, both positive and negative, on the Wobbly element. In a letter to Oliver Sayler, O'Neill notes that the I.W.W. newspaper *Solidarity* praised him for "something I didn't mean" (O'Neill *Selected Letters* 168).[5] It is perhaps a testament to O'Neill's naivete and relative youth as a playwright as well as to the tenor of the times that O'Neill would be so surprised that the I.W.W. portion of his play would steal focus.[6] The very fact that Wobblies appeared on the New York stage not as dangerous radicals but reasonable-looking men who resembled and spoke like the well-educated middle class, and by extension, the audience, was enough for many critics, as well as audience members, to read the physical staging of the I.W.W. as "pro-Wobbly" and "propaganda." Anti-anarchist values of the post–Great War era led audiences to believe that since O'Neill did not seem to be overtly against the Wobblies, he must have been "for" them. Such ideas assisted in the *succes de scandale* of *The Hairy Ape*, but led to, as far as O'Neill was concerned, a profound misunderstanding of his larger picture.

The audience's reading of the I.W.W. in *The Hairy Ape* might at least partially be explained by Daniel Berlyne's categories of variables that work on audience's attention: "novelty, surprise, complexity, and oddity" (qtd. in De Marinis 108–109). The figure of a Wobbly on Broadway was sufficiently novel, and it could safely be noted that a low-key, reasonable-, and, on the whole, "average-looking" and sounding Wobbly was something of a surprise as well as an oddity. These elements would seem to have conspired against the more humanistic message O'Neill wanted to deliver, or at least claimed to want to deliver.

Another element the audience had to "read," either successfully or not, was O'Neill's expressionistic use of exaggerated actors and effects. Much of what was being exaggerated was not too far removed from the day-to-day world of much of the Broadway audience. This visual hyperbole extends to O'Neill's description of the stores on Fifth Avenue, for example, the jewelry shop and its displays: "From each piece hangs an enormous tag from which a dollar sign and numerals in intermittent electric lights wink out the incredible prices" (14). As for the people promenading along the Avenue, O'Neill extends his vision in the same contemptuous vein, after letting both the men and women have it in a show of equality: "A procession of gaudy marionettes, yet with something of the relentless horror of Frankenstein in their detached, mechanical unawareness" (16). What might well have appeared to be a fun house mirror reflection of many of the men and women in the Broadway audience who shopped at those stores and went to the churches the onstage "marionettes" attended probably went a long way toward convincing many of the witnesses in the audience that they were indeed watching broad and blunt anticapitalist propaganda.

At any rate, the daily papers' response to O'Neill's play was largely respectful; O'Neill was already well on his way to earning acceptance as "the" American playwright.[7] Critical response to O'Neill's inclusion of the Wobblies, as well as his perceived attitude toward radicals, however, is worth examining further. Alexander Woollcott, writing for the *New York Times*, for example, while perhaps tellingly not mentioning the Wobbly episode specifically, takes the time to tease the radical sensibility through his discussion of the character of Long, a Cockney malcontent (his accent rendered, the reader can be sure, in full-out phonetic transcription in O'Neill's dialogue) who accompanies Yank on his fateful visit to Fifth Avenue. Woollcott mentions actor Harold West, who played Long, describing him as "a cockney agitator who is fearfully annoyed because of the hairy ape's concentrating his anger against this one little plutocrat instead of maintaining an abstract animosity against plutocrats in general" (Woollcott 22). The critic for *The Dial* flatly, and rather antiintellectually, avers the Wobbly scene to be a mistake and unnecessary: "it must not turn the spectator's mind to intellectual activity," the reviewer warns (G. S. 548). Percy Hammond fairly noncommittally reports that Yank, while in jail, "learns from the prisoners... of the I.W.W. and he determines that that organization shall be instrument of his enmity. But he is thrown out of the I.W.W. headquarters when he applies for membership, being suspected as a spy..." (Hammond "The New Play" 8). The more conservative James Patterson, writing somewhat snidely for the *Billboard*, dismissed the play and O'Neill entirely: "If it is propaganda it is worthless because it lacks penetrative quality. If it is drama it needs climaxes" (Patterson "The Hairy Ape" 19). Both Heywood Broun (in the *New York World*) and J. Ranken Towse (*New York Evening Post*) agreed with dismay that O'Neill was writing I.W.W.-inspired propaganda.[8] Apparently, however, the FBI did not feel that the propaganda should be dismissed right away. According to their report: "The Hairy Ape could easily lend itself to radical propaganda, and it is somewhat surprising that it has not already been used for this purpose."[9]

In examining the scenes referring to and then directly including the I.W.W., the Wobblies themselves perhaps emerge at their most reasonable in O'Neill's "serio-comedy of modern life." A significant part of this reasonableness lies in the casting of the I.W.W. secretary, billed in the program simply as "a secretary." The performer was journeyman actor Harold McGee, who would stage-manage another O'Neill production, and cap his career in 1949 in Maxwell Anderson's *Anne of the Thousand Days* as "Bailiff, Musician, and Royal Servant." McGee, physically speaking, was no outsized working-class tough stomping through an otherwise orderly world and wreaking havoc. He resembled, both in physical appearance and costume, a typical mid-level employee of the period. This embodiment of a recognizable and ordinary business worker, looking like a member of the professional managerial class, directly colluded with the audience's idea of a "Wobbly." Whether O'Neill intended the message or not, Harold McGee's physical presence and performance told the audience, even before his dialogue began, that Wobblies could conceivably be one of them—an idea that was perhaps too much for many theatergoers.

The dialogue that ensues between the secretary and Yank confirms the idea of misunderstanding—both on the part of Yank and, by implication, many audience members. The secretary is to the point, alert, and justifiably suspicious of the oblivious Yank, who has taken an anti–I.W.W. screed from the *New York Times* literally (Yank is not a character to whom one can communicate in metaphors). Yank's mistaken assumptions include thinking that he has to knock at the door, and that there is an initiation ceremony he must pass through—both assumptions that are laughed off by the secretary.[10] Notably missing from this early play that is much more a feature in later plays involving the Wobblies is the passion and anger, although the secretary does give Yank something of a dressing-down once he decides Yank must be some sort of inept spy at the end of the episode. The secretary notes casually that "some guys get a wrong slant on us" (20), and when the subject turns to the purpose of the I.W.W., his tone turns textbook-dry when referring to changing "the unequal conditions of society by legitimate direct action" (21). When the secretary at last has Yank thrown out, thematically repeating the insult of "ape," he offers the supposed "Secret Service skunk" a copy of the manifesto. Yank, in turn, replies with an impotent anti-Semitic slam on the secretary ("yuh Sheeny bum, yuh!") as he is thrown through the door. It is this straightforward, nonjudgmental representation of the I.W.W.'s policies and procedures that led to the I.W.W. approval of this play. O'Neill, a former member, would have been well-acquainted with the I.W.W., and it becomes an interesting facet of *The Hairy Ape* that within O'Neill's often expressionistic experiments, it is the I.W.W. that emerges as the most realistic element.

O'Neill, for his part, quickly took great pains to distance himself from the notion that he had written a radical propaganda play; he had bigger, or at least more humanistic, fish to fry. "Yank," O'Neill insisted, "is really yourself, and myself. He is every human being" (Gelb and Gelb 499). The "every human" attitude that O'Neill insisted upon, rather than a strictly "social" play, becomes a main factor in interpreting O'Neill's tragedies as humanistic, where something essential to life is man's greatest enemy. Raymond Williams, in *Modern Tragedy*, elaborates on O'Neill's take on life as man's antagonist: "The isolated persons clash and destroy each other, not simply because their particular relationships are wrong, but because life as such is inevitably against them" (Williams 116). Or, as Yank himself sardonically explains to a callous police officer who asks what Yank has been doing to warrant an arrest, "I was born, see? Sure, dat's de charge. Write it in de blotter. I was born, get me!" (O'Neill 22). It was this "charge" that ultimately defeats Yank, as well as a number of other of O'Neill's characters. It was also this charge to which, as far as O'Neill was concerned, that organizations such as the I.W.W. were ultimately unequal.

Whether O'Neill's attempt to create a "humanist" story rather than a "social" one was misguided or not proved fodder for critics, both conservative and more radical. Eleanor Flexner's commentary on the play in her 1938 book on American playwrights of the past 20 years (significantly subtitled "*The Theatre Retreats from Reality*") chides the play and O'Neill for a failure of logic: "Just what does all this mean?...Why do the I.W.W. reject him? Why the insane episode at the zoo? From the moment of Mildred's entrance into the stokehole Yank ceases to be a valid symbol and becomes merely a deranged individual incapable of adjustment within the social mechanism" (150–151). Anita Block, for her part, recognizes the markers that audiences looking for social messages picked up on: "an alleged Socialist rails against capitalism... the daughter of a steel-magnate is portrayed as a decadent... Fifth Avenue churchgoers are depicted as shallow, purblind marionettes, and... the I.W.W. is presented sympathetically, as the real answer to a groping Yank" (146). Nevertheless, Block succinctly dismisses the idea that *Hairy Ape* could be a social drama: "O'Neill is not in the least concerned with the social problems of Yank. He is really not concerned with Yank at all. His interest is with the inner conflicts of *man*, midway between the hairy ape he has left behind him and the evolving human race to which he is not yet conscious that he belongs" (146–147).

Yank's information about the Wobblies comes, significantly, from the Sunday *New York Times*; a prisoner reads a florid article denouncing the I.W.W.: "I refer to that devil's brew of rascals, jail-birds, murderers and cutthroats who libel all honest working men by calling themselves the Industrial Workers of the World; but in the light of their nefarious plots, I call them the Industrious *Wreckers* of the World!" (18) Yank's destructive mood is a match for the article's overheated rhetoric, which leads him to the seriocomic misunderstandings of his meeting at the I.W.W. itself. Yank naively echoes the nation's most conservative, antiunion sentiment.

Worth emphasizing is the fact that O'Neill's exaggerations in penning a typical *New York Times* editorial are not as great as one might suppose; nor is Yank's literal acceptance of the *New York Times* editorial such a far-fetched characterization. We have already noted A. Mitchell Palmer's inflamed rhetoric against Communists, which O'Neill (and his audience) were most likely aware of. The I.W.W. was, for many people, including those who read the *New York Times* and saw Broadway plays, a symbol of something fierce and monstrous—indeed, many middle- and upper-class children were told to behave or the I.W.W. would get them.[11] The anti–I.W.W. sentiment emerged with varying degrees of vitriol across the country. In the *Mansfield News* (of Mansfield, Ohio) of 30 November 1920, for example, the editorial writer confidently debunks Bill Heywood's proclamation that the I.W.W. would cooperate with the Bolshevists for peaceful revolution: "But the honest workers of the nation, such as are willing to give a full day's work for a fair day's pay, want none of the I.W.W. and the Bolshevist propaganda.... it is opportune season for the same treatment to be given to [the I.W.W.] that is accorded to any other robber or thief" ("Straining 'Free Speech'" 6).

The phrase the fiery fictional *New York Times* writer gives the Wobblies, "Industrious Wreckers of the World," was also common parlance for anti–I.W.W. sentiment. As noted in a squib in the 10 August 1917 edition of the *Newark Daily Advocate* (of Newark, Ohio), "One paper calls them Industrious Wreckers of the World, and another calls them Imperialism's Willing Workers. Neither of these terms is good enough, because each contains the idea of labor" ("Pointed Paragraphs").[12] The anti-Wobbly rhetoric proves an interesting example of mythmaking and countermythmaking, as Fred Thompson in his I.W.W. compilation points out: "it [the I.W.W.] was ridiculed as a bunch of bums with bombs in hip pockets, advocating violent sabotage. This weird reputation has no relevance to the facts, but it became so widespread and such an influence on its subsequent history, that the history of the myth must be told alongside the history of the actual organization" (Thompson *The I.W.W* 80–81). Indeed, the lines between myth, legend, and fact were fundamentally blurry not only for the I.W.W. detractors, but also for many of the Wobblies themselves. It seems fair to say that the first "uptown" audiences of *The Hairy Ape* might not have "read" the editorial Yank hears in jail as satirical, but rather nodded in sincere agreement with regard to the still-potent Wobbly threat.

A key factor in the popular picture of the Wobbly was violence. A "playful" headline and story in the 31 December 1916 issue of the *Salt Lake Telegram* serves as an illuminating example. The headline read "Plan is Made to Poison Community with Strychnine," and the story continued with instructions regarding how to prepare the poisonous mixture. The punchline revealed what community was to be poisoned: "This is no I.W.W. plot but part of the instructions issued by [the] agricultural agent of Salt Lake City...for destroying sparrows" (qtd. in Conlin 316). The joke on the I.W.W. reveals a great deal about the popular perception of the Wobblies and their agenda, as Conlin continues: "During its heyday before and for a decade after World War I, the IWW had a most unsavory reputation for violence. In the popular eye, the IWW was a conspiracy of desperate villains who set fire to wheat fields, drove spikes into sawmill-bound logs, derailed trains, destroyed industrial machinery, and killed policemen" (Conlin 316). Newspapers heightened this view of the Wobblies even when violence was done against the union. In a brief commentary on the lynching of I.W.W. Executive Board member Frank Little from the *New York Times* of 4 August 1917, the unnamed writer calls for bringing Little's murderers to justice, but adds at the end: "Little was lynched. The I.W.W. has been trying, and is busily trying still; to lynch the United States" ("The I.W.W.," *New York Times*). Small wonder, perhaps, that the naïve Yank would naturally take the hyperbolic editorialist at his word and assume that the I.W.W. could help him dynamite "all de steel in de woild up to de moon" (O'Neill *Hairy Ape* 21). While historians such as Conlin qualify the nonviolent Wobbly philosophy with terms such as "on balance," the evidence shows that the Wobblies were much more violent in the fertile public imagination, fueled by antiunion sentiment, than they were even in their most active and enterprising era.

O'Neill's Yank, in his painfully inarticulate argot, gives us the first of many examples of rejecting the I.W.W., even as the Wobblies rejected him. In the Wobbly scene's climactic monologue, where Yank again assumes the pose of Rodin's "The Thinker," Yank groups the I.W.W. with religion and the Salvation Army: "Dey're in de wrong pew," as Yank puts it (22). For Yank, and for O'Neill, the existential and cosmic problems of man can be cured by neither social activism nor faith—"De same old bull," as Yank puts it. Yank's dismissal of the I.W.W. agenda was most likely what O'Neill hoped the audience would pick up on. Nevertheless, the physicalization of the sensible, onstage Wobbly trumped Yank's ruminations in the public imagination; indeed, audience members might be forgiven if they did not trust Yank as a reliable spokesperson for the author.

Another element with regard to physicalizing the Wobbly onstage is the character of Yank himself. Although Yank himself is never a Wobbly in the course of the play, he does spend significant stage time trying to become a member, enthusiastically parroting the anti–I.W.W. rhetoric of the newspaper article in the play as positive Wobbly attributes—"Wreckers, dat's de right dope! Dat belongs! Me for dem!" as Yank puts it (O'Neill *Hairy Ape* 18). Actor Louis Wolheim, who created the role of Yank for the Provincetown Players and continued the role uptown as well, was very much the titular "hairy ape" as a physical presence. Wolheim's ability to bring O'Neill's detailed description to life—"broader, fiercer, more truculent, more powerful, more sure of himself than the rest," according to O'Neill's stage directions (3)—was commented upon with great admiration by critics. Wolheim's conveying of great brute force, and "stripped to the waist" to boot (Eaton "The Hairy Ape"), might well have signified the images of giant, outsized workers popularized by both the pro- and anti-Wobbly cartoons of the period.[13] While the text and the action of the play are clear that Yank does not belong as a Wobbly, this clarity might have been lost on the Broadway audience. The conflation of Yank's enthusiasm with the prevailing anti-Wobbly sentiment of many Broadway audience members might well have made a scary combination.

The idea that the I.W.W.'s agenda, however ambitious, was insufficient to address the problems of man or the issue of the soul is significant in reading *The Hairy Ape*, and this theme will reappear in nearly all the plays in this study. Indeed, throughout this survey of I.W.W.–themed plays, we see something of a lost cause. The portraits of the Wobblies may vary in degrees of sympathy, wit, and aggressiveness, but the echoing refrains of the plays are remarkably similar in their fatalism—same old bull, won't do any good, man isn't going to change. The notion that men in charge will choose greed and power at the expense of those who work surfaces as a foregone conclusion—an air of pessimism and fatalism that stands in contrast to the social play of the 1930s. It is Yank's tragedy, capped by getting crushed by his "ape" brother, a real gorilla, that he seeks something beyond himself, or "beyond the horizon," to use another O'Neill title.[14] And in Yank's plight, we might discern something of the Wobblies' tragedy as well.

Our first examination, then, of a Broadway Wobbly play finds the playwright shunning the social aspects of the play and the explicit I.W.W. agenda—in many ways, for O'Neill, a defensive response to those observers who saw and heard "I.W.W." and leapt, favorably or otherwise, to the conclusions of propaganda. O'Neill, indeed, had more to be defensive about than the Wobbly aspects of his play—*Hairy Ape* was also the subject of an investigation regarding indecency and impurity, a charge that was soon dropped. "Morons will be morons," O'Neill commented laconically ("O'Neill's 'Hairy Ape' Escapes Charge" 18). O'Neill had more to say about his play and the "modern" world that the play occupied: "If there is anything significant about modernity it is that we are facing life as it truly is. That fact differentiates this age from any other. We have no religion to evade life with. Like all the other evasions, religion is breaking down. We are looking life straight in the eye" ("Young Boswell Interviews O'Neill" 13).

Modernity, evasions, and religion are threads we will continue to follow as we examine the remaining plays. These threads are of particular interest in examining the role Broadway plays in the evolving Wobbly story. For O'Neill, the Wobblies themselves constituted a form of evasion, and with reference to the use of the quote from James Jones at the beginning of this monograph, a form of religion as well. The Wobblies themselves, nevertheless, saw an opportunity to not only look life straight in the eye, but find substantive ways to change that life for the working class of the world. It is perhaps these inconsistencies, or ironies, or paradoxes, as the case may be, that made the Wobbly an intriguing figure on the Broadway stage for a time. The tension between how the Wobblies saw themselves, how the playwrights saw them, and how the audiences saw them, creates an interesting dramatic narrative to what might otherwise be something of an American theatrical footnote.

The next play under discussion also deals with modernity, evasions, and religion in one form or another. The modernity emerges from a fairly simple and logical solution to what, for generations, had been a considerable moral issue. The evasions, including religion, are acted out by the characters themselves onstage, and also, perhaps, by the audiences and even by the playwright in creating a Wobbly play with a strong Wobbly figure that is not necessarily remembered as a Wobbly play. The play appears a couple of years following *The Hairy Ape*, and it encompasses, willingly or not, some more significant I.W.W. backstory before it reveals itself to an appreciative audience. It would give a journalist/playwright his first hit play and launch his career as something of a theatrical realist. Part of that realism, whether audiences particularly noticed or remembered, included its use of another Wobbly.

3. No Kick Coming: The Romantic Wobbly of Sidney Howard's *They Knew What They Wanted* ∾

The year 1924 was a turbulent and, in many ways, a disastrous one for the Wobblies. As Joyce Kornbluh spells out:

> The ordeal of the antiradical campaigns of the war and postwar years culminated in a serious schism in the I.W.W. organization in 1924—exacerbated by disagreements regarding amnesty for political prisoners, rivalries between the lumber workers and agricultural workers unions, and especially the Communist Party, who were making unwanted inroads and advances on the union. (Kornbluh *Rebel Voices* 351)[1]

The Russian Communist group successfully attracted major I.W.W. figures, including Elizabeth Gurley Flynn and Big Bill Haywood, but most I.W.W. members grew increasingly disenchanted with the system in Russia. Nevertheless, the Wobblies lost ground to the Communists, as they would later, to the expanding Congress of Industrial Organizations (C.I.O.) (Kornbluh *Rebel Voices* 351–352).[2]

A further blow to the Wobblies was, as Kornbluh writes, "changing American industrial technology following World War I." Changing technology changed the workforce as transportation and machines replaced many of the kinds of workers who had been good candidates for Wobblies (352). The 1924 audiences may have been following the vicissitudes of the Wobblies with varying degrees of closeness (and accuracy), but it was safe to say that Wobblies continued to mean "trouble" to the readers of the *New York Times* and the other dailies, especially the more conservative dailies. The year 1924 was, after all, the year the United States decided to "keep cool with Coolidge," and the cool, considerate atmosphere led the president to his most famous quote about American business: "The chief business of the American people is business."[3] It was into this fraught atmosphere that the second play under study made its first appearance on Broadway, and by most accounts, the occasion seemed to be a happy one. How *They Knew What They Wanted* managed to place a rambunctious Wobbly in the middle of the action and avoid the accumulated bad feelings surrounding the I.W.W. will be the focus of this chapter. The answer is largely based in several savvy decisions made by the playwright.

Playwright Sidney Howard had been following labor relations for some time as a journalist, and his attitudes were more sympathetic to the workers than not. In 1921 for the *New Republic*, Howard blasted the practice of industrial spying: "He [the labor spy] capitalizes the employer's ignorance and prejudice and enters the plant specifically to identify the leaders of the labor organization, to propagandize against them and blacklist them and to disrupt and corrupt their union" (Howard "The Labor Spy"). Howard also followed the strikes and trials of the Wobblies, and these impressions would find their way into his drama. As Howard prepared *They Knew What They Wanted,* he developed a love triangle in California's Napa Valley—a simple story but with an intriguing I.W.W. twist.

For his entry into the 1924 Broadway season, Howard found a place for, if not the most active of the Broadway Wobblies under discussion, arguably the sexiest. A sexy Wobbly for the Theatre Guild audience was by no means a sure bet for success. Nevertheless, audiences and critics did indeed embrace playwright Sidney Howard's *They Knew What They Wanted*, which would run 192 performances and go on to win the 1925 Pulitzer Prize, making the play the biggest "hit" of the plays under examination, at least upon initial performance. The successful containment of the wild and unpredictable figures of the I.W.W. was an integral element of Howard's first Broadway hit.[4]

By the time John Gassner compiled the "early series" of *Twenty-Five Best Plays of the Modern American Theatre*, published in 1949, Sidney Howard's legacy had already acquired an aura of dullness. This was 10 years after Howard's death in 1939, the same year his most enduring writing credit was released to the public—the screenplay for *Gone With the Wind*. "The adjectives 'solid' and 'sound' are apt to crop up in descriptions of his best writing," Gassner wrote, and he later added the term "reliable" as well (Gassner "Introduction: *They Knew What They Wanted*" 90). Nevertheless, Howard himself might well have been pleased with such a description. For Howard, writing for the theatre meant writing for actors—giving them the most interesting roles he could, and counting on them to make his work livelier. As Howard noted in a 1927 interview:

> An actor—and I don't care how great the part is—can always add to what the author has written. The author gives him practically no more than an indication of what the performance is to be. It is the actor who fills it out. Richard Bennett [who created the role of Tony in *They Knew What They Wanted*] once said to me that he counted no man an actor who could not give an author at least 60 per cent more than he had written. (qtd. in Houseman 13)

The perhaps already quaint plot that Howard devised, which served as the basis for the 1956 Frank Loesser musical *The Most Happy Fella*, follows Tony, a late-middle-aged successful winegrower whose prosperity has grown exponentially in the midst of the government's crackdown on alcohol: "I say pro'ibish' mak' me dam' rich," he proclaims in his rich stage-Italian dialect (Howard *They Knew What They Wanted* 114). He has fallen in love with Amy, a waitress, and woos her by mail—but, fearing that Amy would not find him desirable, Tony has substituted a picture of Joe, the handsome young drifter in Tony's employ. Tony, out of guilt and panic, drinks too much before driving to the train station to pick up his bride-to-be, and we later find out he has had a terrible accident, breaking both legs. In the meantime, Amy has found her own way to the vineyard and meets Joe, assuming he is Tony. The misunderstandings multiply until a hurt and angry Amy nevertheless decides to see the wedding through and tend to Tony. The wedding night brings a conciliatory Joe and a vulnerable Amy together, with the predictably unfortunate result of pregnancy. After Tony furiously threatens the lives of both Joe and Amy, reinjuring himself in the process, he decides upon a more mature, "modern" course of action—since Amy now loves Tony and wants to stay, and since Joe, ever the drifter, wants to leave, and since Tony wants Amy and kids, he forgives Amy and convinces her to stay. "We tellin' evrabody he's Tony's baby. Den evrabody say Tony is so goddam young an' strong he's break both his leg' an' havin' baby just da same!" Tony proclaims in a comic combination of magnanimity and pride (Howard 121). The title is illustrated and fulfilled as Joe contentedly heads on his way, leaving Tony and Amy in a loving embrace. Joe remarks, with "a broad grin spreading over his face," that "there ain't none of us got any kick comin', at that. No real kick" as he exits, employing period slang for not having anything to complain about (122).

The story, as one critic of the revival of the Loesser musical once noted, might well be one that "babies tell to babies" (Kalem 1979).[5] Of interest for the purposes of this chapter is the character of Joe, whom Howard identifies as a sometime (and still card-carrying) member of the I.W.W. It is the "dark, sloppy, beautiful and young" Joe, in fact, who gets the first dialogue of the play—as Howard notes in his stage directions, "he half sings, half mutters to himself the words of 'Remember,' an I.W.W. song, to the tune of 'Hold the Fort,' and the audience hears Joe as he works, preparing Tony's house for the impending wedding: "We speak to you from jail to-day,/Two hundred union men,/We're here because the bosses' laws/Bring slavery again" (Howard *They Knew What They Wanted* 92).[6] Joe's identification with the I.W.W., the other characters' comments about the "Wobblies," Howard's strategies regarding how the audience is meant to receive Joe, and how the audience might have responded to him, provide a significant chapter in the relatively brief history of the Broadway staging of the I.W.W. The fact that the audience meets Joe singing this particular song would color their impression of Joe instantly. Even if the audience did not necessarily recognize the song (although many probably did), the lyrics would indicate Joe's position as a discontented worker of some kind, and for many in the audience, the song would instantly translate as "radical." For playwright Howard, the opening moments of the play was a bold move in terms of risking audience sympathy.[7]

The rhetorical position of the Wobbly in Howard's play is the result of a balance between Joe's physicality and the placement of his pro-I.W.W. arguments within the play's space. Howard, in fact, gives his cast of characters plenty to say about the I.W.W.—most of it negative, in line with the approval of the "moral Americans" in the audience. Amy, for example, purposely getting Joe's goat, speaks of the Wobblies with disdain: "Wobblies? Huh! I never could see much in it myself. Calling in at farmhouses for a plate of cold stew and a slab of last Sunday's pie. Down in the Santa Clara we used to keep a dog for those boys. I guess it's a fine life if you like it. Only I never had much use for hoboes myself" (Howard 109).[8] While it is clear, as noted, that Amy is speaking largely out of spite for Joe, her likeability for the audience—largely a result of actress Pauline Lord's sympathetic portrayal of Amy—gives her words a great deal of weight and power.

For Tony, another character strongly designed to elicit audience goodwill and sympathy, the description is a good deal blunter: "goddam Wobblies" who "ain' got no good sense" (116). Father McKee, who, as Howard describes in his stage directions, is "one of those clerics who can never mention anything except to denounce it," puts in his two cents as well: "I've read a-plenty of your radical literature an' if you ask me, it's just plain stupid.... You radicals... you're always an' forever hollerin' an' carryin' on 'bout your rights. How 'bout your duties? There ain't no one to prevent you doin' your duties but you ain't never done 'em in your life" (116). Howard then has Father McKee pronounce the fatalistic view that will hang over nearly all the plays in this examination. The father continues rather matter-of-factly:

> I come to the conclusion that capital an' labor'll go on scrappin' to the end of time and they'll always be a certain number of people that'll stand up for the underdog. I been standin' up for the underdog all my life...but I learned a long time ago that the dog on top needs just as much standin' up for as the other kind and I ain't got much use for either of 'em because both of 'em's always complainin' an' carryin' on. (Howard 116)

Father McKee's conclusion that things are generally not going to change carries a great deal of thematic and rhetorical power in the world of Howard's play. Such a laissez-faire attitude would have played well with Howard's audience, who would have generally related more to the dogs on top, or at least, dogs on the way up. It is also important in this scene to note that it is only Father McKee who is allowed to make a strong and complete argument, one with a beginning, middle, and end, or in other words, a thesis and a conclusion. Tony, for his part, is pretty much limited to a dismissive "Tak' a pinch-a snuff an' shut up!"—the 1920s' stage-Italian equivalent of "STFU."[9]

Nevertheless, playwright Howard proves if not exactly subversive, then at least willing to problematize the issues he raises about power, government, and the place of radicals in the world. For Howard gives Joe a considerable contribution to the argument—if not necessarily the winning argument, certainly an argument meant to command attention and respect. Joe's argument is inconclusive, unlike the Padre's; further, Joe's points are not always articulate, and, as perhaps is appropriate for the young drifter, rather unformed, but perhaps a bit disconcerting to those who might complacently leave the theatre on the side of Father McKee and Tony. "A man ought to think if he can," Joe insists, "Oh, not tall talk. Just what he could be doin' himself. I think how I could get into the scrap. I ought to have been in on the dock strike at San Pedro, but I wasn't. I don't want to miss another big fight like that, do I?" (Howard 116). Joe is referring to the I.W.W.'s biggest effort to organize the longshoremen, fishermen, and sailors—the Maritime Workers Union strike the year before, in 1923. This same strike would inspire Upton Sinclair to write one of the other plays under study, *Singing Jailbirds*. When Tony and Father McKee warn Joe that he'll wind up in jail (where Joe, in fact, has been before), Joe produces his red I.W.W. card and declares:

> I could go to worse places. A guy went to jail up in Quincy, in Plumas County, awhile back, for carryin' a Wobbly card—like this one, see? His lawyer pleads with the judge to go easy on the sentence. "Your honor," he says, "this chap served in France an' won the Croy de Gaire an' the Distinguished Service Cross." An' right there the guy jumps up an' says, "Don't you pay no attention to that stuff," he says. "I don't want no credit for no services I ever performed for no gover'ment that tells me I got to go to jail to stand up for my rights".... What I say is: about the only freedom we got left is the freedom to choose which one of our rights we'll go to jail for. (Howard *They Knew What They Wanted* 116)

Joe's speech once again echoes similar accounts of the period. Father McKee, "super-sententiously," according to Howard's directions, is about to admonish Joe, but the disagreement is interrupted by Amy's entrance, never to be resumed or resolved (116). Joe's speech also rings true to Wobbly form by his reference to getting "into the scrap"— as noted with regard to the "great" I.W.W. trial, the Wobblies often spoke enthusiastically about scraps and scrapping.

The scene between Joe, Tony, and Father McKee is illustrative of Howard reconciling his support for the I.W.W. and his sense of his audience, and a key to how the pro-I.W.W. sympathies "got by" what would most likely not have been a sympathetic Broadway crowd. Howard was fairly well known as a "radical" reporter—his scathing series of articles for *The New Republic*, "Our Professional Patriots," which offered withering critiques of those who would suppress the rights of individuals' free speech, had appeared just before the play opened. "Patriots," Howard observed in the 15 October edition of *The New Republic*, "succeed in making ridiculous anything they touch" (Howard "Our Professional Patriots VIII" 171). Joe's argument, however, is not the last word; it is the sympathetic Amy with her earthy common sense that ends the discussion with a genial report that all is well in the vineyard. Cultivating one's garden proves, in the end, a higher calling than the fomenting of rebellion.

As was previously evident in O'Neill's *The Hairy Ape*, the humanistic aspect of American drama typically won out over the overtly political in the American drama of the 1920s. As David Savran notes: "Given the decline in leftist activism…and the difficulty of compassing the social and economic complexities involved in the construction of the Fordized subject, it is little wonder that so many artists who catered to elite audiences ended up dematerializing the social, turning politics into psychology and metaphysics" (Savran 262). In Howard's case, "dematerializing the social" meant letting the sympathetic, winning, and plain-speaking heroine enter and shutting the misguided (though undeniably sexy) radical up so the story can resume. The genuine issue, Howard invites his audience to realize, is to enjoy life when one can and appreciate the day-to-day pleasures—a soothing message for the clichéd but nonetheless real "tired businessman" who did not pay good money to hear stump speeches actively criticizing his government.

The fact that Joe does get to actively make pointed criticism was largely mitigated by several key factors, one of which is Joe's physicality—as mentioned earlier, Joe, as played by the handsome young Glenn Anders, was legitimately sexy.[10] This sexiness was Howard's explicit intention as noted in his stage directions: "JOE—dark, sloppy, beautiful, and young—is busy opening a packing case in the center of the stage" (Howard *They Knew What They Wanted* 92).

Joe's physical attractiveness is necessary to make the misunderstandings and the love triangle work—Tony would have little reason to place a photograph of Joe in his letter to Amy if Joe were not, in slang parlance, the bee's knees. It is in part this sex appeal that excuses Joe's I.W.W. leanings—including songs, speeches, and reading Wobbly newspapers throughout his time onstage. It is not uncommon for an audience to forgive a great deal for the sake of physical beauty.

Joe's youth plays an important role in how audiences and critics read him as a Wobbly as well. Percy Hammond, from the *New York Herald*, for example, comments (in somewhat antiquated terminology) that "Joe, the vagrom-man, sets out upon a journey to the horizons," describing Joe further as a "southwestern Peter Pan" (Hammond "The Theaters: 'They Knew What They Wanted'" 16). Burns Mantle in the *New York Daily News* praised Anders's "splendid" performance as "the unstable Tony [Mantle meant 'Joe'], a likable and human wabbly [sic] for all his weaknesses" (Mantle "'What They Wanted'" 24). Stark Young's *New York Times* review gives an even stronger sense of what Anders brought to Joe in terms of sympathy and naturalness:

> He [Anders] understands exactly that kind of shiftless integrity in such a character as this Joe that he plays, a fellow who migrates along from place to place, sometimes talking for the I.W.W., sometimes in jail, sometimes in the orchards and vegetable farms, but honest throughout, and loose and kind, even tender when life comes near to him. Mr. Anders brings to the part his singular gift for a casual naturalness in his readings and inflections… (Young "The Play: Love in the Valley 27)

With the sample critical responses, it becomes fairly easy to put together a profile of how much of the audience most likely received and read Joe. The character read as young, irresponsible, immature, but basically honest and good-hearted. Anders presented Joe as a very young man—a boy, perhaps—whose forays into the I.W.W. were part of a delayed growing up process—hence the Peter Pan reference. It seems safe to say that the satisfied customers excused

Joe's preachier radical tendencies as the result of misguided youthful idealism; as Burns Mantle noted (somewhat comic spelling errors aside), Joe provided the Wobblies with a likeable and human face. Likable and human, however, did not necessarily translate to the audience accepting Joe's Wobbly messages—quite the contrary. Anders's presence as Joe did, however, render the Wobblies not so much as an abstract terror that might well have been verified by Louis Wolheim's Hairy Ape, but as human beings with good intentions who might well turn out "all right" (i.e., non-Wobbly) given enough time to mature.

That the play was not received as a "Wobbly" play, in contrast to the way many saw O'Neill's *Hairy Ape,* is further borne out by the venerable Joseph Wood Krutch in his landmark study *The American Drama Since 1918.* Prefacing his admiring examination of the play, Krutch writes: "The play is not topical; it deals with no specific or recurrent social problem; and in so far as it may be said to have any thesis at all that thesis is a highly generalized one" (Krutch 45).

Krutch's pronouncement is worth another look: a play that features a Wobbly, who in turn directly references a recent major strike as well as real-life imprisonments of I.W.W. members under charges of syndicalism, is neither topical nor one that deals with a social problem. For the collective memory regarding any given play, a topic to which this study will return when discussing *Processional,* the overall "mood" and "atmosphere"—or perhaps, the shape of the stage story—overrides other details that might be written in the text or stated quite plainly in the production. *They Knew What They Wanted* did not "read," for most audiences, as either a social play or a Wobbly play, but rather as a "mature" and "modern" (and for the time, rather racy) love story.

Nevertheless, the play, in fact, did not escape scandal, but not because of the I.W.W. or any real or imagined radical sympathies on Howard's part. The scandal grew from the way Howard resolved the story, with everybody getting what he or she wants. If the reader were to reread the plot summary, he or she might notice that Amy and Joe have, in fact, committed adultery, and Amy is about to bear a child out of wedlock. The surprise and, in some cases, shock, for portions of the audience in 1924, apparently had little to do with Joe's I.W.W. membership, and everything to do with the fact that Joe and Amy are not punished for their sin—Amy is not left a fallen woman, and Joe leaves free of responsibilities. The concept of this kind of poetic or divine justice might seem quaint to the twenty-first-century reader, but Howard's handling of the characters, and the solution he proposed, broke a number of long-standing theatrical conventions—and for some, these conventions, in fact, constituted taboos.

As Heywood Broun succinctly pointed out, "All traditions of the theatre and most traditions of life say that nothing but stark misery can possibly come out of this situation. She [Amy] must slink away with Joe, whom she does not love and who does not love her" (Broun, "Seeing Things at Night"). Krutch writes along much the same lines, referring to some dramaturgical remarks from the one-time "Dean" of American Playwrights, Bronson Howard, who stated rather ominously: "The wife who has once taken the step from purity to impurity can never reinstate herself in the world of art this side of the grave" (qtd. in Krutch 51). Krutch acknowledges the changing times that *They Knew What They Wanted* helped to usher in:

> There is no primary intention to challenge or even shock the spectator but it is plain that audiences even considerably later than those which Bronson Howard had in mind would have been, not only shocked, but so bewildered by the difference between their preconceptions and the preconceptions of the author that the play would have completely failed of its effect and the audience would not even have known in what direction its sympathy was supposed to go out. (Krutch 52)

The tradition Sidney Howard overturned for his happy ending had a long history in theatre, and for many, that tradition was connected to a strong sense of morality—a morality that, for a few, had been violated by the onstage antics of the *They Knew What They Wanted* company. While the shocked few seemed clearly outnumbered, they would indeed be heard, and they would have their day in court, so to speak. This hearing would constitute the scandalous side of the play's history.

Critics, most audiences, and ultimately the Pulitzer committee appreciated the comic common sense of the resolution, but the play ran afoul of those who wanted to clean up Broadway. "Play juries," drawn from diverse Broadway theatergoers, were called upon to judge the decency of Howard's play (as well as O'Neill's *Desire Under the Elms*, which played the same season and indeed shares some story elements). One New York reporter broke down the makeup of this particular play jury as "several professional men, a novelist, a newspaper publisher, a sculptor, an Ethical Culture Society leader and a group of women prominent both for their own civic activities and as the wives of professors, artists or writers." With regard to the findings of the play jury, the reported noted sardonically, "It was a chuckling theatrical world last night when word came that the first citizen play juries ever to function as purifiers of Broadway had found almost nothing about which to complain.... Complaints on these plays were based on their treatment of sex, both plays dealing with the problem in a serious manner" ("36 Play Jurors" 8). As one of a long line of battles between purifiers and theatre artists (certainly neither the first nor the last), the victory was not an insignificant one by any means.

It is worth noting that although *They Knew What They Wanted* was "acquitted" (as was *Desire*), the Will Hays Office was greatly reluctant to allow a filming of Howard's popular play (White 27). Eventually, the play would be filmed three times.[11] Along with Howard's clever positioning of Joe's I.W.W. sentiments in terms of the play's structure and emphasis, this diversionary scandal also took considerable attention away from, and potential heat off of, any "radicalism" audiences might have found and objected to in the production.

As Joe makes his final exit at play's end, Amy and Tony have reconciled, and Joe is free to leave, his next destination left up in the air. He is free to wander, think, or get back in the scrap, as he himself might put it. In turn, Howard invites, or at least allows, his audiences to leave with their views confirmed of Wobblies as "I-Won't-Workers," as Joe's freedom appears to be what he wants—or, as Tony puts it, "Looka Joe. Joe is wantin' go with Wobblies, eh? With goddam Wobblies" (Howard *They Knew What They Wanted* 121). Tony's dismissal of the Wobblies at this point in the play is significant, for it is at this crucial moment that Tony is meant to earn full audience sympathy and support. Tony's solution is meant to be the one of common sense and practicality, two qualities that neither Howard nor his audience would apply to the Wobblies. The picture of Joe, and how the audience is most likely meant to read him, is therefore complete—not unsympathetic by any means, but young, beautiful, and fundamentally rootless and irresponsible. That Joe is the play's Wobbly representative extends the description to the I.W.W. itself. In other words, the rhetorical and sympathetic deck is too stacked against Joe for the play to be "pro-I.W.W.," strictly speaking, even as the play acknowledges Joe's basic decency and humanity. Nevertheless, Howard allows some room for his I.W.W. journalism as well as his desire to let his characters present their sides of the story.

The time of the play also makes Joe's desire to rejoin the Wobblies more significant, because Joe is looking to join a union that had just suffered its most damaging blow. While the I.W.W. continues to argue adamantly that 1924 was not the historical end of the Wobblies, the fact remained that someone like Joe would not be returning to the union he had temporarily left. The free speech fight in San Pedro that Joe refers to would be, according to Fred Thompson, "the last such large scale effort by IWW" (Fred Thompson *The I.W.W.* 141). Joe might not have any kick coming as he leaves, but he would most likely have to either find another cause, or immerse himself in a much weakened I.W.W.

That Howard is cagey regarding any sort of definitive stance is not surprising for a commercial playwright of the 1920s; what perhaps is somewhat surprising is that the I.W.W. angle exists in the play at all—the fact that Joe is a member of the I.W.W. adds comparatively little to the proceedings in terms of plot or even character development. Along with how the character of Joe was generally perceived, this apparent irrelevance to the plot undoubtedly also contributed to the ultimate forgetting, or dismissing, of the Wobbly part of the play for most audiences. In spite of Joe's opening I.W.W. song, few Broadway witnesses could be said to "Remember."

Indeed, Joe's political as well as his union leanings became relics of another world quickly—the references to the I.W.W. and Wobblies were cut in a 1950s television version of the play with the reasoning that no one would know who the Wobblies were or what the I.W.W. had been ("Radio: Drama for an Hour"). Composer-lyricist Frank Loesser, who in 1952 started work on the musical version of the story that would become the popular *The Most Happy Fella*, was enamored with the basic story idea, but, to put the matter in his own words: "I figured take out all this political talk, the labor talk, and the religious talk. Get rid of all that stuff and you have a good love story" (Wilk 330–331). Whatever one might think of Loesser's critical acumen with regard to Howard's work, the man did have a point—make Joe a simple drifter with undesignated political or union affiliation, and the love story would certainly remain intact. Indeed, such reasoning was perhaps not unjustified—the *New York Times* would report on the I.W.W. again as old-timers gathered for the Wobblies' fiftieth anniversary in 1955. The initials "I.W.W.," the article explains, mean "Industrial Workers of the World" ("I.W.W. is 50 Years Old").[12] No such explanation was necessary 31 years earlier, when audiences first got a good look at a "dark, sloppy, beautiful" young man who sang Wobbly songs and had some vague ideas about wanting to change things—a potentially dangerous young man whom Howard tamed (somewhat), then banished from the idyllic vineyard.

If that ending sounds harsh, however, it might be appropriate to keep in mind Joe's "broad grin" as well as Tony and Amy's loving and passionate embrace as the curtain falls. Howard's "sound" and "solid" construction paid off handsomely; the Guild audience took an attitude of paternal tolerance toward the (perhaps temporarily) wayward Joe, as well as an attitude of amused understanding toward what seemed to be a "new morality." While the sexual elements might have shocked a few, for most, any shock most likely wore off in the warmth of three sympathetic characters getting what they wanted with no one having to suffer greatly for any perceived sin. If, as John Gassner opined in his introduction to the play, the new morality and new tolerance was not of primary interest to Howard, it mattered little. The playwright emerged with a hit play, major prizes, and a thriving and respected career until his fatal farming-related accident in 1939.

If Howard found a way to make the Wobbly sensibility acceptable (or tolerable) to a mass upper- and middle-class audience, the event might at least partially verify one of Adorno's observations about mass culture and art. As David Gartman explains:

> The autonomy of high art from the market is destroyed, and it is leveled into a homogeneous, standardized mass culture whose sole purpose is to make money by giving consumers what they want—immediate gratification of desires repressed by the totally administered society. The crude physicality and rebellion of popular culture, which testify to the deprivation of the lower class, are also destroyed, as mass culture sanitizes and "civilizes" the expression of this group to make it acceptable in "polite society." (Gartman 46)

Perhaps it is accurate to say that the "crude physicality" of the Wobblies, along with their rebellion, do indeed become "civilized" in the course of Howard's popular and prize-winning play. The idea could be at the heart of the problematic task of putting the Wobblies on Broadway, which in retrospect makes Howard's successful balancing act all the more impressive. Adorno himself put the issue of entertainment as a form of manufacturing: "The entertainment manufacturers know that their products will be consumed with alertness even when the customer is distraught, for each of them is a model of the huge economic machinery which has always sustained the masses, whether at work or at leisure—which is akin to work" (Horkheimer and Adorno 1972, 127, qtd. in Gartman 45). The Wobblies, whose goal was always to stop the world of manufacturing, were never a natural fit for the commercial realities of Broadway. In other words, setting a Wobbly character in an environment (in this case, a Broadway play with the express and immediate goal of making a profit) meant to sustain the very capitalistic environment that the Wobblies sought to overthrow through sabotage, could well be the height of irony or of folly, and could certainly give the social historian and the theatre critic considerable pause. Or, as Tony suggests, we could always take a pinch of snuff and shut up.

For the next "Wobbly" play, the scene shifts from the pastoral to the urban, with the accompanying sound of that most American of city music, jazz. This play, by John Howard Lawson, did not have the run or the award recognition that *They Knew What They Wanted* had amassed, but the production was still considered a success in its day, and certainly provided a considerable amount of heated (and occasionally acrimonious) discussion regarding where the American drama was headed. How the play works to position jazz and the Wobblies in the emerging American scene presents something of a landmark in the annals of Broadway-Wobbly folklore. This achievement is perhaps all the more surprising, especially given the distinct possibility that the play is not truly a "Wobbly" one at all. The result is the challengingly rough and tumble *Processional*, which, of all the plays under study, might well be the purest attempt to create art which, in Adorno's words, "take[s] up the cause of that which is branded ugly" (Adorno *Minima Moralia* 72).

4. Jazzing the Wobblies: John Howard Lawson's *Processional*

Simply put, 1925 was not a good year to be a Wobbly. Indeed, we have reached the point in our study where many, in the words of the I.W.W. website, "sectarian Leftist historians...end their histories of the IWW." The website goes on in a protesting tone: "Such histories are an injustice to the IWW, particularly following 1924" ("Chronology of IWW History"). One of the key talents of I.W.W. chronologists and historians is making the Wobblies appear to be a constant and active presence long past what might at first appear to be their expiration date. Nevertheless, even indefatigable I.W.W. chronicler Fred Thompson had a hard time writing about 1925, pretty much drawing a blank from the 1924 split until the 1927 protest demonstrations centered around the Sacco-Vanzetti executions. As Thompson admits, "progress was inconspicuous" (Thompson *The I.W.W.* 152). The I.W.W. website fares little better in terms of highlighting 1925, noting that the Philadelphia MTW went to the ILA (i.e., the Marine Transport Workers defected to the International Longshoreman's Association) over the 1924 split, and recording an I.W.W.-led coal miners' strike in Alberta.

Nevertheless, if historians with the tool of hindsight frequently ring down the curtain on the Wobblies post-1924, the Wobblies themselves were determinedly unaware of their demise. Equally unaware, for the most part, were audiences of popular theatre, including the subscription audience of the Theatre Guild. We now proceed to the first month of the year 1925.

By January 1925, the year *Processional* opened on Broadway, the I.W.W., as noted, had just suffered its final major debilitating split the year before. That the schism was largely the result of a political rejection of the growing Communist Party (CP) was somewhat ironic, given that the popular imagination still, and would continue to, link the "Red" and the "Wobbly" ideologies together. (The fact that many Wobbly leaders fled to Russia or became Communists also proved to be a great determining factor in this conception, or misconception, as the case may be.) This popular conflation of the communists and the I.W.W. was evident in the entertainment of the day, including the cartoon features preceding motion pictures that audiences enjoyed around the time *Processional* made its mark on the Theatre Guild.[1]

One of the more interesting Walt Disney creations of 1925 was part of a series of "Alice" cartoon shorts—Alice was played by a real little girl, and she was surrounded by animation. In the episode "Alice's Egg Plant" (a factory where the worker hens laid eggs, hence the "eggplant" pun), Alice's plant is threatened by the diabolical "Little Red Henski," a subversive chicken from Russia with "I.W.W." printed on his suitcase. (The clever and resourceful chicken is able to hide his suitcase under the railroad tracks, but not before we get a good look at it.) The Henski organizes the workers to call for a strike, as henskis are wont to do, and Alice and her foreman (a friendly cat) wind up devising a sporting entertainment where the admission is one egg each. As Alice and the cat collect the admission eggs, their plant productivity problem is solved (until the eggs break in the final, somewhat dark, gag).

Students of Disney history conjecture some parallels between Walt Disney starting a fledgling company (the talkies, where Mickey Mouse truly came to life, were a couple years away yet) and having problems with unionizing.[2] At any rate, apart from the allegorical references to distracting the workers with mindless recreation in an animated example of *panem et circenses*, the short illustrates the casual conflation of strikes, the I.W.W., and the CP. This is the conflation that also permeates the response to John Howard

Lawson's *Processional*—dubbed "a symphony in red" by the *New York Telegram-Mail*'s Gilbert Gabriel. And the symphony, as Lawson added as a subtitle, was a "jazz symphony of American life." This chapter addresses how jazz and the Wobblies came together in what would later, during the Depression under the auspices of the Federal Theatre Project, be advertised as "the first modern American play."[3]

To consider the use of jazz in Lawson's *Processional*, we might begin with Adorno's examination of jazz. Adorno confesses early on that "the question of what is meant by jazz seems impossible to answer with a clear definition" (Adorno *Night Music* 118). The confusion and conflation among commentators regarding jazz, that Adorno appears to share at the beginning of his essay, dates to the early part of the twentieth century. Jazz, depending on the critic and his or her perspective, could refer to any sort of dance music that was fast, syncopated, or, in some way, different. Nevertheless, understanding how Lawson relates "jazz" to the working class in his play necessitates an understanding of how jazz operated in the play and for its audience. Adorno's observations in this case prove enlightening, even if the reader questions whether or not Adorno really "got" jazz.[4]

Returning to Adorno's jazz essay: "One could say that it [jazz] refers to the relam of dance music, whether used directly for that purpose or slightly stylized, since the war, which stands apart from the previous kind through a decided, but still highly ill-defined, character of modernity" (Adorno *Night Music* 118–119). The link between the idea of "modernity" and the idea of an American art form is an important factor in the stage life of *Processional*. In Lawson's preface to the play first published in the *New York Times* in February 1925, he addresses his intentions to "express the American scene in native idiom, a method as far removed from the older realism as from the facile mood of expressionism" (Lawson, "On 'Processional'"). Lawson's definition of "native," closely related to the idea of modern (and the distance from "older realism"), dovetails interestingly with Adorno's observation regarding the "ill-defined character of modernity." How jazz made Lawson's play "modern," and how Lawson related jazz, or his concept of jazz, to the working class, and how the whole picture relates to staging Wobblies makes for a colorful section of our study. How the production was read by the audiences of the then already prestigious Theatre Guild is also worth exploring.

By 1925, the Theatre Guild, or more popularly, simply "the Guild," had been producing some of the most important, experimental, and adventurous American and world drama for the past seven seasons, and had firmly secured its place as, in John Gassner's words, "the foremost theatrical organization in America" (Gassner "The Happy Years" xviii). In the midst of the Guild's quest for innovation was Lawson's wild, difficult-to-classify piece of Americana, and in the midst of Lawson's play was a hint of Wobbly philosophy. This hint, interestingly enough, might not have been as great as many of the eyewitnesses seem to insist.

In fact, whether or not *Processional* fits in the "Wobbly" play category is an arguable point. The play is nevertheless remembered as being "Wobbly" and "radical" in tone and subject, pointing to the interesting differences between memory and content—or, as William Faulkner put it in *Light in August*, "memory believes before knowing remembers." The venerable George Abbott himself, who played the lead role and went on to direct plays and musicals till his hundredth birthday had passed, had this to say about the Theatre Guild's production in his memoirs published some 35 years after *Processional*'s premiere: "The Guild was in its heyday; it produced boldly and made many innovations," Abbott begins. His comments then grow increasingly wry and terse:

> Harold Clurman, Lee Strasberg and Sanford Meisner played members of the Ku Klux Klan. Not type-casting.[5] I played a radical organizer who was hunted by the Ku Klux Klan and blinded by soldiers—it was that kind of play. It was also very poetic, and [theatre impresario] John Golden ridiculed it. 'When a man can't create a real love scene, he writes vague talk about the stars just to cover up his incompetence,' he said. Philip Moeller, who was the director, wasn't very good, but he was artistic. It was a success. (Abbott 108–109)[6]

What is perhaps most notable about Abbott's reminiscences is how the passage of time altered his perceptions of the play and his role in it, and how the play's reception generally shaped Abbott's memory—that is, "it was that kind of play." Abbott was not one to elaborate, but we are free to ask, "what kind of play, exactly?" And, as we are primarily interested in the I.W.W. aspects of *Processional*, we might also ask, "How 'Wobbly' was this play?"

The answer to both questions depends partly on vastly imperfect collective and theatrical memory. The plot itself was not especially complicated; in terms of linear progression, the play tells a fugitive story involving a man on the run and an innocent girl who falls for him. It is in terms of presentation that the play takes on the layers of meaning that might have interfered with the memory of the original participants and witnesses of the event. An interested researcher need only read the script to see how great the gaps are between memory and what Lawson set down in script form. For example, Abbott's character, Dynamite Jim, was not a radical organizer.[7] He was simply an angry drunk caught in the middle of a strike and arrested along with the workers in a general sweep. His longest exposure to union rhetoric happens offstage as he and the play's actual radical organizer, the vocal Pole Jake Psinski, are hiding in the basement of his mother's place. Jim's response to Psinski's union-based exhortations are far from that of a "radical organizer"—Jim pops out of the trapdoor, gun in hand, exclaiming, "gotta breathe, that feller talks his head off, mebbe I could make a run for it!" (Lawson *Processional* 53). If Lawson's goal was a subversion of theatrical and American values, it seems clear that the radicals were as much an object of satire as the capitalists.

Even when the blinded Jim refers to Jake and the miners as "pals" in the final act, his connection to any cause is tenuous at best, and when the workers create the final jazz procession that marches down the aisles of the theatre, Jim and his pregnant bride Sadie are left alone onstage. Brooks Atkinson's remark that the play mentions belief in the I.W.W.—"typical of the folklore of the twenties" (Atkinson *Lively Years* 44)—is also pertinent, as of course is his use of the term "folklore." Belief in the I.W.W.? Readers who peruse Lawson's script will find the term "Wobbly" mentioned exactly once.

That's it. Once.

It happens during a brief exchange between a soldier and the sheriff regarding the fugitive Dynamite Jim.

"Is he a Wobbly?" the soldier asks.

"He ain't a Democrat," the belligerent sheriff replies, "that's all I aim to know about a man" (Lawson *Processional* 30).

This two-line exchange is the extent of the discussion of Wobblies in the play.

The question arises: why would both Abbott and Atkinson, two reliable professionals with a lifetime of theatrical tenure, think of *Processional* as "that kind of play"? The play's "Wobbliness," at least in the script, is rather slight, to say the least. Nevertheless, Atkinson was proven right in a sense; the play strongly entered and added to the "folklore" of the Wobblies on Broadway. Lawson drew on the turbulent history of coal miner strikes in West Virginia (a history which would continue throughout the twentieth century)—strikes supported by the I.W.W.—and it is likely that he could count on his audience to associate striking workers as well as criticism of capitalist institutions with the Wobblies and the I.W.W. Indeed, the 40-odd-year history of the West Virginia mine wars would have been well known to even the casual follower of labor struggle, including the Paint Creek-Cabin Creek Strike and the battles of Matewan and Blair Creek.[8] The I.W.W. itself, through its literature and self-promotion—including its own version of songs and vaudevilles—was, in large part, responsible for this association as well.[9] While there is comparatively little direct connection between the Wobblies and the world of Lawson's play, the collective Wobbly *story* contributed to the way audiences and witnesses, including Atkinson and, most likely, Abbott, received the play, and consequently contributed to the expansion of Wobbly "folklore." The combination of jazz, a multinational aggregation of striking workers, and the mere mention of the word "Wobbly" was unstoppable—willy-nilly, *Processional* became a Wobbly play telling a Wobbly story.

Lawson's ambitious attempts to use "lowbrow" entertainment forms to convey high-minded idealism no doubt contributed to the divided reactions of the Guild audiences as well as the critics. One fan wrote a letter to the *New York Times* not long after the show's opening bearing witness to the diverse reactions of the audience. On the letter-writer's third enthusiastic viewing of the production, he paid close, and amused, attention to some of his fellow theatergoers that best illustrated what might be called the two types of *Processional* audiences. The fan describes the first group of people as straining particularly hard to follow the onstage antics, not wanting to miss whatever it was that was making the production such an important event, and engaging in pointed, if hushed, debate throughout. The writer then portrays another small group of people simply enjoying the show, as well as some candy (unwrapped noisily during the performance, one imagines), not overly concerned about any messages or portents the show might contain. The idea that those who think too much at the theatre are miserable and those who just "go with it" have more fun is perhaps a tired notion, but apparently accurate in this instance (Grainger "In the Dramatic Mail Bag"). The varied and various audience reactions amplify Marvin Carlson's observation regarding audience response to work that could be considered unusual: "Theatre history provides many examples of audiences that have not at all responded to a performed work in the expected manner.... Problems are particularly likely to arise when an experimental work resists the reading strategies of an audience expecting something more conventional" (Carlson 85). The *Processional* fans' accounts seem to confirm that the audience members who garnered the most enjoyment from the experience were those who did not treat the production like a conventional theatre (or Theatre Guild) offering.

Opening night reviewers also noted audience response—in this case, apparently, the consensus was much less divided on opening night than later. According to the reviewers' reports, the final curtain was met with a damning and outraged silence. As an example, sympathetic critic Heywood Broun, in his column "Seeing Things at Night," remarked: "To me this curious and somewhat pretentious experiment is among the most absorbing things which the present season has to offer," followed by, "I have never seen a play received in such sullen silence" (Broun "Seeing Things at Night" A48).

In turn, Percy Hammond, writing for the *New York Herald*, admitted the sheer novelty the evening provided: "The play was different, at least." His fairly faint praise ends there as he proceeds with a plot summary:

> At any rate, it seems that there was a ragtime strike in the West Virginia coal mines, with a stage Jew, his pretty daughter, a Polish anarchist, some burlesque soldiers and a newspaper reporter aimlessly coming and going, and muttering as they did so. Mr. George Abbot as Dynamite Jim, a fire-eating miner, broke jail, murdered a guardsman, made Sadie Cohen a woman, and was strung up by the authorities, losing the sight of both eyes.
>
> The actors seemed to be making it up as they went along. (Hammond "The Theatres: Some Mysterious Proceedings" 12)

That Hammond sets up his summary in the classic structure of telling a joke is not insignificant; many of the critics took Lawson's project as something of a radical lark or leg-pulling. Nevertheless, apart from the questionable, if not downright disturbing, use of the euphemism "made Sadie Cohen a woman" in describing what is in fact a rape, Hammond is not inaccurate with regard to either events or stage types. How these events and stage types were received provided some colorful continued argument and commentary in the pages of the daily papers, and, one may fairly imagine, in the theatres, on the streets, and in a number of homes as well.

It was Stark Young, writing for the *New York Times*, who gave one of the most enthusiastic reviews of the play, while acknowledging that the work did not always succeed and that there appeared aspects of the production that were "full of the amateur." In a burst of praise that seemed very much in tune with what Lawson was attempting, Young wrote: "It was a mixture of the serious, the vaudeville, the halls of jazz, a twisting and turning of the idea, great matter stirred up, passion and blood and revolution thrown into the air and brought down again to the rattle and sigh of drums and sliding horns, life stirred, shaken, dared, outraged, dreamed of and made beautiful, ending always in jazz." Young further appreciated the idea of "jazzing" the American scene and American mores, "well spanked by a writer who seemed a poet, a genius, a college sophomore not yet grown up and a dramatic journalist by turns" (Young "The Play: Jazzing Folly and Beauty" 17).

What is perhaps most striking about Young's observations is that in a broad sense, even those who vehemently despised the play acknowledged many of the same elements—witness, for example, an annoyed theatergoer writing to the *New York Times* a few weeks after the opening: "To begin at the beginning, let us grant in theory that Mr. Lawson had an idea when he wrote his play: to express American life in American rhythms. I say 'in theory,' for I do not think Mr. Lawson can be accused of anything so definite as an idea" (Seaver X2). The public and critics, while disagreeing over quality and success, seemed to agree with the intent and the core concept—American life expressed in uniquely American terms, that is, the stage types of burlesque and vaudeville, and the rhythms of jazz. They also seemed to agree that Lawson was behaving as the amalgam Young describes—part naughty boy, part new artist to watch, part shrewd observer, and part screwball.

The concept of jazz as well as its use also stumped many critics and audiences. "Like jazz," Burns Mantle wrote for the *Daily News*, beginning just as tentatively about the subject as Adorno does, "'Processional' is probably not to be understood.... It is satire and muttered ravings.... They will have their happy endings, these young progressives with cobwebs in their brains. I hope the subscribers like it," Mantle snorts, referring to the Theatre Guild subscription audience, "'Processional' is by the author of 'Roger Bloomer,' busy in a padded cell" (Mantle "'Processional is a Discordant Jumble" 24).[10]

While one might wonder how Mantle pulled a happy ending out of a final scene involving a blind man and his pregnant wife alone onstage as the jazz procession passes them by (it could be that the music fooled him), Mantle is otherwise not necessarily wrong about the play—upon reading, "satire and muttered ravings" does not seem too far off the mark.[11] Lawson was, however, deadly serious in his pranking, and a connection between his dramaturgical aims and the program of the Wobblies might bring his work into a clearer light. For the Wobblies and Lawson might well have had similar agendas in terms of subversion and sabotage.

The world of Lawson's *Processional* sought to be subversive in all aspects of production, in both large and small details. Director Philip Moeller saw the project as an opportunity to work with his cast in "a sort of intellectual democracy—born not free of errors, but equal in intelligence" (Stone C14). (With regard to George Abbott's earlier, rather disparaging, remarks about Moeller as a director, Moeller's ideas of a cast democracy might not have met future director Abbott's approval.) Moeller himself described a pertinent example of subversive staging: "By utilizing the orchestra pit as an entrance and exit for this play we have done something I have never seen done before. But every one [*sic*] seems to accept it without comment, as though it had always been done" (Stone C14). Moeller's comments point to his attempts to creative a subversive piece of work in line with Lawson's imagination, thwarting audience's expectations even at the basic level of actors' entrances and exits. Interestingly, perhaps Moeller inadvertently showed how quickly audiences can accept a convention or the breaking of a convention if it used consistently. Lawson further subverts audience expectations with unusual musical interludes (the onstage jazz band), the use of vaudeville conventions (such as the sets and the stock characters, including the fussy stage Jew with the exaggerated accent and the lazy Negro), and utilizing the newspaperman, Philpotts, as a voice of brutal cynicism (laced with some romantic sentimentality). Philpotts serves as another important subversive figure, as he is directly described by Lawson as a "George M. Cohan" type of newspaperman. Audiences would have been well familiar with the work of Cohan since the beginning of the century. By 1925, Cohan was securely a living and working legend, the Yankee Doodle Dandy who practically invented the unique personification of American morality and integrity in his early musicals. Many of the same audiences further enjoyed Cohan's forays into business farces—filled with heroes who conquered all with their breezy manner and casual conversation that could turn the most outright business frauds into something true and valuable. Lawson employs one of the major embodiments of bright, can-do Americanism to tell the striking workers in the jazz band that they do not stand a chance. (He also gets to observe at Dynamite Jim and Sadie Cohen's "jazz wedding" that she has transformed from a "Yiddishe Rose" to an "American Beauty"—a line Cohan himself would, no doubt, have appreciated.) While the actor in the original production, colorfully named Donald MacDonald, was not a veteran of Cohan shows, he appeared in major roles in his share of comedies and musicals throughout a fairly busy career, including the popular farce *Getting Gertie's Garter*. He would, in other words, have been at home as a Cohan type, and most likely recognized as such a type by the audience.

It is this subversion that marks a possible kinship between Lawson's play and the Wobbly agenda, which, as noted, favored a radical subversion of the owner-worker relationship and a fundamentally jocular, and often musical, approach toward their serious demonstrations of work stoppage, free speech, and attempted social change. *Processional* itself finds a way to enter the world of Broadway, confuse and confound its producers, patrons, and practitioners, and leave audiences in an agitated state. Lawson's (somewhat barbed) sympathy toward workers and his willingness to attack the middle-class verities of the largely middle-class and upwardly striving audience jibes in many ways with a "Wobbly" sensibility. In language that Wobblies would most likely have approved of, playwright Elmer Rice said of the play: "He says, this Lawson, that the noble cult of social justice is largely bunk; he says that the noble cult of patriotism is largely bunk; he says that the noble cult of motherhood (noblest of all the noble cults!) is largely bunk" (qtd. in Chambers 67). Later in this study, we will bear witness to other playwrights crying "bunk" to American ideals of government and justice, often through the mouths of Wobbly characters.

Although the playwright is not always the best source for a clear explanation of intent or concept, Lawson's introduction to the play is quite clear even if the stage picture occasionally (or more than occasionally) was not. "It is only in the fields of vaudeville and review that a native craftsmanship exists," he writes in his introduction. "Here the concern is with a direct contact, an immediate emotional response across the footlights" (Lawson "On 'Processional'" X2). Lawson saw songs, vaudeville, and comic routines as necessary for direct audience contact; the Wobblies used songs, skits, and parody as a backdrop for their idea of direct action. While the comparisons may well be considerably stretched, the ideas may well have contributed to the shared "memory" that *Processional* was "that kind of" Wobbly play. One might take the *Processional*-Wobbly connection a bit further, as Lawson freely admits, "I am not offering solutions. I am not even stating a concise question" (Lawson X2). While the Wobblies thought they were indeed offering solutions (and stating concise questions), both question and answer proved elusive.

While the style of production was strikingly new to the critics and audiences, Lawson's conclusions also strike a similar tone to the bulk of "Wobbly" Broadway drama of the 1920s—not only are the not-too-bright hero and heroine left alone with little but the prospect of the impending birth of their child (conceived, as noted earlier, by way of rape), but, as the character of the newspaper reporter cynically notes to the radical Psinski: "The laugh is always on you" (Lawson *Processional* 79). The comment is prompted by the transparent display of worker peace and harmony engineered by the allegorical "Man in the Silk Hat." The workers may have "the jazz...for the glory of the working class" (11), but the capitalist men in silk hats still call the shots. As is often the case in the plays under study, there seems to be great sympathy for the cause (although the cause itself also comes in for its share of barbs and spanking), but little confidence that the noise and the jazz will have lasting value.

If we argue for *Processional* as a "Wobbly-esque" play, we might also take Abbott at his word regarding his portrayal, that is, quite possibly if he thought he was playing a radical organizer, the audience, or a good portion of it, might have thought the same. If such is the case, the physicality of Abbott is a significant consideration. Abbott was a towering and imposing figure, and remained so well into his later years. It is not inconceivable that Abbott's physical presence also caused audience members to make a connection between the character of Dynamite Jim and the threatening figure of the Wobbly still popular in editorial cartoons familiar to many audience members. Although, as Ryan Jerving points out in his *Modern Drama* article on *Processional,* Abbott's character is ultimately subjected to the lowest forms of slapstick as he is captured, such a towering image might also have contributed to the memory that Abbott played a radical who believed in the I.W.W. (Jerving 531). In following these suppositions, it is also worth remembering that the play does have its own radical, the Pole Jake Psinski, whose speechifying is rendered as something of a joke as Dynamite Jim runs directly into danger in order to get away from the radical's nonstop worker-centered (and possibly Wobbly-style) rhetoric. Again, memory proves selective in terms of just how much belief in the Wobblies the play in fact was advocating.

The physicality of the play's true radical, Jake Psinski, might also be worth considering. The role was created by veteran character actor Charles Halton, who was already in his late 40s by the time *Processional* was first produced. Halton, with thinning hair and appearance sometimes described as "birdlike," specialized in playing officious busybodies. (Movie buffs would recognize him from *It's a Wonderful Life* as the bank examiner—also an officious, "it's my job" type, although he is won over like the others in the overwhelming wave of good cheer that cascades upon Bedford Falls by the end of the movie.) The fact that the anarchist (and possible

Wobbly) of the play is played and embodied by Halton is a fairly strong statement regarding how Lawson and director Moeller meant the audience to read Psinski as a radical force. Psinski is positioned in the play through his dialogue, the hero's response to him, and his physicality as someone not delivering a message meant to sway a capitalistic audience, but rather as someone one would very much like to shut up already. This particularly salient element of the play's dramaturgy is not commented upon by those who remember the play as one with a Wobbly heart and soul.

Also worth noting is the maintaining of the characters' physicality in the 1937 Federal Theatre Project revival. Dynamite Jim, in continuing the model set by Abbott, is played by big, burly character actor George Matthews (just a couple of inches shorter than Abbott, but somewhat bigger-featured). The radical Psinski was played by Joseph Kramm, by his own admission a once-promising actor who never advanced beyond promising, and who would later gain fame and a Pulitzer Prize as a playwright for his 1952 play *The Shrike* (Kramm "A Personal History"). While Kramm most likely lacked the distinct birdlike presence of Psinski's original interpreter (Kramm once played David Garrick in a short-lived 1932 comedy about Jane Austen), it seems safe to say that the *Processional* revival retained a good deal of the physical dynamics of the 1925 production.

There is also a case to be made for the similarities between the often brutal Dynamite Jim and our first (anti-)hero under examination, *The Hairy Ape*'s equally brutal and perhaps equally confused Yank. As Jonathan L. Chambers illustrates, like Yank, "Jim is a brutish antihero who has been plucked from the fringes of society, thrust into the midst of an excessively violent civilization, and forced to commit acts of irrational cruelty and unimaginable violence in order to exist" (Chambers 62). Admittedly, the reader might argue as to whether either Yank or Dynamite Jim are truly "forced" to commit their most brutal acts, or what forces are truly acting on the characters. Nevertheless, the suggestion of kinship between the two characters is a valid one, and one might also find similarity in the two characters' intimidating physicality, which most likely had a lasting effect on audiences, as well as the fact that while both antiheroes interact tenuously with the Wobbly world, neither quite belong there—although both plays had the reputation of being "Wobbly" in nature. In a sense, both Yank and Dynamite Jim search for where to get off at, and the Wobblies are either unable or unwilling to provide even a temporary home.

Another element of Lawson's dramaturgy that is either remembered or misremembered, touching on another part of the growing "folklore" surrounding the play, is the element of "expressionism." Part of the confusion is Lawson's own doing, as he explicitly distanced himself from the notion of expressionism in his introduction, as noted earlier. It is probably fair to say that elements of expressionism, in the sense that the set and the mood reflect the feelings and inner conflicts of the character under examination, are present in *Processional*, and even most critics who found fault with the play found themselves impressed with the overall look and the set design. [12] It is perhaps a notable comparison that just as Lawson sought to distance himself from the foreign (German) idea of expressionism even though audiences and critics even vaguely familiar with the term saw the expressionistic elements fairly clearly, the Wobblies, whose philosophy was closely aligned with the foreign (French) idea of syndicalism sought to distance themselves from that notion as well. The need for American playwrights and American radicals to identify as American was by no means a small one, whether one was an artist searching for a new kind of American theatre, or a discontented worker searching for a way to build a new society "in the shell of the old."

At length, the arguments, both good-natured and otherwise, continued through the moderate run of *Processional*—indeed successful, as Abbott correctly remembered, if more of a scandalous success than a "long run" (it ran 90 performances). As with most arguments regarding a theatrical production, and indeed with all arguments regarding matters of pure opinion, all sides were right and wrong. What the audience was supposed to take away from *Processional* most likely had less to do with Wobblies and their agenda and more to do with challenging the way a comfortable Broadway audience looked at what they considered "prestigious" theatre. Nevertheless, as previously noted, the air and atmosphere of Wobblies clung tenaciously to the play even if, perhaps, such a result was not the intention of anyone involved. As a testament to the connection people made between the 1920s' "social" drama and the I.W.W., *Processional* stands as a unique monument to the widespread perception of Wobblies and their attendant folklore. Whether or not one agrees with the more effusive estimations of Lawson's work, and whether or not one reads the play as "Wobbly" in nature, the play is a fascinating contribution to the Wobbly legend.[13]

The idea of the jazz symphony might best be summed up by a return to Adorno, who noted, "If people actually listened to jazz properly, it would lose its power; rather than identifying with it, they would identify the music itself" (Adorno *Night Music* 170). It may well be that audiences and critics, as well as Lawson, were unable to listen to jazz properly. But it made for a colorful evening of theatre. Lawson would go on, in the next phase of his career, to help found the New Playwrights Theatre, who would later produce Upton Sinclair's *Singing Jailbirds*.

It took an especially dark chapter in the history of American justice—certainly an incredibly controversial one—to inspire the next Wobbly play under study. The case was the notorious Sacco and Vanzetti affair, a case that would sufficiently haunt coauthor Maxwell Anderson to inspire two plays. The second play was by far the more successful and honored in its time, 1936's verse drama *Winterset*. It was the first of these plays, however, *Gods of the Lightning* from 1928, that wore an angry, romantic, and perhaps sentimental Wobbly heart on its sleeve. The notable attempt by Anderson, along with his partner Harold Hickerson, to make a familiar type of American stage hero into a proud member of the I.W.W. provides an interesting chapter of labor struggles as the Wobblies on Broadway take another heroic, if futile, stand against injustice.

5. Dead Hand of the Dead: Anderson and Hickerson's *Gods of the Lightning*

In many ways, the turbulent history of anarchy in the United States reached a climax with the case of Sacco and Vanzetti. In turn, the fate of Sacco and Vanzetti seemed to confirm and validate the pessimistic strain of the social protest plays under study. Maxwell Anderson and Harold Hickerson set out to capture the outraged sentiments of the time with what John Gassner called "the strongest drama of social protest produced in the 1920s" (Gassner "Introduction: *Gods of the Lightning*" 530). It is perhaps in this play that the anger and the fatalism that the age seemed to consistently evoke came together to make as close as the period comes to a definitive statement on Broadway—a statement that encompasses and acknowledges the growing resentment against the Great War, as well as the anger and gallows humor that accompanied the activism and anarchy of the I.W.W. The deaths of Sacco and Vanzetti, by extension, also reinforced the ultimate grimness and fatalism accompanying the rage.

By the time the play opened in late October 1928, the Wobblies were some four years past the great organizational split that separated many Wobblies from their brothers and sisters. The infamous case, with its roiling controversy surrounding the familiar targets of anarchy and radicalism, was something of a natural fit for a Wobbly revitalization. The I.W.W. was, along with many sympathetic voices, movements, and leaders around the world, deeply involved in the cause of Sacco and Vanzetti. It is also notable that the Wobblies had also just scored a major victory in the Colorado coal fields, thanks in large measure to the groundswell of feelings involving the Sacco-Vanzetti case. As Kornbluh recounts: "When the I.W.W. called a two-day protest strike in the summer of 1927 against the execution of Sacco and Vanzetti...half of Colorado's 12,000 miners stopped work. Their protest led to a strike which started on October 18, 1927, against company domination and lack of outlet for miners' grievances" (Kornbluh *Rebel Voices* 352). While the I.W.W. suffered loss through state police and company guard violence, the Wobblies also made modifications and improvements in their strike strategies: "Striking miners used car caravans to carry their message to other communities to persuade workers to come off their jobs" (Kornbluh *Rebel Voices* 353). "Rebel girl" Milka Sablich went on a fund-raising tour of the United States, and "Junior Wobblies" chapters were formed by and for the strikers' children. In the end, the miners won a wage bump of a dollar a day, along with "union pit committees in the mines and enforcement of all state mining laws" (353). The Wobblies were still, both rightly and wrongly, tied in the general imagination to the radical and anarchist ideas and idealists of the world, including the two Italian anarchists who, depending upon one's point of view, were either justly executed as threats to the American way of life, or flagrantly and fatally railroaded simply because they were anarchists.

The actual case became and remains famous the world over. Nicola Sacco and Bartolomeo Vanzetti were charged with a holdup and murder at a shoe factory in Brockton, Massachusetts. As Howard Zinn sums up:

> They went on trial, were found guilty, and spent seven years in jail while appeals went on, and while all over the country and the world, people became involved in their case. The trial record and the surrounding circumstances suggested that Sacco and Vanzetti were sentenced to death because they were anarchists and foreigners. In August 1927, as police broke up marches and pickets lines with arrests and beatings, and troops surrounded the prison, they were electrocuted. (Zinn 376).

Articles, books, plays, songs, and movies grew from the ongoing story of the two men, including an epic novel, *Boston*, by one of the writers represented in this study, Upton Sinclair. This outpouring of literary, journalistic, and dramatic activity represented the kind of mythmaking and folk hero creation that forms one of the major threads of this study. While, as years have passed, experts have disagreed regarding the probable guilt of at least one of the men, the trial still stands as an iconic moment that encapsulates the widespread fear of anarchy, particularly foreign anarchy.[1]

A year and two months following the execution of the pair, Maxwell Anderson and Harold Hickerson's *Gods of the Lightning* opened in New York City's Little Theatre. Wounds were still fresh, and the timing, combined with the indignation and the skill of the playwrights, should likely have created a notable sensation in the annals of American theatre history. Before the play's Broadway opening, *Gods* had already run afoul of Boston authorities. As Anderson biographer Alfred S. Shivers reports: "Boston, near which the Sacco-Vanzetti trial had taken place and where passions still ran high, was incensed at the prospect of seeing *Gods of the Lightning*...John M. Casey, chief of Boston's Licensing Division, ruled that the text was practically 'anarchistic and treasonable...'" (Shivers 311). "Anarchistic and treasonable" was quite the promising start for a Broadway-bound show, and the stage would seem to have been set for a whale of a theatrical scandal.

Indeed, reports of possible trouble led the Department of Justice to attend the premiere—no arrests, but a fair amount of note-taking, as some daily reviewers would point out. Nevertheless, the long-lasting scandalous sensation never quite materialized despite early and vivid signs of flames of unrest getting fanned. While there was some controversy and brushes with the police, the play has settled into semi-obscurity, nestled in Gassner's *Twenty-Five Best Plays of the Modern American Theatre*, without a major production since an Equity Library Theatre performance off-Broadway in the early 1960s.[2] Later critics, while generally kind to the play and especially to Anderson's intentions, mustered little more than faint praise after the fact. Edith J. R. Isaacs, writing in the December 1936 issue of the *English Journal*, refers to the play as "an admirable failure" and "not a good-enough play to do the job it set out to do. The story is not well told... The characters are slim and angular, most of them made out of one and the same cloth and not defined in color or in scale. It is too full of black and white, of hurt angels and triumphant devils..." (Isaacs 803). The play might fall under the category of propaganda, but, as has often been the case with these plays under study, the call to action was distinctly muted by an underlying fatalism.³

The Sacco and Vanzetti figures in *Gods of the Lightning* become James Macready and Dante Capraro, thus half-Americanizing the iconic real-life duo. Tellingly, Anderson and Hickerson give Macready, or "Mac," no physical description in the stage directions, while Capraro is described only as a "gentle young Italian" (538). The career criminal Suvorin (whose daughter Rosalie loves Mac) is given the more compelling description: "a solid bulk of a man, with a satanic, dominating face" (532). Together, Macready and Capraro not only stand in for Sacco and Vanzetti, but represent the gamut of nonviolent antigovernment philosophy and action, but the playwrights emphasize Suvorin's physicality for the reader at the expense of the two "principal" characters.

When Anderson and Hickerson made one of the Sacco-Vanzetti duo into an American Wobbly, they converted the play from a pure Sacco-Vanzetti allegory into one of the most blunt I.W.W. statements of the plays featured in this monograph. While the real-life Wobblies worked diligently on behalf of Sacco and Vanzetti through the Sacco and Vanzetti Defense Committee and through strikes, it was Anderson and Hickerson who chose to place the Wobblies front and center in their version of the controversial trial. The playwrights made a significant choice in making one of the radicals a rough-and-ready American heroic type that audiences could conceivably identify with. In utilizing an American Wobbly figure, the playwrights made several strong statements to its Broadway audience.

For one, dissatisfaction with the government was not just a "foreign" anarchist sentiment; hardworking Americans had legitimate gripes. And, ideally, the hardworking Americans had the right to speak freely—a long-standing theme of I.W.W. activity—but often had to face subsequent arrest. Another statement was something of a matinee move—exciting young actor Charles Bickford was advertised as having the "principal role."[4] The ultimate failure of the production, as well as the considerable spurts of furor the play aroused during its brief tenure, both speak to the interesting attempts to Americanize and humanize the radical viewpoint through the lens of the I.W.W.

Indeed, Charles Bickford created something of a strong physical presence for the Broadway audience. He was described as burly, with a powerful voice, and was groomed to be a Hollywood leading man in the James Cagney mold (Cagney and Bickford had made their Broadway debuts together in another Anderson play, *Outside Looking In*). While Bickford was not an especially successful leading man, he did score later in his career as a versatile and well-regarded character actor. The production's use of Bickford as the personification of the Wobbly is significant in terms of how the audience was meant to "read" Macready—a breezy, snappy, man-of-action type with whom the audience was meant to sympathize, despite the many inflammatory statements Anderson and Hickerson have Macready make.

Anita Block's almost breathless description of Macready's character amplifies this intention: "Macready... understands the capitalist system and the conflicts it breeds, and he expresses himself in a breezy vernacular that is a joy to the ear. Indeed, Macready is one of the unforgettable characters of contemporary American drama" (Block 231). While one might take issue with, or at least be somewhat less enthusiastic about, Block's full-throated approbation, she does seem to articulate the specific bodily and vocal type the playwrights and producers were attempting to stage.

The bodily image of Bickford was also meant to contrast with his onstage partner, Dante Capraro, played by Horace Braham. Just as Capraro is the gentler and more passive of the onstage pair, Braham's slight build made him less likely to lead or cause a fight. Later the same year, Braham would play in Elmer Rice's highly successful *Street Scene* as the sensitive, dreamy Sam Kaplan, who cannot significantly handle himself in a fight.[5] While both Bickford and Braham received strong notices from critics, it is significant that both men were completely absent from the third act, as Mac's girlfriend and a motley collection of friends and hangers-on wait for news of the impending execution. The Sacco and Vanzetti figures do not return, but improbably, Suvorin does, having made something of a superhuman (or at least unexplained) escape from prison.

Throughout the play, I.W.W. sentiments and anarchist philosophy are given full and powerful voice; the anarchists are noble and heroic, whereas those who would preserve American corporate capitalism are portrayed as craven, dishonest, and often bluntly stupid—the "angels and devils" remark by Isaacs was by no means entirely unjustified. Capraro, in the trial scene of Act II, self-identifies as an anarchist. "You would destroy all government?" the district attorney asks. "It will not be necessary. I would rather wait till it was so rotten it would rot away. That would not be so long now," Capraro replies with a smile (Anderson and Hickerson, *Gods of the Lightning* 556). Capraro similarly does not throw bombs, but he fled Italy to avoid the Great War: "It was a war for business, a war for billions of dollars, murder of young men for billions" (557). Of interest in Capraro's response is that the intended audience is meant to sympathize with the anarchist—he is not only gentle, but in the world of the play, irrefutably innocent of the crime for which he and Macready are charged (killing a paymaster). Some seven years later, Odets in *Waiting for Lefty* and *Awake and Sing* would also feature characters with jaundiced positions on the war to end all wars, but in plays that would gain considerably greater popular acceptance.

In Macready, Anderson and Hickerson create a representative Wobbly, the last such major representative on Broadway under study until O'Neill's postmortem Wobblies in *The Iceman Cometh*. Early in the play, Macready is warned by the union representative,

Bauer ("a self-important busybody"), that I.W.W. and anarchists are no longer welcome in the labor lyceum (Anderson and Hickerson 535–536). Later, during the trial, "Mac" espouses I.W.W. philosophy in an exchange with the fundamentally dishonest, and exceptionally shrewd, District Attorney Salter:

> *Salter*: Were you guilty?
> *Mac*: I was of being an I.W.W.
> *Salter*: What are the principles of the I.W.W.?
> *Mac*: One big union, organized to break the capitalistic stranglehold on natural resources.
> *Salter*: Does the I.W.W. advocate violence?
> *Mac*: Only when expedient, which is seldom.
> *Salter*: When does it consider violence expedient?
> *Mac*: Listen, we're taking up time here. If you're interested in the I.W.W.
> I've got a book I'd like to lend you. You can read it in fifteen minutes, and when you get through, you'll know something about economics. (Anderson and Hickerson 554)

Mac further denigrates the courts, the constitution ("I believe it was made by a little group of hogs to protect their own trough"), and authority in general ("Respect for authority is a superstition. And the sooner everybody gets over it, the better") throughout his examination (Anderson and Hickerson 554–555). Again, the audience is meant to be sympathetic toward several distinctly "anti-American" sentiments; in the play's most propagandistic elements, the anarchists are the ones throughout speaking most sensibly. Bickford's physicality and distinctive voice would also go a long way toward "selling" the material for the potentially unsympathetic audience.

Further, while the trial and characters are fictionalized, the playwrights place Mac in situations that were historically significant in terms of I.W.W. activity. "I was in Bisbee, Arizona, at the time of the deportations. I was in Everett at the time of the I.W.W. massacre.

You heard about that, I suppose?" Mac testifies, and later throws out an accusatory line, the significance of which could well be lost on most twenty-first-century audiences: "Who killed Salsedo?" Contemporaneous audiences might well have been largely unsympathetic to Wobbly causes, but they most likely would still have been familiar with Mac's pointed references.

To proceed in the order of Mac's testimony, the Bisbee deportations took place in July of 1917. The deportees consisted of some 1,160 striking mine workers and their supporters. As Kornbluh explains: "An armed vigilante committee raided the homes of striking miners, loaded... them into cattle cars, and deported them to the town in the desert where they were retained until September, following the end of their strike" (*Rebel Voices* 309). Mac, not proceeding in chronological order, next refers to "Bloody Sunday," a tragic confrontation between Wobblies, who were in Everett, Washington, to support striking shingle workers and local authorities. The I.W.W. reported somewhere between five and 12 members killed, with two local deputies killed, resulting in the arrest of 75 Wobblies (who were eventually acquitted).[6] Finally, Mac asks about anarchist Andrea Salsedo, arrested in New York and held by the FBI for two months. Salsedo's body was found on the pavement below the building where he was held; the official report was suicide, but there were understandable doubts (Zinn 375–376). The Salsedo line is also of interest as a piece of meta-theater, since *Gods of the Lightning* significantly features a Salsedo figure—the unseen Nick Bardi, who is killed in the initial confrontation between the strikers and police. Anderson and Hickerson effectively smudge the line between the fictional trial and the real-life events—or, as Edith Isaacs described the play, "history relived as news" (796).

The maelstrom of antiwar activity and the violence toward anarchists and suspected anarchists during this time was still fresh in the minds of Anderson and Hickerson's intended audience. The antiwar rhetoric spoken by both Macready and Capraro in the play echo the sentiment of the oft-quoted anonymous Wobbly speaking in court against the Great War in 1918:

You ask me why the IWW is not patriotic to the United States. If you were a bum without a blanket; if you had left your wife and kids when you went west for a job, and had never located them since; if your job had never kept you long enough in a place to qualify you to vote.... if every person who represented law and order and the nation beat you up, railroaded you to jail, and the good Christian people cheered and told them to go to it, how in hell do you expect a man to be patriotic? This war is a business man's war and we don't see why we should go out and get shot in order to save the lovely state of affairs which we now enjoy. (qtd. in Zinn and Arnove 291)

The makeup of the audience that actually saw the play seemed to provide for lively debate and argument. As Newspaper Enterprise Association syndicated columnist Gilbert Swan noted in his column of 7 November 1928, "the audience refused to leave for 15 minutes after the curtain fell, and then went out into the night with the Sacco-Vanzetti question very much alive" following, in Swan's words, "the most startling, stirring and 'radical' theatrical exhibition Broadway has seen in many a year" (Swan "Sacco and Vanzetti Return in Guises to Give Broadway a Thrill").

The short run of the play, as noted, belies some notably sympathetic reviews from the major critical voices of the day. The usually acerbic Robert Benchley praised the production as a "production we shall be proud to remember for our grandchildren." Benchley joined Swan in taking a jab at Boston, which would not allow a production of the play there: "We doubt very much, however, that the august courts of the Commonwealth of Massachusetts will permit it to open" (Benchley 14).

The unnamed (probably student) reviewer of the *Barnard Bulletin* dated 16 November 1928 was also alive to the unusual presence of the play on Broadway: "a play with the two Italians as protagonists has been produced on Broadway, not usually the scene of realities." The reviewer goes on to refer to the production as "dramatic dynamite" and that "the play unrolls in an atmosphere as dangerously live as a third rail" ("Second Balcony: *Gods of the Lightning*" 2). Walter

Winchell, in his "Your Broadway and Mine" column that ran on 3 November 1928, also acknowledged, if somewhat dismissively, the atmosphere of danger the play provided: "James Sinnott, representing Mayor Walker, was an interested spectator the opening night, as was a man who sat with an attentive ear and jotted down notes—for the Department of Justice, they were saying. No matter, it is an incessantly intense and compelling drama, that will move all who witness it, and it contains a great cast of players" (*Harrisburg Telegraph* 8). Winchell, as did Swan in his write-up, noted that much of the testimony in the trial scene, according to some audience witnesses, was verbatim from the actual Sacco-Vanzetti testimony, adding to the atmosphere of verisimilitude.[7] Brooks Atkinson, writing for the *New York Times*, referred to a "strong, harrowing drama...bravely played at the Little Theatre..." ("The Play: Based on the Sacco-Vanzetti Case" 27).

The reviewers often noted the strong audience response to the play—clearly, the play had the capability to move those who saw it. Principal actor Bickford, reminiscing about the play in his memoirs, extensively quotes Robert Garland of the *New York World-Telegram*, who noted the audience response and provided a sketch of the audience as well:

> From curtain to curtain we worshippers of, as the phrase goes, law and order, are permitted no word of protest. From curtain to curtain Sacco and Vanzetti are martyrs in a great crusade—holy men who live, suffer, and burn for a holy cause...
>
> ...where a croupy and uncomfortable audience is concerned, Sacco and Vanzetti are on every tongue. In the lobby, between the acts, it's Sacco and Vanzetti this, Sacco and Vanzetti that, Sacco and Vanzetti the other thing. "Sacco and Vanzetti are dead," says one. "Why not let well enough alone?" says another. "Let the dead bury its dead." "Sacco and Vanzetti are not dead," says a third. "Sacco and Vanzetti have just begun to live." (Garland qtd. in Bickford 152–153)

Garland's observations point to the freshness of the case for audience members, as well as their discomfort with the plays anarchic viewpoint. Notably, Garland does not identify Macready as a Wobbly, although the play is very clear on this point. He continues:

> As Macready, Charles Bickford is the strong, bold, outspoken, acrid anarchist.... You believe in his Macready without believing in his point of view. We are wise, we tell ourselves, to get the Macreadys out of our way. But, as we hang them and burn them, we respect them. If they really are mistaken, they're mistaken magnificently...
>
> Last night, as I left the Little Theater, a well-dressed, well-fed, hundred percent anti-anarchistic audience was cheering...the tremendously effective play which has been fashioned from the life, death and resurrection of Sacco and Vanzetti. (Garland qtd. in Bickford 153)

Actor Bickford himself also noted that along with the cheers, "some fifty or more indignant customers had hissed, booed and stomped their way out of the theater" (Bickford 153). The two views of the audience are not necessarily incompatible; the play touched on emotions just beneath the surface of the Broadway audience in ways both positive and negative. The effect of the play was something akin to lightning itself, both in its ability to generate a great deal of light and heat, while at the same time disappearing fairly quickly. As Bickford ruefully noted, "It should have been a smash hit. It wasn't" (154).

Not insignificantly, the production also captured the attention of the Wobbly press. In a somewhat prematurely titled article, "Radical Play Goes Well on Great White Way," the anonymous writer reports with great satisfaction how the I.W.W. is represented onstage: "The I.W.W. organization and its members are used to re-enact the most dastardly frame up of this age. Unlike other plays on the street this play gives the working class point of view of the capitalistic courts.... the play is well worth seeing" ("Radical Play" 3). At 29 performances, the play proved a disappointment, but as many of the reviewers and witnesses noted, there was evidence of a certain limited success in terms of engaging what would ordinarily be an unsympathetic audience. Certainly, it was a play that inspired and thrilled those segments of the audience who were sympathetic. As

Gassner poetically enthuses in his introduction to the play, it "communicates pity and anger, crackles with contempt for connivance and time-serving, and flagellates the coward heart and the mean spirit" (Gassner "Introduction: *Gods of the Lightning*" 530).[8]

Nevertheless, despite the martyred status of both the anarchist and the wobbly in the world of *Gods of the Lightning*, and the angry outcry that the play represents, it is once again the cold voice of pessimism that seems to prove the voice of reason. Rendered in the criminal Suvorin's often heavy-handed English, the themes of skepticism against all revolutionary activity that have permeated the plays under study are all given full voice here as well. Thus Suvorin speaks to the dismayed Wobblies who have just discovered a spy in their midst: "I tell you there is no government—there are only brigands in power who fight for more power! It has always been so. It will always be so. Till you die! Till we all die! Till there is no earth!" (Anderson and Hickerson 542). After a romantic self-affirmation as the only man alive who has the capability to be dangerous, Suvorin elaborates on the workings of the government with regard to the worker: "You are whipped before you start. The government sets a little game for you, and you play it with them, and the government wins because it is their game" (542). Again, a notable comparison could be made with Odets's *Waiting for Lefty*, which also uses a fixed poker game as an extended metaphor for the helpless and hapless position of the worker—except, of course, that the workers do find their voice and their power by the end of Odets's drama.

Suvorin, as Gassner points out, is something of a fanciful and romantic figure in contrast to those elements of the play that stick closer to the known facts (Gassner 530). He is also, however, a stand-in for the real-life Celestino Madeiros, who confessed to the murder for which Sacco and Vanzetti were eventually executed, and as Gassner astutely notes, stands in for the authors' viewpoint as well. Suvorin spells out the connection just as he is about to be arrested in the trial's climax: "That would be like you, too! To kill us all three, innocent and guilty together—burn us in your little hell to make your world safe for your bankers—you kept Judge, of a kept nation, you dead hand of the dead." The appropriate stage direction following this outburst reads, "General confusion" (559).

To further underline the connection between the stage trial and the real-life anarchists, Capraro's final statement to the judge echoes Vanzetti's well-publicized statement to the court at the time of sentencing: "Those who know these two hands will tell you they have never needed to kill to earn bread," Capraro states earnestly (Anderson and Hickerson 561). Vanzetti's words in his closing statement were similar enough to indicate that Anderson and Hickerson were consciously appropriating Vanzetti's overall tone and echoing specific cadences, words, and rhythms. An excerpt from Vanzetti's speech bears this out: "Everybody that knows these two arms knows very well that I did not need to go into the streets and kill a man or try to take money."[9]

While the time span between the crime and execution in Sacco and Vanzetti's case was seven years, the time frame in *Gods of the Lightning* is somewhat more ambiguous. Judge Vail, the Judge Thayer stand-in, gives the date of execution as Monday, 10 August 1927, in his sentence, and characters in the third act note that the execution has been delayed once, bringing the fictional characters' execution date very close to that of Sacco and Vanzetti—23 August 1927. What is less clear is how much time has elapsed since the crime in the play; the stage directions simply read "The restaurant as in the first act." We read that one supporting character, Milkin, is "bent, grey, and more wizened" (561), and later, Mac's love interest, Rosalie, cries that "we've had all day to help—we've had days and weeks—and years!" (565). One might assume that the audience is meant to understand that the time frame is that of Sacco and Vanzetti's, especially given the other efforts to encourage identification with the real-life anarchists. Anderson and Hickerson also plant clues so that the reader and audience could assume that the "Macready-Capraro" case caused similar international outpourings of support and protest to their real life counterparts. As another supporting character, the rundown academic Sowerby, holds forth in the third act:

> It would be a gigantic error, from a tactical point of view to kill these men now when the whole world is watching them. They will pursue a safer and more dastardly course of action. They will execute Suvorin and commute the sentences of Mac and Capraro to life imprisonment. They will do this and then they will sit back and laugh at us, having drawn the sting from all our arguments. That was what they did in the Mooney case. Trust any government to choose the safe and dastardly course. (Anderson and Hickerson 562)

Sowerby is proven wrong by the play's end, of course, but his speech is not meant to be dismissed by its audience. "The Mooney case" is a direct reference to Wobbly Tom Mooney, convicted of bombing a Preparedness Day parade in San Francisco on 22 July 1916.[10] The bomb would kill 10 and wound 40 more, and Mooney was convicted on flimsy (as well as perjured) evidence. His death sentence, as the character Sowerby notes, was indeed commuted to life imprisonment, and, some 11 years after *Gods* opened and closed on Broadway, Mooney at last received a pardon.[11] Mooney's imprisonment was still ongoing at the time of the play's production, and, much like the names dropped earlier in the course of the play's three acts, would have most likely struck a chord with audiences on either side of the labor issues.

The play, as noted earlier, was a financial failure, and indeed stands as the least successful play in this study—the others were at least modest hits or scandalous successes. The variables that make up a play's financial success or failure are perhaps too numerous to speculate upon, but it is of some interest to note that at least two observers felt that the play fell short directly because of the underlying fatalism, or negativism, of the play's tone. As Gassner points out in his introduction, " he [Anderson, to whom Gassner gives the primary writing credit] may be seen straining to shift the emphasis on to Suvorin, the proponent of negativism. It is curious how the 'Sacco' and 'Vanzetti' characters, who should have stood in the center of this drama if it was to have maximum emotion as well as relevance to the case, are overshadowed and given an essentially passive role" (Gassner 530). It is worth remembering at this point that Charles Bickford, in the "Sacco" role, had been advertised as playing the principal part—perhaps if he had indeed been the center of the play, there would have been a longer succession of sympathetic audiences. The other somewhat disappointed observer was Arthur Ruhl from the *New York Herald Tribune* who felt the events were too recent for its intended audience: "It is a good deal like putting a volcano or a battlefront on the stage for those who have just been through an earthquake or a battle." After noting that "indignation, after all, is not enough," Ruhl tellingly comments that the play should have ended a bit sooner, that the curtain "should have been brought down a few seconds earlier, at the line which said, in effect, 'Shout it to the world! Shout it to the world!'" (Ruhl "Off Stage and On").[12]

Anderson, for his part, rather rankled at the idea that his work was defeatist—an accusation leveled at him by the *Liberator* editor Max Eastman, among others. Anderson felt that as a poet, it was his station in life to envision "man as he must and will be, man a step above and beyond his present." Anderson maintained that such a view was the truly brave view of mankind: "To hold to this... requires more courage than to cherish illusions that man with all his present limitations could save himself by revolutions—political or scientific" (qtd. in Wall 355). Anderson's fundamental doubt in the efficacy of revolution to solve mankind's problems is underscored throughout the play, and especially so in the ending about which *New York Tribune* critic Ruhl complained.

It is, in fact, Rosalie who gets the last line of the play, delivered as she receives the news of the executions and hears the raging crowd just outside: "Shout it! Shout it! Cry out! Run and cry!" is where Ruhl would have had the play end. The final part of the final line, nevertheless, is extremely significant in that it reiterates one of the recurring themes of this study: "Only—it won't do any good—now"

(565). The line could indeed be the ultimate summation of the "Wobbly" plays we are examining—the first part evoking the call to shout, to cry, to protest, to respond with outrage. Along with the call to action, however, is the second part of the message—it will not do any good now. Indignation was not enough, and perhaps, neither was outrage. Or, perhaps, as Gassner opines, "The underlying social framework is, moreover, romantic by comparison with the closely analytical quality of the later social drama" (Gassner "Introduction: *Gods of the Lightning*" 530). The problem with the Wobbly drama of the 1920s might have been a surfeit of romance. Since we are dealing, in the I.W.W., with one of the most doggedly romantic of unions, the statement of the problem in romantic terms makes a certain poetic sense.

Another problem might well have been as simple as the wrong play meeting the wrong audience. Lewis Rogers, writing in *New Masses* about *Singing Jailbirds*, which New Yorkers would see for the first time later the same year, found a direct comparison with *Gods of the Lightning*, about which he noted: "There was a play never intended for the Broadway theaters and the pot-bellied brokers and their silk-shod mistresses. It was intended for a workers' theatre. The American playwrights who want to tell the truth must learn that they cannot flirt with Times Square" (Lewis qtd. in Knox and Stahl, 197). Lewis's bluntness may bring the historian to the heart of the matter—O'Neill managed to flirt with both the downtown and the uptown audiences, but he was not so much interested in the "truth" of the worker but in the "truth" of all mankind. Sidney Howard scored the biggest popular hit by, purposely or not, leavening (and in many ways overshadowing) the truth of the Wobblies with the racier truth of human sexual relations. John Howard Lawson also had "truth" in mind in his own way, but his was the way of jazz, vaudeville, and wild improvisation, leaving the workers to either follow the music or stumble blindly behind. And tracing the path of the "Wobblies on Broadway" back to the Paterson pageant, perhaps even the Wobblies themselves learned that the commercial end of mass entertainment was not an appropriate bedfellow. If, as Adorno writes, "the need to lend a voice to suffering is the condition of all truth" (*Negative Dialectics* 17–18, qtd. in Helmling 169), then Broadway might not be the most ideal environment for truth.

At any rate, the Great White Way would see its share of protest and social drama during the Depression, but the players would change just as America's perceived economic villains had changed. While the answers might come in the form of strikes, as in the final audience-fueled chants of *Waiting for Lefty*, the audience would not be asked, nevertheless, to come face to face with Wobblies and the Industrial Workers of the World. A depression would come and go, as would World War II, before Broadway audiences heard some of the old familiar Wobbly epithets again—only this time, perhaps, the audience did not find the expressions as familiar.

Also worth noting, with regard to the social drama of the 1930s, is that Maxwell Anderson was not quite finished with the Sacco and Vanzetti case. In his verse drama *Winterset*, Anderson had found the right, or at least most successful, combination of distance, both in terms of time and dramatic form. Anderson's 1935 play dealt with the son of an executed anarchist seeking revenge, and finding love just before meeting his violent death. The shadows of Sacco and Vanzetti still remained, but the drama focused on the plight of the son (named Mio, a nod to Vanzetti's first name), and the audience was not necessarily asked to pick sides. In this sense, perhaps Anderson did indeed find a way to bring Sacco and Vanzetti onstage while flirting with Times Square, but that way was no longer the way of propaganda or of anything resembling workers' theatre. As Anita Block writes with extreme disillusion: "Finally, after the audience, or the reader, has floated over this poetic sea of unreality, Mio and his love are mowed down by the gangster's machine gun, and the play ends with a long speech in blank verse, expressing the utter defeatism that has supplanted the playwright's former responsive understanding of the implications of the Sacco-Vanzetti case" (Block 241). What is interesting about Block's bitter response is not so much that one might disagree regarding the merits of *Winterset*, but that Block seems to either forget or ignore the similar defeatism of Rosalie's final lines in *Gods of the Lightning*. As we have seen throughout this study, anger, activism, and defeatism battle for the souls of many of the Wobbly plays.[13]

Later the same year that *Gods of the Lightning* made its short-lived Broadway stand, another Wobbly play set its sights for downtown. The play had been kicking around for awhile—Upton Sinclair had first published the work himself some four years earlier, in close temporal proximity to the events he was writing about. Although the ensuing years provided some distance, as well as some foreign productions, the play still blew into the space of the Provincetown Players with an impressive force. Rather than admit defeat, Sinclair even dared to give his play an ending set in a worker-friendly utopian future. The tone and approach of *Singing Jailbirds* provides an interesting contrast and comparison with the Wobblies of Broadway.

6. "We Even Sing 'em in Jap and Chink": Upton Sinclair's Workers' Theatre Contribution ⁂

Upton Sinclair's contribution to the Wobbly play oeuvre is a bit misleading, as noted in the introduction, since it was not a Broadway play in the sense that the others included were. (*The Hairy Ape* did not begin life as a Broadway play, but it did move uptown.) Although a researcher can find *Singing Jailbirds* on the Broadway database, most likely because of the production at the Provincetown Playhouse, the play was a distinctly different animal, a production of the New Playwrights Theatre, dubbed "the revolting playwrights" (credit, or blame, for the nickname generally goes to critic Alexander Woollcott), and it courted a radical, downtown, "revolting" audience.

As George Knox and Herbert Stahl explain in their study of the New Playwrights Theatre, *Dos Passos and "The Revolting Playwrights,"* the dissatisfied radicals who formed the company were "revolting" against a Broadway that had become representative of "The Interests" and "The System" (Knox and Stahl 7). Indeed, one of the tensions throughout this study has been the attempt to tell Wobbly stories through a popular commercial vehicle. The New Playwrights felt that it was futile, and, in fact, fundamentally wrong, to make such an attempt. The ideal audience for this company was "educable," as Knox and Stahl spell out: "The audience, let us say a 'labor audience,' or a class-conscious white-collar audience, would be enlightened and stimulated through both variety and familiarity. As this process continued, the New Playwrights would insinuate themselves into a growing sector of theatre-alert public and their repertory would become a vital part of its cultural equipment" (11). The tenure of the New Playwrights was short-lived; they disbanded two years later, in 1929. Nevertheless, they are of interest to this study as a company producing a play as "workers' theatre" for a "workers' audience" (as well as a worker-sympathetic audience) in contrast to the era in which they found themselves—generally considered the "boom" years before the Depression, and in contrast to the kinds of audiences sought by the Broadway practitioners.[1]

The popular conception of such an audience, as opposed to a close social study of these audiences, was well defined by the end of the 1920s—in a similar fashion to the combination of "intellectuals" and uptowners who went downtown to see the first performances of *The Hairy Ape*, New Playwrights audiences were seen as a combination of "pale, intelligent-looking young people with horn-rimmed glasses, and capitalists (a few) who drove away in shiny, new sedans" (Knox and Stahl 181). The theatre solicited a subscription audience, with five dollars paying for a season of four plays (64). In many ways, therefore, this particular production of *Singing Jailbirds* comes closest to what De Marinis refers to as a "closed performance"— the kind of performances that "anticipate a very precise receiver and demand well-defined types of 'competence' (encyclopedic, ideological, etc.) for their 'correct' reception. This is mostly the case with certain forms of genre-based theatre: political theatre, children's theatre, gay theatre, street theatre…" (De Marinis 103). It would seem that *Singing Jailbirds* in its New York incarnation found as close to an ideal American commercial audience as possible.

Nevertheless, there are connections to be made with the Broadway Wobblies, besides the fact that the Wobblies constitute the principal characters and that the prevailing of the Wobblies' agenda is the principal theme. One connection has to do with origin—the 1923 San Pedro Marine Transit Workers Strike that inspired the character of Joe in *They Knew What They Wanted* gave rise to Sinclair's play as well. The second connection resides in the play's use of music, particularly jazz, thus linking *Singing Jailbirds* to Lawson's *Processional*. How Sinclair uses the Wobblies, the San Perdo strike, and jazz is quite different from the dramaturgical strategies of both Howard and Lawson, but worth remarking upon by virtue of comparison and contrast with the Broadway use of Wobbly subject matter and agenda.

Just as Anderson and Hickerson wrote *Gods of the Lightning* quickly after the debacle of the actual Sacco and Vanzetti executions, Sinclair was also inspired to put his impressions of the San Pedro strike and the treatment of Wobblies in the area into dramatic form in something of a hurry. The journey of Sinclair's *Singing Jailbirds* began, and nearly ended, with a promise made to his wife, Mary Craig Sinclair. That promise entailed not getting involved in worker activism and concentrating instead on writing once the pair had settled in California. However, the Marine Transit Workers port strike in San Pedro, California, beginning in April 1923, convinced Sinclair that he could not keep his promise. While evidence suggests that Sinclair had a tendency to romanticize his experiences and exaggerate his importance in the affairs that followed, the accomplishments that resulted from Sinclair's interventions were real enough—most notably, the creation of the Southern California American Civil Liberties Union.[2] Sinclair's arrest, for attempting to read the First Amendment before the enthusiastic crowd of strikers, was also real, and provided him a firsthand account of prisoner treatment (augmented by accounts from prisoners whose trust and admiration Sinclair had gained) that would fuel numerous fiery articles, novels, and correspondence.[3] The strike also spurred Sinclair in the field of drama, leading him to create perhaps the most heroic and messianic stage portrayal of the Wobbly to be found in New York.

Singing Jailbirds survives as a fascinating, frequently powerful, and just as frequently clumsy, historic artifact of Wobbly activism and I.W.W. mythology, as well as an often brutally journalistic account of one example of the violent suppression of free speech.

Sinclair's shortcomings as a dramatist were remarked upon by sympathetic and unsympathetic reviewers alike, both in the United States and abroad (the play had been performed in Germany before the New Playwrights Theatre finally took it on roughly four years after Sinclair self-published the script). The *Wall Street Journal*, for example, praised the "robust and ambitious" production, but went on to say that the production itself was "defeated by their author" (S.B., 4). The *New York Herald Tribune*'s Arthur Ruhl commented on "the somewhat too infrequent bits of action" the play had to offer (Ruhl "I.W.W. Wobbly Glorified"), and German critic Alfred Kerr simply threw up his hands and concluded that Sinclair was not only a "half artist" but a "queer fellow" to boot (McPherson "Germans Discover America" F2). Knox and Stahl sum up the strengths and weaknesses of the play and the theatrical event: " Sinclair shared the fatal propensity to oversimplify, to enslave oneself to stereotyped ideas. The ungoverned passion of utterance, the bald labelling, and diatribe and soap-box oratory, unfortunately beclouded the 'facts' on which the play was built.... Here was exciting, although revolting, theatre. But, again, good theatre is not necessarily good play" (Knox and Stahl 180).[4]

The daily critics also knew what they were getting into with the New Playwrights, who had been producing radical-minded, worker-friendly, and distinctly left-leaning plays for the past year, and their reviews revealed a jaundiced attitude toward their agenda. Ruhl of the *New York Herald Tribune*, for example, begins in a fairly barbed tone: "The diminutive stage of the Provincetown Playhouse rocked again last evening to the drama's attacks on a capitalist order, as the New Playwrights Theater presented Upton Sinclair's *Singing Jailbirds*" (Ruhl "I.W.W. Wobbly Glorified" 33). The more sympathetic *New York Daily News* noted that the play "finally reached the American audience," and favorably noted that "the element of truth always to be found in Sinclair's writings is evident in this grim tragedy of the labor classes." The unnamed writer also praised the performance of Grover Burgess, who played the principal Wobbly,

"Red" Adams, as "splendidly convincing" ("Village Views Upton Sinclair I.W.W. Drama" 35).

The casting of Grover Burgess is significant as the key personification of the Wobbly in Sinclair's play. Burgess, as a physical type, was another nonthreatening presence, as opposed to the "sexy" Glenn Anders or the towering George Abbott, but closer in type to the distinctly ordinary-looking I.W.W. secretary from *The Hairy Ape*. Burgess's "Red," while possessing enormous energy and fortitude, was presented as a man of inner strength rather than brute muscle. This presence, no doubt, lent additional pathos to Red's scenes of solitary confinement and his imagined reunions with his deceased wife that permeate the play's story.

Contextualizing Sinclair's play requires some background on the specific strike that spawned *Singing Jailbirds*. The Wobblies, as noted, often found themselves and placed themselves at the center of a number of cases involving free speech and the right of assembly. Many Wobblies spent considerable time in jail thanks to the national criminal syndicalism laws—a bitter return of the term "syndicalism" for a group of radicals who tried so diligently to distance themselves from it. These laws, which presumably were intended to protect law-abiding citizens against those who advocated political or industrial change by means of terrorism, sabotage, and other criminal conduct, were enacted and enforced during and just after the Great War, and provided an ongoing and troubling challenge to free speech that may have disturbing parallels to our more recent policies on terrorism.[5] In a sense, the criminal syndicalism laws were the illegitimate offspring of Justice Oliver Wendell Holmes Jr.—the source of the famous "shouting fire in a theatre" analogy, a point he was making as he upheld the Espionage Act of 1917 (deciding that it was a clear and present danger to distribute antidraft flyers during World War I).[6] Sinclair, passionately involved in the protection of free speech, championed, and indeed lionized, this organization even though he did not agree with its agenda.[7] Historian Richard B. Fisher attributes Sinclair's interest in and affection for the group as a tribute to "their romantic individualism [and] their lack of organization" (Fisher "The Last Muckraker" 351; see also Zanger "Politics of Confrontation" 386).

"The impulse to write the play came as a result of an experience in the strike of the Marine Transport Workers at San Pedro, California, the harbor of Los Angeles, in May, 1923," Sinclair noted laconically in his postscript to *Singing Jailbirds*, written "for the benefit of those readers who ask to what extent conditions pictured in this play really exist" (Sinclair *Singing Jailbirds* 84). His address to "readers" is significant, as Sinclair published the play himself in 1924, and it was not staged in this country until December of 1928. Sinclair's copious notes, quotes, and statistics follow, bearing out his descriptions of labor prisoner abuse that in turn are brought to life in his play. Exactly a year after the strike began, Sinclair had finished the play and was working on the notes, keeping his statistics as up to date as he could: "At the time this play is completed, May 1924, there are in the prisons of the United States 114 men and women, whose only offense—the only offense charged—has been the holding and advocating of certain political ideas. Four or five years ago there were between 1,000 and 1,500 such prisoners" (Sinclair 88). "Class war prisoners," as Sinclair called them, typically pulling no punches, were generally arrested on accusation of criminal syndicalism, along with occasional trumped-up charges of vagrancy, picketing, or blocking traffic (90). Sinclair had attempted to show the public the truth of the I.W.W.'s plight through novels and journalism—and in this instance, he took to the stage in what was, according to Robert J. Cadigan in "The Drama and Social Problems," his "only good play" (Cadigan, "The Drama and Social Problems" 567).

Upton Sinclair flatly distanced himself from the I.W.W. agenda: "As a Socialist, he disapproves of the I.W.W.," he wrote, rendering himself in third person (88).[8] Nevertheless, the same righteous passion and fury that drove Sinclair to get arrested with the San Pedro strikers and to help form the Southern California ACLU drove him to write a powerful anticapitalist screed in play form—one that presents the I.W.W. in only the most positive and heroic (and oppressed) light. Sinclair dramatizes a war of wills and ideology through heated arguments, expressionist fever dreams, I.W.W. hagiography, long speeches, and a great deal of music. The play stands as arguably the most pro-I.W.W. play to be produced in the New York City commercial theater, running some 79 performances at the Provincetown Playhouse and later the Grove Street Theatre. Sinclair's strategies to stage and glorify the I.W.W. intertwine, not always neatly, with his relentlessly muckraking expose of the brutality against the class war prisoner.

The key prisoner in *Singing Jailbirds* is Bert Adams, better known as "Red," a nickname that can speak for itself. As Red is questioned by the D.A. (Red refers to him contemptuously as "Mr. 'Cutor"—that is, short for "Prosecutor"), we learn that he has been an I.W.W. leader for three years. The questioning is punctuated throughout, as is the entire play, with lusty singing of I.W.W. songs by supportive strikers outside the jail as well as by the prisoners inside. While the D.A. seems contemptuously amused by the singing, Red references one of the key I.W.W. folk heroes, Joe Hill, credited with writing many of the songs used in the play. A major element of I.W.W. solidarity that Red voices in his scene with the D.A. is its inclusiveness—through terms that are now cringe-worthy in their racial and ethnic connotations, Red educates the D.A. (and a large section of the intended audience) with regard to how the songs have gained popularity throughout the country: "But now Joe Hill's songs are all over the land. We sing 'em in Dago and Mex, in Hunkie and Wop, we even sing 'em in Jap and Chink!" (Sinclair *Singing Jailbirds* 10). The ethnic terms, usually meant as slurs in common parlance, here serve as a kind of code of inclusiveness and rough affection.[9]

As Red only answers the D.A.'s leading questions in repetitions of I.W.W. slogans and rhetoric ("We nail the I.W.W. preamble to the wall: 'We are forming the new society within the shell of the old'"), he is taken to the prison tanks, in a horrifying scene illustrating deadly overcrowding and suffocation of prisoners. It is this scene that made the most positive impression on the *New York Times* reviewer, but as we will see, even this admiration was qualified by a fundamental disbelief that such a situation could possibly exist.

In the overcrowded prisoner scene, the flamboyant Presbyterian clergyman, the Dominie, makes his entrance. The Dominie enjoys a privileged position among the I.W.W.—while the workers regale him with the same terms they use for all men of the cloth (Bible-shark, sky-pilot, etc.), they welcome him because the Dominie is on their side. The Dominie's colorful (and loud) prayers stir up the prisoners and the strikers outside, conflating and combining Christian and Wobbly doctrine: "I proclaim unto you Christ and Him crucified! Not the stained glass window saint of the fashionable churches, but the working-class revolutionist, the rebel carpenter, the First Wobbly of the World!" (22) The disparagement of religious doctrine and hymns combined with the appropriation of the same doctrine to promote and extol the "One Big Union" is a recurring theme in Sinclair's play, and an important element in the I.W.W. self-mythology. Indeed, scenes such as this one constitute a strong argument for the Wobblies as a form of religion.[10] While the I.W.W. consistently mocked the idea of religious belief and held with the philosophy that religion was primarily a tool to keep workers underpaid and docile with the promise of heaven, the evangelical fervor and messianic fervor of the preaching of the One Big Union (O.B.U.) definitely conveyed a kind of religious intensity.[11]

The prisoners continue to sing defiantly ("Sing, you Jailbirds, sing!" becomes the play's most repeated line and gives the play its title) as the guards suffocate them by turning on the steam heat and crowding them beyond endurance. The Dominie is released for causing a scene, and Red is relegated to the dreaded "hole"—solitary confinement—where he spends the rest of the play (except in his dreams). As the act ends, Sinclair indicates that the audience should sing along as well. As previously noted, the I.W.W. leaders well knew the value of music and entertainment in spreading its message of worker solidarity and equality, and Sinclair extends the I.W.W.

outreach through his use of the sing-along and through his inclusion of many titles from the (in)famous Little Red Songbook—indeed, *Singing Jailbirds* functions as something of a Little Red Songbook jukebox musical.[12] The singing reinforces the heroic and popular status of both Red and the I.W.W. throughout the play.

As Act II opens, we find Red alone in solitary—a slop pail is his toilet, and he gets white bread to eat (with fewer vitamins and nutrients than regular bread) and water. Red's fights to stay sane and healthy echo the plight of many real-life Wobbly prisoners. According to reporter Winthrop Lane, "For a year and a half these men had been idle in body and brain. They spent their days in crawling from cell to bull pen and from bull pen to cell.... Their muscles, once strong, grew flabby and their minds, once alert, grew dead" (qtd. in Kornbluh *Rebel Voices* 321). Sinclair, making sure the audience understands the disintegration of healthy mind and body suffered by such prisoners, has Red comment directly on the process throughout his time in the cell.

In a long monologue, one of many, Red tries to keep his spirits up through singing and exercise—then he lets his mind roam to happier times, particularly a worker's restaurant where many of his friends are gathered together for a big meal, served by the accommodating, I.W.W.-friendly and English-language-mangling One Lung, otherwise known as "the Chink." As Red imagines the scene, he enters the restaurant to much singing and dancing, and Sinclair brings to life one of the most common "Wobbly" origin stories—One Lung unsuccessfully tries to say "I.W.W." and it comes out "I-Wobble-Wobble." "Us boys took up the Chink's word, we got to calling ourselves wobblies when we came here to a meal," one of Red's friends explains (Sinclair *Singing Jailbirds* 39). This scene, with its legendary origin story, further serves to mythologize the I.W.W. while emphasizing solidarity and inclusiveness—Red and his fellow workers embrace "the Chink" as they simultaneously make fun of him. Red leaves the imaginary scene and begins to think of his late wife, Nell, and they are together in the hole (in Red's mind) as the act ends.[13]

The third act of *Singing Jailbirds* reveals Red back in the hole, trying to come to terms with his environment, and in the process name-checking a self-help method grounded in mental repetition that was popular at the time: "I suppose I ought to give that old French guy Coué a chance at me.... He says to be monotonous, and by heck, that's made to order for wobblies in solitary!" (47) (Apparently, Wobblies were not necessarily out of touch with the popular culture.)[14] Red soon imagines Nell again, this time reliving their difficult life on a California ranch-house, dealing with a failing farm and falling produce prices. They have two children and assure each other that they're still in love even though they dare not risk having another child. In the play's most graphic scene, Nell discovers her pregnancy and tries to give herself an abortion, dying in horrible pain. It is this memory that drives Red's fevered imagination beyond the realistic. He next "sees" the D.A. from the first scene and Muriel, a stenographer, enjoying a lavish dinner at a road house with jazz music in the background. Red confronts the D.A. with the line "Here's the end of your debauchery!" (Sinclair notes that the melodramatic tones are intentional as this is "Red's imagining of the life of the ruling classes" [55]). In a striking interlude, Red sings one of the key I.W.W. songs, "Solidarity Forever," but the D.A. counters musically as well: "Well, we have a way to drown their songs.... Open the doors! We want music! Our kind! Leisure-class music! (*the waiter runs off, and the strains of the jazz orchestra rise loud. MURIEL leaps into activity, enacting the music, pressing herself into the DISTRICT ATTORNEY's arms, kissing him, cajoling him; they abandon themselves to a sensual orgy*)" (58–59) As Muriel sings a particularly vapid version of a jazz song ("Quack, quack, ducky duck! I'm your chick, cluck, cluck!"), the D.A. threatens Red explicitly with jazz: "This is our music! Join the chorus—or we put you in the hole!" (59).

The sequence bears mentioning for its commentary on music and how different forms of music correspond to virtues or lack of virtue. In this scene, the "folk" music of the I.W.W., often appropriating familiar melodies ("Solidarity Forever," for example, is sung to the tune of "John Brown's Body" and, of course, "The Battle Hymn of the Republic"), represents integrity, personal strength, and union (as well as the O.B.U.). The I.W.W. songbook is the music of the working class. Jazz, in sharp contrast, is, as the D.A. tauntingly proclaims, "leisure-class music"—the music of capitalist oppression, amorality, and worker subjugation. It is a particularly striking scene to include in an entertainment that appeared at the height of the Jazz Age, and, as noted, to provide interesting contrast with the jazz that permeates Lawson's *Processional*. While Lawson appropriated jazz rhythms and terminology to create his version of an impudent American tapestry, Sinclair's jazz world is thoughtless and hedonistic—a form of escape that only the leisure class could afford or even enjoy. Sinclair highlights the supposed mindlessness of jazz by giving the music the most childish and downright silly lyrics imaginable. Indeed, an interesting comparison might be made between Sinclair's version of jazz music and another generation's making fun of rock and roll.

Red hallucinates further and imagines a wild and phantasmagoric trial in the Hall of Hate, with corrupt lawyers, judges, and police wearing animal heads and spewing legalese double-talk. The workers cannot win the trial, but they get the last word in through song, again with the suggested help of the audience.

In the final act (Sinclair wrote the play in four acts, but it was apparently produced by the New Playwrights Theatre in three), Red tells the imaginary Nell that he intends to starve to death and that it won't be long before he succeeds. Red and Nell visit their Wobbly friends in the jungles and give them words of encouragement. Red's messages are explicitly Christ-like in language and context as he becomes an I.W.W. martyr: "This message I give unto you; write it in your hearts, take it with you into the blackest dungeon—that even there is unity, even there, in the midst of affliction and despair, brotherhood works its miracles of life and resurrection. Remember my words" (Sinclair *Singing Jailbirds* 81). Sinclair also provides a ten-year flash forward when Red's children, now grown, help to commemorate the new Industrial Commonwealth that Red's death helped to bring into fruition. Back in solitary (in the "present"), the prison guards find Red's body with his eyeballs devoured by the prison rats. Despite, or perhaps because of, Red's gruesome end (another parallel with many of the saints), the audience and the workers triumph through song in a final chorus of "Solidarity Forever."

Perhaps not surprisingly, it was not the United States that gave Sinclair's play its premiere. Sinclair's theatrical strategies well suited Berlin's Lessing Theatre, which first produced *Singing Jailbirds* in April 1928—director Ernst Lonner, following Piscator's lead, used revolving stages and motion pictures to stage Sinclair's epic visions, apparently with considerable success ("Upton Sinclair Abroad"). When the New Playwrights Theatre produced the play in New York City at the end of that year, the unnamed *New York Times* critic found positive things to say about the production, but equally notable is his response of incredulity and skepticism with regard to the treatment of the I.W.W. portrayed onstage. The critic's attitude is probably best summed up by the second part of the headline: "Company Makes Good Showing with an Absurd Situation".[15] "If it was not convincing it was not the fault of the direction or of the actors. It was because the idea of the manual laborer as an oppressed creature in this tenth year after the Great War in these United States is so patently absurd that all the art of stage-craft and all the fervid indignation of the author are wasted in the effort to give it the similitude of truth" ("'Singing Jailbirds' Called Propaganda"). That a theater critic writing for the *New York Times* could not take the plight of the onstage workers seriously because he did not believe such conditions existed tells us a great deal about class and much of the Broadway audience's perceptions of the labor movement during the late 1920s.

Sinclair did not accept the critical drub, or the implication that he might have been exaggerating, quietly. In a letter to the editor written on 10 December, five days after the review appeared (it was printed in the *New York Times* on 23 December, on page 86), Sinclair flatly told the *New York Times* and the critic where they could get off: "It must have been a very young dramatic critic whom you sent to witness

'Singing Jailbirds,' and I cannot, in the space of a letter, attempt to remedy his extreme naivete, but please permit me to make this one explicit statement: Everything that I have described in 'Singing Jailbirds' actually happened in Los Angeles Harbor in May of 1923" (Sinclair, "From Upton Sinclair"). After further noting that such treatment of prisoners and strikers are still happening, Sinclair notes that he has enclosed the postscript to the published version of the play, "hoping that you will place it in the hands of your young dramatic critic." While Sinclair's response was somewhat acidic, he was not exaggerating with regard to labor struggles. As Lee Papa points out in his introduction to *Staged Action: Six Plays from the American Workers' Theater*, the year before the production of *Singing Jailbirds*, a mob in Walsenburg, Colorado (led by the town's mayor) destroyed the I.W.W headquarters when the Wobblies threatened a miners' strike, and as of January 1928, it was common practice in Pittsburgh for employers to use "hired thugs" to beat any suspected union agitators (Papa 6).

The comparative success of *Singing Jailbirds* for the "revolting playwrights" of the New Playwrights Theatre throws into perspective the importance of audience and approach with the plays under study. In Lewis Rogers's enthusiastic review of the play for *New Masses* (in which he makes an interesting and important comparison to Anderson and Hickerson's *Gods of the Lightning*), he writes: "Such plays as *Singing Jailbirds* will someday inspire the creation of a revolutionary American art. And such theatres as the New Playwrights will undoubtedly play a major role in the creation of that art" (Lewis qtd. in Knox and Stahl 197). While *Gods of the Lightning* was a play with many of the earmarks of "workers theatre" that would fail uptown, *Singing Jailbirds* was geared toward and marketed to the ones who knew and supported the "revolting" agenda.

The play's presence was such that it even landed on a list of Christmas holiday theatergoing ideas. In "Listing the Attractions for the Holiday Trade," featured in the 23 December 1928 edition of the *New York Times*, the writer recommends the play for those looking for some activism in their holiday fun: "Singing Jailbirds is a play by the militant Upton Sinclair, and on his own testimony pictures events which actually took place in Los Angeles about five years ago. It has been staged successfully in Berlin; at the Provincetown Playhouse the New Playwrights Group has mounted it with considerable shrewdness and ingenuity" ("Listing the Attractions" 84). The Christmas advertisement might call into question the usefulness of putting the plight of the worker, and the Wobbly in particular, on stage as, roughly speaking, a form of entertainment. As Adorno noted in *Minima Moralia*, "In the end, glorification of splendid underdogs is nothing other than glorification of the splendid system that makes them so" (Adorno *Minima* 200). Adorno further warns: "When society... is presented as if good-will were enough to remove its faults, it is defended even when it is honestly attacked" (202–203). While the Wobblies themselves would be the first to argue that "good-will" was not enough to stop the world, it could also be argued that the play itself was meant to generate good-will for the I.W.W.—perhaps a fundamental issue with all the "Wobblies on Broadway" works under study. Whether Adorno's observations are true even when the underdogs are doing the glorifying is an ongoing question, one that the "revolting playwrights" were unable to answer to the satisfaction of enough paying audiences. As Colette Hyman notes in *Staging Strikes*, "As the 1920s drew to a close, the curtain fell on the New Playwrights Theatre as well. Incapable of attracting its intended audience of workers, the group was also unable to compete with commercial entertainment for middle-class theatregoers." It fell to the burgeoning groups of workers' theatres, such as the Brookwood Labor Players, to bring together workers theatre with its intended audiences (Hyman 24–25).

If Sinclair did not strictly share the faith of the I.W.W., he did, at least at the time of his writing the play, have some hope for the country's future, especially in its young people. As he has Red say toward the end of the play: "There are lots of young people that have understanding—boys and girls in the colleges" (Sinclair *Singing Jailbirds* 79). This faith, however, was tempered with his journalistic duty to report the reality of the situation in the final grim words of the postscript to his play—Sinclair reported a mob of 300 raiding the I.W.W. hall in San Pedro in the midst of some "peaceful entertainment." Many Wobblies were tarred and feathered, and a little girl at the hall was thrown into a boiling vat of coffee, "not expected to live." Sinclair concludes: "The most determined agitation on the part of the American Civil Liberties Union cannot persuade the public authorities to give any protection to the working people at San Pedro, or any pretense of justice" (95).[16] *Singing Jailbirds* represents an interesting and historically significant attempt to redress this miscarriage of justice through the means of vibrant and spirited workers' theatre. Sadly, the notion that such atrocities could not happen "in these United States" was perhaps stronger than Sinclair's most concerted efforts to show otherwise, and our collective history is the darker for it. Nevertheless, it is unique in this collection because of its lack of defeatism—certainly, Red's end is a painful one, but by the end of the play Red is not merely vindicated, but venerated through the ceremonies headed by the denizens of a new, Wobbly-based society. As critics noted, Sinclair's piece was something of a dream play—perhaps even a pipe dream, to lift an expression from O'Neill's play that will be examined next—but the unfettered optimism of the ending proves something of a welcome. The notion of defeat becomes even more relevant when we turn to Eugene O'Neill's epic barroom drama.

As O'Neill began our look at the I.W.W. on the Main Stem, it seems fitting that his play delivers the elegy. We travel almost 20 years ahead in terms of date of production, as O'Neill in turn goes back to the 1910s for his time and place. It is perhaps ironic that O'Neill's wobbly postmortem is set when the I.W.W. was a fairly young seven-year-old and in the midst of considerable productivity, but such sincerity was no match for O'Neill's idiosyncratic combination of ultimate human comedy and tragedy. In O'Neill's last chance saloon, at least, the Wobblies were already doomed just as they were getting started.

7. You I-Won't-Work Harp: I.W.W. Elegy in *The Iceman Cometh* ∾

Adorno wrote, perhaps too famously, that "to write poetry after Auschwitz is barbaric" (Adorno *Prisms* 34). He amended the sentiment later, although in terms no less harsh: "Perennial suffering has as much right to expression as a tortured man has to scream; hence it may have been wrong to say that after Auschwitz you could no longer write poems. But it's not wrong to raise the less cultural question whether after Auschwitz you can go on living—especially whether one who escaped by accident, one who by rights should have been killed, may go on living" (Adorno *Negative Dialectics* 362–363). Adorno was getting at the morality of producing artistic monuments to a culture that produced an Auschwitz; he then brings up the impossible situation of using the same "basic principle of bourgeois subjectivity" (363) to survive an Auschwitz as the principle that created the death camps in the first place.[1]

While Eugene O'Neill did not write *The Iceman Cometh* after Auschwitz, he did wait until after World War II to have the play produced. Sometimes a study will provide its own symmetry—or, if not precise symmetry, poetically satisfying bookends. Eugene O'Neill was praised by the Wobblies for his fair and balanced depiction of their organization in the early 1920s, although this was not praise that O'Neill accepted graciously. Some 20 years later, O'Neill weaves I.W.W. activity throughout his last play to make it to Broadway in his lifetime, the massive *The Iceman Cometh*. O'Neill's take on the Wobblies is, in many ways, consistent with the previous plays under study, and perhaps serves as a fitting epitaph for its representation on Broadway.

The play also serves as something of a condensed prehistory of I.W.W. activity, as well as a telling critique on the disposability of those radicals broken by prison, who were, in the words of "Remember," the song Joe sings in *They Knew What They Wanted*, "in here for you." Obviously not everyone remembered, nor was everyone remembered. The forgotten found a home in O'Neill's "last chance saloon"—the dismal yet welcoming bar that serves as the center for *Iceman*.

"I knew 'em all," O'Neill observed in a *New York Times* interview shortly before *Iceman* opened. "The man who owns this saloon, Harry Hope, and all the others—the Anarchists and Wobblies and French Syndicalists, the broken men, the tarts, the bartenders and even the saloon itself—are real. It's not just one place, perhaps, but it is several places that I lived in at one time or another... places I once knew put together in one" (Schriftgiesser, "The Iceman Cometh" XI). Some of the broken men O'Neill refers to might well have seemed identified by ghost labels to many readers of the 6 October 1946 article. It is perhaps also interesting to note that the "anarchists, Wobblies, and French Syndicalists" are mentioned first, or at least just after Harry Hope in order of importance. The emphasis O'Neill meant to place on the anarchists seems to been largely lost on future audiences as well as future producers of the play.[2]

Further, O'Neill not only drew on his own experiences with radicals and anarchists from his youth, but apparently put in a fair amount of research on the subject as well. As O'Neill historian Doris Alexander points out, not long before O'Neill began work on *Iceman*, he requested information from his friend Saxe Commins on Bakunin, Kropotkin (both of whom would be name-checked in *Iceman*), or anything referring to the kind of "utopia" the anarchists and syndicalists hoped to one day effect. Commins granted the favor and then some, providing O'Neill with a clearer understanding of the anarchist and syndicalist agenda than most (Alexander *Eugene O'Neill's Last Plays* 40).

O'Neill's use of the term "French Syndicalist" might be somewhat puzzling to those familiar with seeing or reading *Iceman*—while characters of various nationalities converge on Harry Hope's saloon, the only French reference is made by the distinctly Germanic Hugo Kalmar, singing in his "guttural basso" the French revolutionary song "Carmagnole" (104). The use of the song might have confirmed the darkest fears of an anarchist-panicked public in the era the play was set, the summer of 1912—"Let us dance the Carmagnole...long live the sound of the cannons!" In the context of the saloon, and perhaps in the context of the initial 1946 performance, the song becomes a genial part of the general background noise.

Nevertheless, the concept of syndicalism is French in origin, as F. F. Ridley notes in his introduction to *Revolutionary Syndicalism in France*: "The French word *syndicalisme* means no more than trade unionism. The French described their movement as *syndicalisme revolutionnaire*. When we talk of syndicalism we really mean revolutionary syndicalism" (Ridley 1). The idea—more accurately described as a "movement" than a theory, as Ridley notes (1)—would have had a profound influence on the German Hugo and the Irish Larry as they found their way to America. Indeed, their beliefs and former actions are often referred to as "The Movement" in the course of *Iceman*, often in sardonic terms, as when Harry Hope threatens to evict both Hugo and Larry for failure to pay their rent (something all the boarders have in common): "Bejees, you'll pay up tomorrow, or I'll start a Harry Hope Revolution! I'll tie a dispossess bomb to your tails that'll blow you out in the street! Bejees, I'll make your Movement move!" (O'Neill *The Iceman Cometh* 54). Hope's tone sets the level of casual indifference and mockery most of the characters share regarding the idea of the Movement and of anarchy in general.

In the *Times* interview, and throughout the course of the play itself, O'Neill touches on anarchist history as he presents his final variation on the Broadway stage Wobblies. The trade union–centered concept of syndicalism, or anarcho-syndicalism, can be fixed roughly from the formation of the *Confederation General du Travail* (C.G.T.) in 1895—"From then on to the aftermath of the World War, the C.G.T. was colored officially with an Anarchist tendency that gave a theory and program to the trade unions and developed into Anarcho-Syndicalism" (Weisbord, *The Conquest of Power*). In a sense, therefore, the term "French Syndicalists" could apply to all the radical characters in the play; even though the Wobblies avoided being labeled as such, they consistently found themselves subject to anti-syndicalism laws and painted with the syndicalist brush. One of the interesting points of tension in *Iceman* stems from O'Neill's nuanced understanding of anarchist distinctions and the lack of this understanding from most of his characters—as well as most of the audience.

O'Neill further provided distance between his intentions and the idea of a "labor play," much as he had done a generation before at the opening of *The Hairy Ape*. As *New York Times* writer Karl Schriftgiesser notes (not with complete historical accuracy, perhaps): "The time of which he writes, [O'Neill] recalls, marked the end of one of the great labor movements in America: the days of the old Knights of Labor[3], the Syndicalists, the Wobblies. Although much of this comes into the play, and more than one of his characters was in the thick of the violence, 'The Iceman Cometh' is not a play about Labor as such. Its philosophy is eternal and universal, O'Neill thinks: 'It will take man,' he says, 'a million years to grow up and obtain a soul'" (Schriftgiesser 11). As has often been noted about O'Neill, he was quick to place the "larger," humanistic concerns above those of the believers of the One Big Union. Man's ongoing struggle to obtain a soul, for O'Neill, was always at the heart of what man truly needed, as opposed to the search for better wages, working conditions, and hours per week. Or, to recall, Yank's words from *Hairy Ape*, radicals, including the Wobblies, were in the wrong pew, throwing the same old bull.

In many ways, the established view toward the Wobblies and the I.W.W. was firmly rooted in the past tense in the 1940s. An amused and decidedly tongue-in-cheek 13 January 1943 *New York Times* obituary of Carlo Tresca, one of the leaders of the Paterson silk strike, sets the appropriate mood:

His name carries one's memories back to days which were certainly turbulent enough but also gayer than those through which we are now living. Tresca was at various stages an Italian Socialist, a leader of the I.W.W. and a self-styled syndicalist. He was best known a generation ago, when he was likely to turn up wherever there was a strike, always, of course, taking the side of the strikers. Those were the days when people like John Reed, Elizabeth Gurley Flynn and Big Bill Haywood seemed a menace to the established order, and when the I.W.W. were looked upon much as the American Communists are now—though in justice to them it must be said that, unlike their successors, they had a sense of fun. ("The Death of Carlo Tresca" 22)

A cursory search of the *New York Times*, by this time long established as "the paper of record," gives a sense of how far the Wobblies had fallen off the radar of national consciousness. Between the years 1910 and 1920, a casual searcher can find over 1,300 mentions of the I.W.W. in *Times* stories. In contrast, the number of mentions drops to just over three hundred between the years 1940 and 1950. Even allowing for random configurations of the letters "I.W.W.," the difference speaks to a sharp decline of interest and shift in perspective. By 1943, Reed and Haywood were long dead; only Elizabeth Gurley Flynn, Joe Hill's inspiration for the song "The Rebel Girl," was still rebelling, but as a full-fledged Communist. The national fear of "Reds" would remain profound, of course, and by the time O'Neill's play opened on Broadway, the foundations of the long-ranging Cold War had been set. The term "Wobblies," however, seldom figured into anticommunist rhetoric as it once did—the Wobblies were now a "colorful" group with some "wild" ideas in turbulent but gay times. This attitude toward the Wobblies extends to the later O'Neill play, and most likely to O'Neill himself.

Nevertheless, the Wobblies themselves insisted upon not only their continued existence but also their relevancy. Fred Thompson rather defiantly titled his section on the years 1930–1940 "The Stimulus of Depression," insisting that "the IWW made a tremendous propaganda effort.... This propaganda effort was constructive, educational, and put on by flat-broke members of a flat-broke union," while admitting once again that "the IWW had never recovered from the 1924 split. It lost its building and printing plant into which it sunk all its resources" (Thompson *The I.W.W.* 156). The current "iww.org" website lists notable strike achievements in Cleveland and Philadelphia, as well as reestablishing the Chilean IWW Administration during this period ("IWW Chronology 1932–1944"). Nevertheless, even the generally upbeat website admits to "Bleak Years for the IWW" from 1945 to 1971 ("Chronology of IWW History"). Before long, the Wobblies would be placed on the list of subversive organizations, and at length deemed by the website as "near extinction" in 1955—the year of the Wobblies' fiftieth anniversary and the publication of Thompson's study ("IWW Chronology 1946–1971"). It was doubtful that O'Neill's audience was giving a great deal, if any, thought to the Wobblies by the time *Iceman* premiered.

By the summer of 1946, when the first production of *Iceman* was in rehearsals, O'Neill's attitude toward radicalism and "movements" in general had mellowed to a bemused tolerance similar to that of the character of former old-time radical, Larry. Addressing an eager young actor in the production, O'Neill reportedly described himself as "a philosophical anarchist...which means, 'Go to it, but leave me out of it'" (Bowen 461).[4] The energy and work required of anarchy was, O'Neill seems to imply, the work of the young—and certainly, as Sinclair makes clear in his anti-drinking sequence in *Singing Jailbirds*, the work of the sober.

The theatergoer interested in observing O'Neill's latest in October 1946 could see the show for as low as $1.80, or $5.40 for the most expensive seats (Zolotow "'Iceman Cometh' to Start at 5:30" 17). For economic context, the movies were 55 cents, a new car was about $1,125, and the average annual income came to $2,600, or $50 a week (www.afcea.org). One might possibly have had time to have dinner at home during the 6:30–7:45 dinner break to save money on a night out, depending on how close one lived to the theater (Zolotow 17). A middle-aged crowd might well have remembered something of the Wobbly heyday, and their attitudes might well have mirrored O'Neill's. As for *New York Times* theatre critic Brooks Atkinson, the Wobblies and anarchists and other–ists do not bear mentioning, except for perhaps an implication of their place in history when Atkinson characterizes O'Neill: "Look back over his career that began thirty years ago in Provincetown and you realize that the affairs of the world have not influenced it much. He has never been a topical writer" (Atkinson "Four-Hour O'Neill 11). The Wobblies and their ilk were, in fact, no longer topical for many people.

The attitude toward such activity pervades the play as the other equally down-and-out denizens of Hope's saloon patronize (though not without affection) the outbursts of Hugo Kalmar, driven to sing revolutionary songs and recite his favorite revolutionary quotation: "The days grow hot, O Babylon! 'Tis cool beneath thy willow trees!"[5]

Hugo's oft-repeated (in a play where repetition is a primary rhetorical tool) phrase bears some examination, particularly as it relates to O'Neill's play as an extensive Wobbly postmortem. The lines, as Winifred Frazer points out in her article "'Revolution' in *The Iceman Cometh*," come from *"Die Revolution"* by German romantic poet Ferdinand Freilgrath, who published the 40-line poem in 1851. Freilgrath aligned himself with Marx and become well known and respected by some notable Americans (such as Whittier and Longfellow) for his antislavery stand (Frazer 2). Apparently, O'Neill remembered the lines well, but despite the help of editor friends and the services of New York libraries, never satisfactorily traced the source, which did not bother O'Neill particularly at the time (3). For O'Neill, the more important source was a personal one, his radical friend Hippolyte Havel. Havel's physical bearing and checkered career served as the prototype for *Iceman*'s Hugo, as did contributions from the popular media. As O'Neil notes in his stage directions: "There is a foreign atmosphere about him, the stamp of an alien radical, a strong resemblance to the type Anarchist as portrayed, bomb in hand, in newspaper cartoons" (O'Neill *Iceman* 4).

The type of cartoons O'Neill references has a traceable beginning. Such cartoons began their heyday with the Haymarket Affair of 1886, when a bomb exploded amongst a group of policemen trying to disperse a labor protest meeting, wounding some 60 policemen and killing seven others. The swift aftermath involved the arrests of eight known Chicago anarchist leaders—four were hanged, one killed himself in prison, and the others languished in jail. Along with the resultant increase in class conflict, the image, fueled by the national newspapers, emerged in the public consciousness of the bomb-throwing radical O'Neill describes. Historians often appropriate the phrase William Preston uses in his *Aliens and Dissenters: Federal Suppression of Radicals 1903–1933* in describing the classic anarchist figure: "ragged, unwashed, long-haired, wild-eyed fiend, armed with smoking revolver and bomb—to say nothing of the dagger he sometimes carried between his teeth" (Preston 26).[6] The fear of radicals and their tools of destruction was amplified in the public imagination through the cluster of destructive anarchist activity in the United States and Europe ranging from the assassination of Italy's King Umberto, to the attempted assassination of Henry Frick during western Pennsylvania's Homestead Strike, to the assassination of President McKinley in 1901 by Leon Czolgosz (Goldstein 58). The cartoons proliferated throughout the early part of the twentieth century and through the Great War, distributed through newspapers across the country, and in the case of Walter Bradfort's "Fitzboomski the Anarchist," the caricatured anarchist became a comic strip character as well.[7]

O'Neill made a wholesale appropriation of Havel's salient characteristics, including the thick accent (one of many accents and dialects O'Neill would painstakingly transcribe in his scripts throughout his career), the detailed physical description included in the stage directions, and the drunken repetitions of snatches of songs and poetry, including the lines from "Revolution."[8] The lines effectively connect the debunking of two of the major "pipe dreams" in which the roomers at Harry Hope's indulge, that love can conquer all, and that revolution can bring forth a new world (Frazer 3). In this way, the recurring theme found in nearly all the plays under analysis in this study but for Sinclair's can be summed up accordingly—what the Wobblies had to offer were as much pipe dreams as the "pie in the sky" mocked in the Wobbly songs. Of interest for our study is the fact that O'Neill presents these conclusions in the time frame of much of the most successful Wobbly activity.

The physical presence of the other longtime anarchist, Larry, is also worth noting in terms of O'Neill's embodiment of "the Movement" and its members:

> Larry Slade is sixty. He is tall, raw-boned, with coarse straight white hair, worn long and raggedly cut. He has a gaunt Irish face with a big nose, high cheekbones, a lantern jaw with a week's stubble of beard, a mystic's meditative pale-blue eyes with a gleam of sharp sardonic humor in them.... his clothes are dirty and much slept in.... From the way he methodically scratches himself with his long-fingered, hairy hands, he is lousy and reconciled to being so... his face [has] the quality of a pitying but weary old priest's. (O'Neill *The Iceman Cometh* 4–5)

Like Hugo, Larry also has a real-life counterpart in O'Neill's past—the colorful former anarchist Terry Carlin, who is usually credited with facilitating the historically significant meeting between O'Neill and the Provincetown Players.[9] As Malcolm Cowley writes, Carlin was a "gaunt, benign Irishman who had retired from gainful occupation after a working career that lasted one day.... He... lived to be nearly eighty, on a chiefly liquid diet. Terry was a mystic of sorts who had been a radical syndicalist in his early days and then a philosophical anarchist" (Cowley 42). That Cowley uses the same term O'Neill used to describe himself to the young actor is not necessarily a coincidence—the image of someone still fond of the idea of syndicalism but who has replaced his direct action with drinking laced with occasional "foolosophy," in *Iceman*'s terms, is one of the major images of O'Neill's ultimate barroom play.[10] Further, the description of "benign" applies to both Larry and Hugo in the play—the radical as tired, drunk, and faintly comical older men.

The final staging of an actual Wobbly in the play is in the character of the young, guilt-ridden Don Parritt. O'Neil's description also disqualifies Parritt as a potential threat to society: "He is eighteen, tall and broad-shouldered but thin, gangling and awkward" (O'Neill *The Iceman Cometh* 21). Thus the anarchist contingent of *The Iceman Cometh* brings precious little of the vitality the Wobblies themselves actually exhibited in the era in which *Iceman* is set. For Parritt, who reveals himself as a traitor to the Wobblies, the members of the movement were primarily layabouts who invaded his childhood home and frequently took turns sleeping with his married-to-the-cause mother.

O'Neill's play is set in 1912, before the repressive Espionage Acts of the Great War had its great weakening effect on the I.W.W., and the year before the Paterson silk strike that brought the Wobbly pageant to Broadway. O'Neill simultaneously presents his characters' attitudes toward the Wobblies as of their time and as a rueful look back at idealistic activity and great times that, O'Neill seems to imply, never quite were. Nevertheless, worth keeping in mind is the well-documented history of O'Neill's radical-influenced youth, including submitting revolutionary poetry to the same magazine that published a translation of Freiligrath's poem in 1910.[11] O'Neill's opinions on the Wobblies, of course, were highly personal, and quite likely a part of a long-standing pattern of distancing himself from the world of radicalism as well as, perhaps, an understandable attitude of a man who was starting to feel the effects of advancing age and debilitating disease.

In the world of the play, the characters' attitude toward the Wobblies is mostly dismissive—as the drunken failed lawyer Willie Oban comments to the unfortunate Parritt, "Go away and blow yourself up, that's a good lad." Oban also directs a good-natured jibe at the unconscious Hugo a moment later: "A dangerous terrorist, Hugo! He would as soon blow the collar off a schooner of beer as look at you!" (O'Neill *The Iceman Cometh* 39). The characters also display a carelessness regarding what sort of anarchism the characters represent—indeed, even the anarchists themselves display such carelessness.

O'Neill's characters conflate the disparate threads of "the Movement" the way many Americans would have at the time.[12] The doomed Parritt self-identifies as a "Wobblie" (O'Neill *The Iceman Cometh* 27), while he recognizes both Larry and Hugo as longtime members of "the movement" who held meetings at his mother's house. Larry, in turn, is referred to as I.W.W. through the various taunts thrown at him by irascible saloon-owner Harry Hope: "You bughouse I-Won't-Work harp..." (87). One notable element about this I.W.W. identification, which Larry does not bother to correct or modify, is that Larry left the Movement some 11 years before the action of the play, which would be 1901 (29–30). Larry, therefore, would have left the Movement about four years before the I.W.W. was formed. While the discrepancy could also be explained as a chronological error on O'Neill's part, his knowledge and intimacy with the down-at-the-heels radicals (after all, he knew them all, as he said) renders this possibility less likely. Nevertheless, it is clear that Larry feels kinship with the Wobblies even as he elaborately protests indifference to "the cause," as well as to any causes. Larry and Hugo serve in the play as representations of the divergent radicals who would soon compromise, not always smoothly, by converging and forming the I.W.W.

The sometimes muddled and muddy thinking among the anarchists regarding where they stood and what their movement meant is borne out by the speeches and literature of the period. In 1913, a year after *Iceman* takes place, Emma Goldman published a pamphlet titled *Syndicalism: The Modern Menace to Capitalism*. In it, she teases the misconceptions of the well-meaning American radicals: "To the indefinite, uncertain mind of the American radical the most contradictory ideas and methods are possible. The result is a sad chaos in the radical movement, a sort of intellectual hash, which has neither taste nor character.... Syndicalism is the pastime of a great many Americans, so-called intellectuals. Not that they know anything about it..." (Goldman *Syndicalism*). Small wonder, then, that opponents of the radicals seldom bothered to keep the players straight when the radicals themselves could not manage the job.

Similarly to *The Hairy Ape*, the I.W.W. representatives in *Iceman* fail to offer answers to the fundamental questions of what it means to be a human being. As Eric Bentley notes in his November 1946 *Atlantic Monthly* review, an impression of the script, rather than the performance, "Politics provide a background for a 'timeless' theme, thus annoying the Marxists who look in vain through O'Neill's work for a social message" (Bentley "The Return of Eugene O'Neill" 65). The character with the clearest sense of distinctions between the various "ists" and "isms" that made up the movement, interestingly enough, is Joe, the itinerant former gambler and only person of color in the play. Joe's disparagement of the movement, and distinctions and disagreements within the movement, are on full display in a sardonic anecdote:

> If dere's one ting more'n anudder I cares nuttin' about, it's de sucker game you and Hugo call the Movement. (He chuckles—reminiscently) Reminds me of damn fool argument me and Mose Porter has de udder night. He's drunk and I'm drunker. He says, "Socialist and Anarchist, we ought to shoot dem dead. Dey's all no-good sons of bitches." I says, "Hold on, you talk's if Anarchists and Socialists was de same." "Dey is," he says. "No, dey ain't," I says. "I'll explain the difference. De Anarchist he never works. He drinks but he never buys, and if he do ever get a nickel, he blows it in on bombs, and he wouldn't give you nothin'. So go ahead and shoot him. But de Socialist, sometimes, he's got a job, and if he gets ten bucks, he's bound by his religion to split fifty-fifty wid you. You say—how about my cut, Comrade? And you gets de five. So you don't shoot no Socialists while I'm around. Dat is, not if dey got anything. Of course, if dey's broke, den dey's no-good bastards, too." (O'Neill *The Iceman Cometh* 20)

While Larry appreciates this story told early in the play, the arc of Larry's belief system throughout Iceman reflects the theme of the ultimate hopelessness of trying to effect major change through "direct action." Larry's consistent refrain throughout most of the play is that he left the Movement "after thirty years' devotion to the Cause" because men were too low and corrupt to create an Ideal

Society: "When man's soul isn't a sow's ear, it will be time enough to dream of silk purses" (30). Larry's autobiographical speech dates his radical activities back to roughly 1871.

Here, O'Neill's tale hints at the probable turbulent pasts of Larry and his contemporary, Hugo, by dating the anarchists' activity during one of the first modern waves of American class struggle and violence. For historical perspective, people of Larry's anarchist bent might have attended a meeting at New York's Cooper Institute "organized by trade unions and the American section of the First International... [that] drew a huge crowd, overflowing into the streets" (Zinn 243), where workers demanded an eight-hour day and that no one individual should own an excess of money or property—in this case, no more than $30,000 (Zinn 243). Along with other demonstrations in New York and Chicago, strikes emerged in textile mills in Massachusetts as well as the coal districts of Pennsylvania. The Irish Larry undoubtedly knew of the fate of the "Molly Maguires," members of the Ancient Order of Hibernians found guilty of acts of violence—quite possibly (probably?) framed because of their status as labor organizers (Zinn 243–44). He would almost certainly have been close to many members of the Western Federation of Miners, acknowledged as an important I.W.W. predecessor. Both Larry and Hugo, moreover, would have known of and perhaps associated with the Knights of Labor, whose successes against the railroad made them, for a while in the 1880s, the nation's most powerful union. Indeed, the similarities between mottoes of the KOL and the I.W.W. are striking—the Knights of Labor insisted that "an injury to one is the concern of all," and the Wobblies modified the saying as "an injury to one is an injury to all."[13]

As for the German Hugo, partially named, as Frazer notes, for Karl Marx himself ("Karl Marx" = "Kalmar"), his real-life counterparts helped organize their own 1876 American centennial celebration in Chicago, a coming together of German socialists and the Workingmen's party. In language echoing the original Declaration of Independence, the party declared its independence from the capitalist system with rights to "make our own laws, manage our own production, and govern ourselves, acknowledging no rights without duties, no duties without rights" (Zinn 244–45). With some 30 years of robber barons, strike-breaking, and the seeming indestructability of "the combination of private capital and government power" (Zinn 251), the theatergoer might well understand Hugo's delusions and Larry's weariness, even if they would not necessarily agree with their old anarchist agendas.

The power of American corporate capitalism is, however, for both Larry and O'Neill, only one side of the story. For Larry makes his views particularly clear that he has grown disillusioned with those in the Movement itself—ones who begin as idealists and world-changers, and who prove just as greedy for power and recognition as those against whom they fight. As Larry puts it early in the play: "I saw men didn't want to be saved from themselves, for that would mean they'd have to give up greed, and they'll never pay that price for liberty" (O'Neill *The Iceman Cometh* 11). Parritt, in the midst of laughing off his too-vehement reaction to being called "stool pigeon" by a drunken Hugo, notes his admiration for the now-fallen anarchist whose friends and associates have apparently left him behind: "I've always stood up for him when people in the Movement panned him for an old drunken has-been" (34). That a movement supposedly dedicated to the uplift of all working-class individuals could treat those who gave their lives and health to the cause so callously must have particularly rankled O'Neill, and the rancor is palpable in such seemingly casual statements that pepper the characters' conversation.

Further, Larry and his contemporaries would have had plenty of opportunities to see union corruption, power plays, exclusivity, and opportunism. Unskilled workers, American Negros, women, and foreigners were excluded from union activity and benefits, and union leaders often prospered at the expense of the workers.[14] As Zinn writes regarding the American Federation of Labor (AFL): "The well-paid leaders of the AFL were protected from criticism by tightly controlled meetings and by 'goon' squads—hired toughs originally used against strikebreakers but after a while used to intimidate and beat up opponents inside the union" (Zinn 329). Whether or not Larry left the movement due to disillusionment or due to an unhappy affair with Parritt's mother, Rosa (referred to in the play primarily as "Mother," possibly a nod to the indefatigable Mother Jones), he certainly had enough examples to back up his misanthropic thesis. Hugo, for his part, is awakened periodically from a drunken fog to relive the singing, declaiming, and speech-making of an earlier generation, dropping names from a turbulent past: "Damned bourgeois Wop!" he declaims to befuddled bartender Rocky, "The great Malatesta is my good friend! Buy me a drink!" (O'Neill *Iceman* 11). During such moments, Hugo shows traces of the commanding orator he possibly once was, even though his powers of persuasion are currently used to procure another drink.

Notably, as Hickey goads the men in the saloon to, at least briefly, face the truth about themselves, Hugo's own conflicting attitudes toward the cause and those for whom the cause was supposedly meant come to the surface as well. Hugo reveals his contempt for the common people—"always a high-toned swell at heart, eh Hugo?" as Hickey jokingly (and accurately) remarks. Hugo, deep down, perhaps was one of Larry's examples of how greedy for power the most militant anarchists could be. By 1946, audiences would have been well aware, and wary of, leaders who self-identified as champions of the working class who became ruthless despots.

Hugo, Larry, and Parritt further provide *Iceman* with another historical thread to the I.W.W. through quick references to anarchist philosophy sometimes appropriated and sometimes debated by Wobblies and their compatriots. Along with Italian anarchist Malatesta, names from the roots of anarchism, socialism, syndicalism, and communism abound in the play, including Bakunin and Kropotkin, regulars at international labor conferences when Larry and Hugo were much younger men. Through this use of names perhaps only vaguely familiar to his 1946 audience, who were more engaged with the ghost of Lenin and the very-much-alive Stalin, O'Neill illustrates and at least partially dramatizes the 40-odd years of anarchist history and activity that Larry and Hugo evoke. Some background regarding these names, seemingly treated as casual throw-away moments in the course of the play, might serve to illustrate O'Neill's use of the anarchist, and perhaps more specifically, the Wobbly agenda.

Michael (or Mikhail) Bakunin is considered the father of Russian nihilism—hence Larry's teasing (with serious undertones, as is Larry's wont) lines to Hugo in Act II: "Be God, it's not to Bakunin's ghost you ought to pray in your dreams, but to the great Nihilist, Hickey!" (O'Neill *Iceman*). For Bakunin, nihilism meant, roughly speaking, "an insistence that one should not believe in anything that could not be demonstrated to be true.... More than anything else, nihilism was a form of literary and political criticism based on a broad definition of science" (Leier 227). Bakunin knew and at least to a degree admired Marx, while he chiefly disagreed with Marx's conception of the proletarian dictatorship. Bakunin candidly admitted, "He called me a sentimental idealist, and he was right; I called him vain, perfidious, and cunning, and I also was right" (Bakunin "Recollections on Marx and Engels"). Bakunin also championed the commune over the state: "I believe...equality must be established through the spontaneous organization of voluntary cooperation of work freely organized, and into communes federated, by productive associations and through the equally spontaneous federation of communes—not through and by supreme supervising action of the State" (Bakunin "Where I Stand").

For Peter Kropotkin, who emerged as Bakunin's chief successor, anarchy was a natural result of man's evolution; just as science adjusted to the discoveries that proved that the earth revolved around the sun instead of the other way around, man's relationship with politics and government would similarly evolve: "[Political economy] cares less to know if such a nation has or has not a large foreign trade; it wants to be assured that bread is not wanting in the peasant's or worker's cottage. It knocks at all doors—at that of the palace as well as that of the hovel—and asks the rich as well as the poor: Up to what point are your needs satisfied both for necessaries and luxuries?" (Kropotkin "Anarchism"). Kropotkin took the idea of the decentralization further, championing the communization not only of the means of production but also the product (Crabtree "History of Anarchism").

Notably, Errico Malatesta, evoked by Hugo in the play in order to get Rocky the bartender to give him a free drink, befriended both Bakunin and Kropotkin, and would later break with Kropotkin and other anarchists on the issue of taking sides in the Great War ("Errico Malatesta"). In sum, such distinctions between the anarchists mentioned in *Iceman* may well have been subtle to the outsider, and perhaps all but nonexistent to the characters in the play as well as audience members who grouped all anarchists together. Nevertheless, the differences were clear enough to cause major disagreements between anarchist movements, and many of these disagreements found their way into I.W.W. meetings as well. O'Neill took great pains to plant these names and their historical baggage in the play; it would be a major production and directing error to ignore them entirely. But, paradoxically, the names and their respective histories have little bearing in the world of Harry Hope's saloon, as Larry acknowledges through his attitude of amused indifference. The challenge in plumbing the depths of the anarchist and Wobbly aspects of O'Neill's play is to acknowledge the indifference of the majority of the characters, while not mistaking that same indifference for that of O'Neill, and not assuming such indifference with regard to matters of production and study.

It falls to truth-telling salesman Hickey, who has disrupted the peace of Harry Hope's saloon, to expose Larry's cynical talk as a front for a sentimental fondness and belief in the Cause: "That's another lie you tell yourself, Larry, that the good old Cause means nothing to you any more" (118). The audience gets to see this old faithfulness briefly stirred in Larry as Parritt confirms that the arrests of the Wobblies out west from which he is fleeing was the result of inside information: "By God, I hate to believe it of any of the crowd, if I am through long since with any connection with them. I know they're damned fools, most of them, as stupidly greedy for power as the worst capitalist they attack, but I'd swear there couldn't be a yellow stool pigeon among them" (O'Neill *The Iceman Cometh* 27).

As Larry comes to learn well before Parritt's confession that he was the stool pigeon, Larry faces his biggest conflict—a desire for justice for Parritt for selling out his comrades, and a desire to stay "in the grandstand of life" neither knowing nor caring to know any of its business. It is Larry's last vestiges of faith that are killed with Parritt's suicide, when neither causes nor life itself means anything to Larry anymore: "I'm the only real convert to death Hickey made here" (258). Also dead, O'Neill seems to tell his audience, is the spirit of Wobbly activism, as the three representatives of such philosophical anarchy meet their respective fates: a "convert to death," a literal suicide, and a raucous, living joke who might in fact recognize his uselessness, but can still hide from the truth through booze, unlike his friend Larry. Perhaps fittingly for the end of the I.W.W. on Broadway, that admission of death is surrounded by raucous, cacophonous singing, led by a particularly wide-awake and lively Hugo—just the way, one imagines, the Wobblies would want to go out.

While this play, as noted earlier, could stand as a "Wobblies on Broadway" epitaph, it is also, paradoxically, the play that perhaps most keeps Wobbly characters alive on the world's commercial stages. Of all the plays under study, it is *Iceman* that most often enjoys major revivals in New York, Chicago, and other major theatrical centers, featuring major actors such as the late Jason Robards, Brian Dennehy,[15] Kevin Spacey, and Nathan Lane in the plum role of Hickey. It is through this play that perhaps audiences get their only exposure to such once-common terms as "Wobbly," and "I Won't Work." The Wobblies on Broadway might well be a dormant theatrical footnote, but one occasionally awakened with the sound of song, laughter, and just perhaps, a hint of sabotage.

8. Postscript: Not Time Yet

The plays examined in this study were a mixed lot that garnered, on the whole, mixed success. The high points of the plays, like many I.W.W. rallies, were vibrant and colorful events, and the staged Wobblies certainly kept the Big Stem lively. In terms of advancing Wobbly causes or even producing long-lasting, evergreen theatre that audiences would return to, the Wobblies on Broadway fared less well—the obvious exception being the Eugene O'Neill plays (particularly *Iceman*), as O'Neill's name value as an important playwright still looms impressively large.

The questions revolving around the study of these plays echo the question Susan Duffy asks in her final chapter of *American Labor on Stage*: "One might rightly ask, why would anyone today want to read these plays?" We might extend the question further to ask about seeing or producing the plays as well. With respect to the plays Duffy examined in her study, her confident answer is that "in their respect for the worker, the laborer, the common man and woman, they transcend the modern political movements that spawned them" (Duffy 137). What, exactly, have the Broadway Wobbly plays transcended as we examine them in the twenty-first century? The answers might well still be worth exploring further, but I would submit that unlike plays that more directly fit the definition of labor play—worker themes and characters for worker audiences—the Broadway plays were constantly straddling, with varying degrees of success, the line between political polemic and mainstream commercial entertainment. The writers, directors, and producers of these plays sought to create a play that could, pretty much by definition, transcend the social and political while at the same time somehow embracing those elements. As previously noted, there were many observers and critics at the time who felt that the goals of Broadway success and the goal of delivering a pro-Wobbly message to the Broadway audience were, also pretty much by definition, mutually exclusive. It is also worth remembering, however, that while some of these plays could be considered "workers' theatre" in the sense of their content and themes, other plays sought to turn the Wobbly into a palatable Broadway "character." As such, the plays under study present an interesting, imperfect, and often fascinating glimpse of the labor struggles and class shifts of the period. Patrick J. Chura asks regarding the career of O'Neill in the 1920s, "Could a middle-class radical/dramatist first seamlessly cross classes and 'be' a worker, then interpret workers' lives in ways that ultimately aided them in the class struggle? What are the real effects—for both downclasser and working-class subject—of class barrier transgression?" (Chura 525). We might adjust those questions to encompass all the examples of the Wobblies on Broadway—what were the real effects for the Wobblies, the playwrights who appropriated the Wobblies, and the audiences of class barrier transgression? Whatever the artistic merits of such transgression, and whatever the obstructions in message delivery the combination of commercialism and Wobbly-ism entailed, the plays and their Wobbly characters represent what is largely a forgotten segment of Broadway history.

The other non-O'Neill plays under study showed sporadic signs of the occasional rebirth. *They Knew What They Wanted* managed a few major revivals, the latest one occurring in 1976—some 20 years after *The Most Happy Fella* graced the Big Stem. *New York Times* critic Walter Kerr found the evening disappointing and artificial, and there is no mention in his review of Joe being any sort of Wobbly (Kerr "Stage View" D5). *Processional* managed a lively return under the production of the Federal Theater Project in 1937, but the play has pretty much kept under cover since, much like Dynamite Jim in his mother's cellar. *Gods of the Lightning* and *Singing Jailbirds* each had their one-and-only shot on or near Broadway, with *Gods*, as noted earlier, making a brief reappearance in the early 1960s, and *Singing Jailbirds* attempting to take flight as a full-fledged musical, appropriately in San Pedro, California, in 2009.

The plays as plays will most likely remain hard-to-produce curios, although not just because the plays deal with Wobbly themes and characters. *They Knew What They Wanted* would probably no longer offend the delicate sensibilities of those who would see adultery always punished, although the repeated use of the word "wop" (for the many Italians in the play, including Tony) might potentially cause some discomfort. Even if a revision-minded revivalist excised the various epithets aimed at the Italians, Howard's play has also been greatly eclipsed by Frank Loesser's musical adaptation—as noted earlier, without all the political, religious, and otherwise Wobbly discussions. The play is nevertheless rather underrated by twenty-first century standards, and perhaps could well stand another look.[1] *Processional*, with its mad jumble of styles, tones, and themes, was always a hard sell; *Gods of the Lightning* would need several pages of footnotes in the theater programs; and *Singing Jailbirds* is perhaps best experienced as a written journalistic record with Sinclair's pointed background notes intact. It is generally left to the O'Neill plays, when they periodically come around to Broadway or the major metropolitan theatre centers, to briefly bring back the I.W.W. slang and a ghost of the old music and spirit.

Occasionally, workers' theatre as workers' theatre scored on Broadway, most notably in the productions of *Waiting for Lefty* and the revue *Pins and Needles* in the 1930s—the latter emerging as the biggest "hit" of the labor stage, running on Broadway for three years. More commonly, and perhaps more appropriately, workers' theatre came to thrive in labor colleges and similar environments where workers could perform education and outreach. Away from the commercial, profit-seeking demands of the Broadway stage, such plays could present, in Colette Hyman's words, "visions of optimism. By affirming the experiences and values of their audiences, the plays transformed the ordinariness of working people's everyday lives and struggles into the tangible possibility of successful collective action" (Hyman 80).[2] In turn, Lee Papa, in his introduction to his collection of workers' theatre plays (which include *Processional* and *Singing Jailbirds*), astutely notes the workers' theatre influence continuing through the plays of Arthur Miller, David Mamet, and August Wilson, and cites the work of Moises Kaufman's Tectonic Theatre and the extended monologues of Anna Devere Smith as carrying on the tradition in the decidedly capitalist world of commercial theatre (Papa x). Workers' theatre found stages not only in the United States but internationally. The seemingly indestructible Manny Fried found audiences, primarily in Buffalo, New York, for his fiercely human workers' plays into his nineties. Even the Wobblies found some stage representation in plays such as *The Man Who Never Died*, Barrie Stavis's chronicle of Joe Hill, and Stewart Bird's *The Wobblies: The U.S. vs. Wm. D. Haywood, et al.: [A Play]*.[3] Hints of the workers' spirit did, and still do, find voice on stages—and occasionally, on the biggest and most commercial of stages.

The Broadway Wobblies, however, both fed this particularly lively stream of theatre and flowed apart from it. The plays under study serve as a distinctly prickly subset and offshoot of workers' theatre—as noted earlier, some of these plays fit the category much more comfortably than others. Their presence on the Great White Way directly challenged the experiences and values of their audience on a stage where there was never quite an ideal fit. And while the actual Wobblies themselves occasionally took the opportunity to cheer their Broadway counterparts, they did so with the recognition that Broadway was not their home base or their most likely bully pulpit. One might feel free to speculate how the Wobblies would respond to audiences paying the highest Broadway and Chicago prices for all-star revivals of *Iceman*. One might also wonder how a Broadway audience of the twenty-first century might respond to the staged world of the I.W.W. The story of the Wobblies on Broadway, nevertheless, is not quite complete.

In the spirit of a Broadway Wobblies "postscript," the early 1990s brought to New York one more variation of the Wobbly in a segment of epic theatre inspired by an actor-turned-playwright's eye-opening journey through Kentucky. Broadway audiences, unfortunately, did not particularly welcome this ambitious project; in fact, the production closed in less than a month. In many ways, the play, Robert Schenkkan's *The Kentucky Cycle*, was highly regarded; it was the winner of the 1992 Pulitzer Prize for drama, and the second Pulitzer Prize-winner examined in this study (after Howard's *They Knew What They Wanted*). More accurately, Schenkkan's work was, as the title indicates, a cycle of nine short plays that staged a span of 200 years in the interlocking lives of struggling, and often vicious, Kentucky families. In a sense, therefore, we return to the world of the pageant that brought the Wobblies to Broadway in the first place. This "almost" Wobbly play featuring an "almost" Wobbly character requires a bit of background information.

In the nearly 50-year span between the premiere of *The Iceman Cometh* and the opening of *The Kentucky Cycle,* the I.W.W. had entered and crawled out of its bleakest period—by their own account, the 25-year period spanning 1946–1971. The website, generally quite positive and upbeat about I.W.W. activity throughout history, notes that by the Wobblies' fiftieth anniversary (1955), they were "near extinction" ("IWW Chronology 1946–1971").[4] The antiwar protests of the 1960s found the peace-loving Wobblies some new welcome attention among students. By the early 1990s, the Wobs were particularly active in their ongoing quest to remain lively and relevant. While the I.W.W. website frankly admits several failures as well as partial successes, the Wobblies found environmentally-minded allies in creating the Redwood Summer project in Northern California in 1990 as a protest against liquidation logging and the exploitation of the timber workers, a branch of workers who had a long history with the I.W.W. (It is worth remembering that the I.W.W. made their first big splashes out west—it would take the eastern part of the country several years to start paying fearful attention to the Wobblies.) The

Wobblies also assiduously protested the Iraq War the following year, calling for a general strike. Perhaps most significantly, the mid-1990s brought the I.W.W. into the internet age, as they became the first international union to create a website presence ("IWW Chronology 1990–1995"). While these activities might not have been widely known to *The Kentucky Cycle*'s Broadway audience, the projects suggest a liveliness impressive for what was still a greatly misunderstood organization as it entered its nineties. This liveliness would come to infuse the union-themed episode of Schenkkan's drama.

When *The Kentucky Cycle* opened in November 1993, audiences were experiencing the early stages of the "Disneyfication" of Times Square—the old adult theatres were being cleaned up and torn down, Disney's *Beauty and the Beast* would open in April of the following year, and *The Lion King* would settle in for its run, presumably forever as of this writing, a few years later.[5] Potential *Cycle* customers would pay top prices of $100 a ticket for this special event, the same as top prices for an earlier epic production, the Royal Shakespeare Company's 1981 production of *The Life and Adventures of Nicholas Nickleby*. The production of the *Cycle* cost $2.5 million to produce, a record sum at the time, and the production in fact offered a fairly wide spectrum of ticket price choices—the side mezzanine seats were the cheapest, selling for as low as $20 on Wednesday matinees (Collins, "On Stage"). Seeing the play also necessitated negotiating a somewhat complicated viewing schedule, including dinner breaks, hearkening back to O'Neill's *Iceman*. Indeed, the *Times* had to print a correction of the schedule shortly after they first printed it.

The end of 1993 was also significant in terms of theatre production, as Tony Kushner's massive *Angels in America* was proving that there were indeed audiences for large-scale (and multipart) epic drama.[6] Why there was comparatively little audience for Schenkkan's drama was a question the playwright was still wrestling with some 13 years later, as evidenced by a *New York Times* interview regarding a new project: "You've really got to know your audience in New York... When I produce, the very first question I say to myself is, what about this piece is going to make two people from New Jersey who work in Manhattan go home, arrange for babysitters, shower, change, get back in their car and come back into the city? You've got to have a hook or an appeal for them to do it..." (Irene Lacher "Go West" A8). While Schenkkan was not necessarily speaking as a social historian, or perhaps even saying anything new, the observation still has some relevance. For audiences at the end of 1993 at least, who certainly included the people Schenkkan described, along with those from the other boroughs and the requisite number of tourists, the appeal of *The Kentucky Cycle* was, for one or more reasons, decidedly lacking. Negotiating time and opportunity to see the production, with its previously noted somewhat complicated schedule, would take rather more effort than usual, which probably did not help the play's final Broadway fortunes.

Another "strike" that the play had against it was the unusual conditions under which it won the Pulitzer—it had not yet been produced in New York, the first time that a "regional" play won the prize without validation from the Broadway or off-Broadway audiences.[7] As *New York Times* theatre reporter Alex Witchel observed: "The New York theater world was shocked...when Robert Schenkkan's 'Kentucky Cycle' won the Pulitzer Prize for drama. Why? Because the 6-hour, 40-minute epic about three families from 1775 to 1975, which has been produced at the Intiman Theater in Seattle and the Mark Taper Forum in Los Angeles, has never attracted a New York producer." At the time of the announcement, there were still "no firm plans for a New York production" (Witchel, "On Stage, and Off"). So what was this mysterious play that New York producers were so slow to get their hands on, and how did the Wobblies fit in?

The "Wobbly" part of *The Kentucky Cycle* is the segment "Fire in the Hole," which takes place in 1920. The I.W.W. representative in this case is a fictitious Jewish organizer named Abe Steinman. The physicality Schenkkan had in mind for Steinman was, according to the stage directions, "tall, intense" (Schenkkan 1993 215). The actor playing Steinman in this production, Tuck Milligan, in his early to mid-forties at the time, had something of the weathered "character actor" look that a number of the earlier stage Wobblies had. Schenkkan also makes Steinman a talker, in some ways similar to the radical Psinski of Lawson's *Processional* in his verbosity. The talkative tendency of Steinman is commented upon by another character: "Don't you never shut up?" (225). One could also make an apt comparison between Schenkkan's project and O'Neill—as critic Robert Brustein pointed out, O'Neill himself had planned on a nine-play cycle of family plays staging the dark side of American development (Brustein, "Robert Brustein on Theater").[8] The "Fire in the Hole" playlet follows a number of familiar patterns from earlier Wobbly plays as well as conventions that would be clear and familiar to most Broadway audiences.

While Steinman is Schenkkan's creation, he references the Paint Creek, West Virginia Mine War of 1912–1913, where he met the legendary labor organizer Mother Jones.[9] Mother Jones, one of the initial organizers of the I.W.W., still active and well into her eighties when the play takes place, makes appearances in the play as well as Steinman recalls her, singing appropriate union songs[10] and threatening soldiers and mine bosses: "You muzzle that damn mug of yours up. I ain't afraid of ninety-nine hundred of you! I would clean you up just like a sewer rat!" (230).[11] It is Mother Jones' spirit, along with that of Abe (who does not survive the play), that inspires the miners' union at the play's close.

Steinman seeks to unionize the miners, and in his rhetorical arsenal are many of the Wobbly sentiments noted throughout their history. Steinman insists upon the inclusiveness of the union, offering the Negro rum and gun-runner Cassius the opportunity to join, and he evokes the distinctly Wobbly notion of Jesus as "a workin' man," reminiscent of the speech of the Dominie's in *Singing Jailbirds* identifying Jesus as the first Wobbly (Schenkkan 1993 249). He further extends the metaphor of union as family to the impressionable 10-year-old Joshua, who is already following his father into the mines (251).[12] And while he does advocate violence, he does so as a last resort and primarily for self-defense—all tenets of the Wobbly platform.

Schenkkan also finds ways to echo and subvert the Wobbly message as it becomes clear that the central character, Tommy, will sell out the others and the strike will fail. The mining boss, Andrew, sells Tommy over to his side by denouncing the "agitators" like Steinman: "These agitators come in here, talkin' that talk, promisin' you people this and that and pie in the sky" (254). Thus Andrew takes the expression originated in the parody song by Joe Hill, "pie in the sky," and appropriates it for a vastly different context. Clearly, Schenkkan intends this segment of his pageant as a glimpse of Wobbly activity, the sort of glimpse that had been absent from the Broadway stage for quite some time.

The play's outcome—not only the "Fire in the Hole" segment but of the entire production—also echoed the major recurring theme of the Wobbly plays under discussion. As Schenkkan himself articulates the dilemma in his author's note to the play: "How do we bring an end to these seemingly endless cycles of violence and loss? If family is not the answer and class is not the answer and social movements are not the answer, what is? It must be something larger..." (Schenkkan 1993 338). The questions that the playwrights of the Wobblies on Broadway had been asking since the 1920s were still pertinent some 70 years later, and the conclusions seemed similar as well. A social movement, or a labor movement, was not sufficient to solve the deepest and most desperate problems of mankind. Fair working conditions and enough food were important, but in the world of these plays, there was always something more that the most enthusiastic and determined union organizers could not touch. Schenkkan's refrain, while not as overtly fatalistic or negativist as the themes of many of the predecessor plays, nevertheless is somewhat familiar; Schenkkan's questions are not far removed from the voices of characters past—people in power will keep their power; top dogs and underdogs will keep "scrapping," and we are all guilty of being born, get me?

The *New York Times* critic, Frank Rich, in a rather withering review of the production that might well have contributed to its swift closing, commented, "I wish I could add that 'The Kentucky Cycle' offered either one startling insight into American history, one original turn of phrase, one novel theatrical moment or one character of tragic size who is deeply moving as an individual rather than as a generic representative of some sociopolitical development. But I can't" (Rich, "200 Years"). Rich's dissatisfaction, and perhaps ultimately that of the mainstream audience, might in many ways be tied to the very notion of folk drama and folk heroes that the Wobblies created—workers were generally heroic, capitalists were generally villainous, and the songs, jokes, tragedies, and heroics followed accordingly.[13] The "story" and "myth" aspects of the play were more appreciated by others, including in a counterpoint response to the production that ran almost a week after Rich's initial review: "If 'The Kentucky Cycle' falls short of great playwriting, it qualifies as a vigorous piece of popular storytelling, filled with the kind of surprises, reversals and sudden revelations that were standard fare in the theater when the theater made a point of reaching out to a broad range of customers" (Richards, "Smashing America's Favorite Myths"). At the heart of Wobbly history was a great deal of vigorous, popular storytelling, and in that sense, Schenkkan's work mirrors and extends the equally vigorous world of workers' theatre. While, as noted, the "Wobbly" portion of this play is a relatively small one, *The Kentucky Cycle* might have been another verification of the notion that a "workers'" play could not "flirt" successfully with Broadway.[14]

Nevertheless, there is one more element of the "Fire in the Hole" segment of the *Cycle* that is of considerable significance. Despite all of the "Wobbly" markers the play features, the terms "Wobbly" and "I.W.W." are never mentioned. The doomed Steinman, who is shot by the mine boss at the end of the play, and for that matter, Mother Jones, are both described as "union" organizers, and Steinman speaks exclusively of the "union," but not the I.W.W.[15] So, the "tall, intense"

Steinman did not directly present as a Wobbly figure to its audience, even though Schenkkan places Steinman in a distinctly Wobbly historical context, and has him do and say what a Wobbly of the time would do and say, although the songs Schenkkan calls for in the script were not, strictly speaking, Wobbly songs.[16] Further, Steinman has young Joshua read a union speech while Steinman whittles: "The next generation will not charge us for what we have done, they will charge and condemn us for what we have left undone. Your children will be free. Freedom or Death" (Schenkkan 234–235). The speech, in Wobbly fashion, appropriates religious language—in this case, a penitential confession of sins (that is, what we have done and left undone)—for the purpose of rousing a crowd. More specifically, the speech is a slight variation of a Mother Jones oration given to the striking West Virginia miners: "It is freedom or death, and your children will be free.... We are not going to leave a slave class to the coming generation, and I want to say to you the next generation will not charge us for what we have done; they will charge and condemn us for what we have left undone."[17] Indeed, the fact that Steinman introduces the subject of Mother Jones and the strike as something of a bedtime story for Joshua is also very much in the Wobbly vein—storytelling, mythmaking, and the creation of heroes and heroines, as noted, was long a part of the I.W.W. platform. For all intents and purposes, Steinman is a Wobbly despite the missing label; he looks like a Wobbly, talks like a Wobbly, and quacks like a Wobbly. The omission of explicit naming, therefore, is an interesting choice on Schenkkan's part. Nevertheless, perhaps given previous commentary about the obscurity of the Wobblies for audiences post-1950 or so, the choice is also an understandable one. It seems fair to assume that Schenkkan would have had to devote at least a few minutes to explaining what Wobblies were in expository dialogue, whereas audiences of the early 1990s would more likely have understood the concept of "union organizer" more readily.[18] The play failed, however, to capture the Broadway audience, although the play has been granted something of an afterlife in university theatre, as well as the smaller theatres that found and championed the play in the first place.[19]

As for the Wobblies themselves? Yes, they are still around. They are even capable of making news, as their recent efforts at unionizing the powerful coffee chain Starbucks attests.[20] A visitor to the website can see updates, information about upcoming rallies, and how to join. The card is still red—old-timers used to maintain that the Communists stole the color from them. If there ever were a heyday of Wobblies on Broadway, we would seem to be long past it in the twenty-first century. Nevertheless, the Wobblies themselves still know how to perform. It could well be that Wobbly plays (both past and future) could find themselves following the old models of workers' theater—where the audience was distinctly the worker and distinctly interested in the causes old and new. The *Daily Masses* writer was most likely correct—Broadway and the Wobblies were probably never meant to flirt, unless the Wobblies are shrouded in booze and regret.

Since author James Jones got the first word in, we shall let him return in the final chapter as well. Here again is *From Here to Eternity*, and former I.W.W. member James Malloy speaking: "Of them all," he begins, never getting around to defining "them" more clearly (radicals? Religions?), "I think the Wobblies came the closest. Nobody ever really understood them. They had the courage, and whats [*sic*] more important, they had the soft heart to go with it. Their defeat was due to faulty technique of execution, rather than to concept. But also, I don't think the time was right for them yet" (Jones *From Here to Eternity* 644). Perhaps an interesting aspect of the Broadway Wobblies under consideration is to what extent their characterizations jibed with Jones' description—to what extent did the Wobblies on Broadway display courage and soft hearts? (It would seem that Jones is referring not to being a "softie" or a pushover, but of having compassion for one's brother and sister workers.)

The nameless *Hairy Ape* Wobbly secretary displays a matter-of-fact style and possibly some courage when it comes to handling the intimidating presence of Yank—although Yank is subdued by force with considerable help. He is not particularly soft-hearted with Yank, in any case. Joe, our rambling Wobbly from *They Knew What They Wanted*, qualifies to some degree with soft-heartedness, at least toward the heroine Amy, and he displays bravery when confronted with his responsibility, although he is clearly none too anxious to tie himself down with a family. As for the characters in *Processional* who might or might not qualify as "Wobbly," we have one misguided drunk who attains a measure of dignity in the end and a radical Pole whose chief trait that he will talk your ear off—neither courage nor soft-heartedness are immediately evident. Perhaps not surprisingly, with *Gods of the Lightning* and *Singing Jailbirds*, we see characters that come closest to embodying the tough-minded but compassionate ideals discussed in the James Jones novel. Mac, in the Anderson play, for all his tough talk, as well as his genuine willingness to fight, clearly has a romantic side when it comes not only to his girlfriend, but also to the stubborn workers who cannot or will not come around to the Wobbly way of thinking. Capraro is, of course, also quietly sweet and brave (if little else in terms of characterization) throughout the play. In *Singing Jailbirds*, Red is given full rein to display his courage and his soft-hearted side through his numerous soliloquies and flashbacks, as well as through a great deal of classic Wobbly music.

The later iterations of Broadway Wobblies in *Iceman* retain their soft hearts in their sentimental affection for "the Cause," but years of living "at the bottom of the sea" have clearly blunted their courage just as booze had drowned their resolve. Finally, as something of a Wobbly throwback, Abe Steinman of *The Kentucky Cycle* does indeed get to display the classic Wobbly attributes as he helps to nurse Joshua back to health and makes withering wisecracks while facing the gun that will kill him. In shaping the figure of the Wobbly into a viable Broadway character, the playwrights and directors who brought these plays to life were not necessarily inaccurate with regard to the Wobbly agenda. Rather, it could be said that while the Broadway Wobblies mostly got to speak their respective pieces, the I.W.W. agenda was overshadowed by a larger agenda—one of reconciliation, romance, resignation, and ultimately, defeat, with Sinclair's play standing as the most notable exception.

How much additional production life these plays receive going forward is, of course, up in the air—the only fairly sure bets, as noted, are the O'Neill plays. Nevertheless, I would submit that a production team needs to try to get inside the Wobblies to do the plays justice—Wobbly history, and at least some of the ins and outs of the various "-isms" and "-ists"—socialists, anarchists, nihilists, and so on—that collided and colluded with I.W.W. growth, decline, and persistence. Even if love stories and survival stories and good versus evil stories can do without all the "political stuff" and "labor stuff," actors, directors, designers, and dramaturgs lose a great deal of the world of the play if they do not explore and analyze why, in O'Neill's words, some people get a wrong slant on the Wobblies. Or why, for Joe, getting into another "scrap" with the "goddamn Wobblies" would be so important—and perhaps, not so likely by the time he makes his exit. Or why the obtuse sheriff and his cohorts make assumptions regarding Dynamite Jim's Wobbly affiliations. Or the years of Wobbly protest and persecution evoked by Macready on the witness stand. Or the songs, speeches, and gospel fervor of the Wobblies who enter Red's tortured thoughts in solitary confinement. Or the dreams of a new society still nursed and reminisced upon in Harry Hope's saloon. Or even Abe Steinman's memories of Mother Jones, powerful enough to bring her onstage. The playwrights of the 1920s chose to include a vibrant part of their world in their plays; in the later plays, they include a not incidental piece of American labor history. Our theatre, as well as our theatre practitioners, shrinks in stature if these elements are ignored or dismissed.

At long last, did no one understand the Wobblies? And by "no one," can we include the theater practitioners and artists who tried to bring them to life, as well as the audiences with their varying degrees of sympathy and interest, as well as, perhaps, many of the Wobblies themselves? Such a conclusion is entirely plausible. Nevertheless, the presence of the Wobblies on Broadway, entirely understood or not, provided an interesting look at class and labor struggle as well as class development through the lens of popular commercial theatre. The message might not have always translated across the footlights, and might not have always survived the mindsets of the many artists needed to put a show together—a defeat due to faulty technique of execution? Certainly, however, *something* was sure happening. And, perhaps, it is happening still. Furthermore, as Schenkkan noted in a 2012 interview, "A certain presidential candidate was discovered saying in private that 47 percent of the country was not going to support him because they're lazy…this is an attitude that is all too prevalent" (Trussell, "Small Theater Company").[21] The issues that inspired the Wobblies to song, strikes, and sabotage have by no means left us, even if the Wobblies on Broadway have faded. Onstage in the commercial realm, an audience's only opportunity to hear the ghost of a ghost's voice might well be to see a production of O'Neill. Nevertheless, on smaller stages geared toward the worker and those who sympathize with the working position, or on stages claimed by companies with a sense of adventure, one might still hear the echoes of echoes of the Wobblies getting into another scrap, most likely to the tune of one of the songs that are meant to fan the flames of discontent. The time might just be right, even if Broadway might not be the ideal place. And maybe, some running and shouting will in fact do some good.

Notes

1 TO STOP THE WORLD: THE MOST STUPENDOUS IMPOSSIBLES

1. Susan Duffy in fact misidentifies the I.W.W. as the "International Workers of the World," rather than "Industrial" in *American Labor on Stage: Dramatic Interpretations of the Steel and Textile Industries in the 1930s* (Westport, CT: Greenwood Press, 1996), (67). According to the I.W.W. website (http://iww.org), "this mistake is made so often, most IWW members simply take it in stride. A former General Secretary Treasurer of the Industrial Workers of the World, Fred Chase, once jokingly remarked that the *Industrial* Workers of the World should ask the *International* Workers of the World to join up, since they're obviously a large and influential organization!" ("Myth #1").
2. The classic I.W.W. story involves a farmer reflecting on his experiences with the Wobblies: "All the I.W.W. fellers I've met seemed to be pretty decent lads, but them 'alleged I.W.W.'s' must be holy frights." Originally included in the fifteenth edition of *I.W.W. Little Red Songbook*; quoted on the Industrial Workers of the World website http://www.iww.org/history.
3. See, for example, John Pietaro, "Solidarity Forever: The IWW and the Protest Song," http://theculturalworker.blogspot.com/2010/12/solidarity-forever-iww-and-protest-song.html, noting that "many, many of its early organizers were writers, musicians or visual artists..." and that "accounts of Wobbly musicians have been recorded as early as 1906, but one year after the IWW's founding." John Reed's description of the Wobblies as musical from a 1918 article in *The Liberator* is also relevant:

    Remember, this is the only American working-class movement which *sings* [Reed's emphasis]. Tremble then at the I.W.W., for a singing movement is not to be beaten.... When you hear these songs you'll know it is the American social revolution you are listening to... I know no other group of Americans which honors its singers. (John Reed, "The Social Revolution in Court," *The Liberator* 1.7 [September 1918])

4. Along with songs and speeches, the I.W.W. also wrote their own theatricals for their own benefit as a way of mocking the bosses, raising spirits and solidarity, and sharing some rueful laughter at an ongoing, uphill struggle. John Reed, in his 1918 article "The Social Revolution in Court," remarks that "there are playwrights in the I.W.W. who write about life in the 'jungles,' and the 'wobblies' produce the plays for audiences of 'wobblies'"(22–24). Among the plays collected by Joyce Kornbluh in her I.W.W. anthology is a sketch by Walker C. Smith titled "Their Court and Our Class," which shreds the anti-Wobbly machinations of the courts of Everett, Washington. The sketch opens with the court clerk addressing the jury: "Do you solemnly swear to hear no evidence in this case favorable to the accused and to render a verdict of Guilty?" (Smith, qtd. in Joyce Kornbluh, *Rebel Voices*, 113).

5. Zinn points out that "the IWW never had more than five to ten thousand enrolled members at any one time... and perhaps a hundred thousand were members at one time or another" (*A People's History of the United States* [New York: Perennial Classics, 2003], 331).

6. American corporate capitalism, for the purposes of this study, will refer to the structure of what we would now consider modern business enterprise, that is, a business entity containing distinct operating units, with each unit managed by a structured hierarchy of salaried executives. See Alfred Chandler Jr., *The Visible Hand: The Managerial Revolution in American Business* (Cambridge, MA: Belknap Press of Harvard University Press, 1977).

7. Hill was convicted of murder in Salt Lake City, Utah. The trial engendered a great deal of controversy and protest, which largely contributed to the Hill legend.

8. While the phrase "pie in the sky" seems to have originated with Hill's song, it can be fairly said that the observation regarding the Church and class distinctions is an old one. It can be argued, for example, that one of the chief functions of morality plays in the late Middle Ages was to encourage serfs to embrace their hard life on earth for reward in heaven, thus not disrupting the feudal system that benefited those

who owned the land. Tensions, and occasional cooperation, between organized religion and labor fuel a number of Wobbly stories, and is a key strand in Upton Sinclair's *Singing Jailbirds*.

9. Hill was also often known as "Hillstrom"; his given name was Hagglund.

10. Reed also wrote passionately and eloquently about the Paterson strike, as evidenced by this story from the June 1913 issue of *The Masses*:

    There's a war in Paterson. But it's a curious kind of war. All the violence is the work of one side—the Mill Owners. Their servants, the Police, club unresisting men and women and ride down law-abiding crowds on horseback. Their paid mercenaries, the armed Detectives, shoot and kill innocent people.... Let me tell you what I saw in Paterson and then you will say which side of this struggle is "anarchistic" and "contrary to American ideals." (Reed, "War in Paterson")

11. See also Anne Huber Tripp, *The I.W.W. and the Paterson Silk Strike of 1913* (Urbana: University of Illinois Press, 1987) and Ann Larabee, "'The Drama of Transformation': Settlement House Idealism and the Neighborhood Playhouse" in *Performing America: Cultural Nationalism in American Theater*, ed. Jeffery D. Mason and J. Ellen Gainor (Ann Arbor: University of Michigan Press, 1999) for accounts of the strike pageant that quote from the *New York Times* editorial.

12. In a special report to the *New York Times*, "Paterson Strikers Anxious for $6,000," the writer states point-blank: "It is openly charged in this city today that the Paterson strikers have been exploited by the I.W.W." The story also notes the response of the Paterson newspapers referring to the pageant as "one of many 'lemons' handed to the strikers by the 'I.W.W.'... but this last one is the biggest and sourest of the lot" (*New York Times* 24 June 1913: 1.)

13. See Brenda Murphy, *The Provincetown Players and the Culture of Modernity*, pp. 5–6, for a detailed account of how the pageant moved theatrical artists.

14. See provincetownplayhouse.com for their history along with their seasons, plays, and authors.

15. See Robert Karoly Sarlos, *Jig Cook and the Provincetown Players: Theatre in Ferment* (Amherst: University of Massachusetts Press, 1982), 19, as well as provincetownplayhouse.com.

16. The preamble is posted on the I.W.W. website, and is quoted extensively in I.W.W. literature, including Fred Thompson's *The I.W.W.: Its First Fifty Years (1905–1955)* (Chicago, IL: Industrial Workers of the World, 1955).
17. Brissenden's account corroborates the importance of the Western Federation of Miners in I.W.W. history, noting that they "may well be ranked as the chief predecessor of the I.W.W" in Paul Frederick Brissenden, *The I.W.W.: A Study in American Syndicalism*, PhD diss., Columbia University, 1919, p. 40, http://archive.org/details/iwwstudyofameric00brisuoft.
18. The Wobblies would find their way into motion pictures as well, sometimes in unlikely places. In the 1914 Mack Sennett short subject "The Fatal Mallet," Charlie Chaplin, as the tramp, conspicuously enters a shed with "I.W.W." marked on a door. Whether or not this was a deliberate addition to the film's set design is unknown, but both the tramp's (and Chaplin's) anarchy suggests that the addition was not out of character. See "'The Fatal Mallet' or Was Charlie Chaplin's Tramp in the IWW?," in *Cinema, Movies and Motion Pictures*, http://picturesmove211.wordpress.com/2013/09/28/the-fatal-mallet-or-was-charlie-chaplins-tramp-in-the-iww/.
19. Taylor is most famous for his *Principles of Scientific Management*, published in 1911. While Scientific Management had and still has its fair share of critics, the principles Taylor outlined were highly influential in the running of American business. As Taylor noted in his introduction, he set out:

> to prove that the best management is a true science, resting upon clearly defined laws, rules, and principles, as a foundation. And further to show that the fundamental principles of scientific management are applicable to all kinds of human activities, from our simplest individual acts to the work of our great corporations, which call for the most elaborate cooperation. And, briefly, through a series of illustrations, to convince the reader that whenever these principles are correctly applied, results must follow which are truly astounding. (Taylor, *Principles*)

20. As will be noted, many witnesses and historians cite particular catastrophic and divisive events in the I.W.W.'s history, particularly in the early 1920s, as "the end." This blunt epitaph, for example, from James B.

Cannon, writing in 1955 (which was the Wobblies' fiftieth anniversary year): "The whole record of the IWW—or at any rate, the best part of it, the positive revolutionary part—was all written in propaganda and action in its first 15 years. That is the enduring story. The rest is anticlimax" (James B. Cannon 1955"The I.W.W.", *Fourth International*, Summer 1955, http://www.marxists.org/archive/cannon/works/1955/iww.htm.). While, again, I do not mean for this monograph expressly to contribute to I.W.W. propaganda, part of the overall point is to illuminate the Wobblies' power over the imagination of the average theatergoer well past the time many historians denoted as the end.
21. See Thomas S. Hischak, *The Theatregoer's Almanac* (Westport, CT: Greenwood Press, 1997), 3.
22. See also Michael Schwartz, *Broadway and Corporate Capitalism: The Rise of the Professional-Managerial Class, 1900–1920* (New York: Palgrave Macmillan, 2009) for an examination of PMC class development and its relation to Broadway entertainment.

2 WHERE DO I GET OFF? THE WOBBLIES I.W.W. SPURN *THE HAIRY APE*

1. See Adorno on "splendid underdogs" in *Minima Moralia: Reflections from Damaged Life* (1951), trans. E. F. N. Jephcott (London: Verso, 1984), as well as his *Aesthetic Theory* on the necessity of art using "the ugly."
2. Historians frequently describe the pacifist Wobblies as essentially destroyed due to war fervor that gripped America during World War I—see, for example, The Oregon Encyclopedia, "Industrial Workers of the World (IWW)"; and Howard Zinn, in *A People's History of the United States 1492–Present* (New York: Perennial Classics, 2001) noting that "the war gave the government its opportunity to destroy the IWW" (372), among others.
3. At this time, educational cartoons were used to warn workers about the I.W.W. menace, including the Ford-produced cartoon "Uncle Sam and the Bolsheviki I.W.W. Rat" from 1919, in which a hardworking farmer brains a rat with a shovel. The rat wears the label "Bolsheviki I.W.W." The farmer tells the audience, "Bolshivists [*sic*] are the rats of civilization." See "A Reality Check from a Century Past," ABC News, 16 October 2007, http://abcnews.go.com/ Politics/Vote2008/story?id=3733457.

4. See Ross Wetzsteon, *Republic of Dreams, Greenwich Village: The American Bohemia, 1910–1960* (New York: Simon & Schuster, 2002), 4, on the subject of tourists accosting people in the village and asking "Are you a merry villager?" as early as 1916.
5. Fred Thompson, in a footnote to his "Those Bomb-Throwing I-Won't-Works" chapter of *The I.W.W.: Its First Fifty Years (1905–1955)* (Chicago, IL: Industrial Workers of the World, 1955) mentions O'Neill's play in an affirmative light: "Eugene O'Neill's 'Hairy Ape' has a scene in IWW maritime workers' hall that realistically dramatizes the conflict of myth and reality" (88).
6. Further evidence of O'Neill's exasperation with the focus on the Wobbly element of his play appears in an interview with Louis Kantor in 1924: "Why ... was I made an apostle of revolution by the I.W.W. and proper timber for the Republican Party by conservatives as a mocker of the I.W.W. when my *Hairy Ape* was produced? ... What bearing had such comment on my function as a dramatist?" (Kantor, "O'Neill Defends his Play of Negro," in *Conversations with Eugene O'Neill*, ed. Mark Estrin [Jackson: University Press of Mississippi, 1990]).
7. See David Savran, *Highbrow/Lowdown: Theater, Jazz, and the Making of the New Middle Class* (Ann Arbor: University of Michigan Press, 2009) for a compelling narrative culminating in the widespread acceptance of O'Neill as "the" important American playwright.
8. See S. E. Wilmer, "Censorship and Ideology: Eugene O'Neill (*The Hairy Ape*)." *Cycnos* 9 (12 June 2008), http://revel.unice.fr/cycnos/?id=1250, as well as Arthur Gelb and Barbara Gelb, *O'Neill* (New York: Harper & Row, 1973), 757.
9. Quoted in, among others, John Patrick Diggins, *Eugene O'Neill's America: Desire Under Democracy*(Chicago, IL: University of Chicago Press, 2007) and a PBS *American Experience* documentary on O'Neill. <(Arthur Gelb & Barbara Gelb, Rick Burns, *Eugene O'Neill: A Documentary Film*. Film, directed by Rick Burns. 2006, WGBH Educational Foundation and Steeplechase Films, Inc.
10. There is evidence that early in the Wobblies' history, there were initiation ceremonies. See, for example, Jim Crutchfield's I.W.W. Page, http://www.workerseducation.org/crutch/constitution/ritual.html, for transcription of the July 1905 initiation ritual.

11. See Verity Burgmann, *Revolutionary Industrial Unionism: The Industrial Workers of the World in Australia* (New York: Cambridge University Press, 1995).
12. The *Daily Advocate* attributed the paragraph to the *Cleveland Plain Dealer*.
13. A generous collection of I.W.W. cartoons is available on the internet, including *Visual Propaganda: Ideology in Art* (http://ideologicalart.wordpress.com/labor-movement/labor-movement-gallery/).
14. In "The Hairy Ape: A Serio-Comedy of Ancient and Modern Life," *Current Opinion* 72 (June 1922), the editors summarize the final scene by noting, "Yank is apostrophizing a gorilla," a sentence one probably does not read every day (776).

3 NO KICK COMING: THE ROMANTIC WOBBLY OF SIDNEY HOWARD'S *THEY KNEW WHAT THEY WANTED*

1. Not insignificantly, Kornbluh's *Rebel Voices: An I.W.W. Anthology*, edited by Joyce Kornbluh (Ann Arbor: University of Michigan Press, 1968) ends with a chapter lumping the I.W.W. activity of 1924–1964 into "miscellany."
2. Fred Thompson, in his *The I.W.W.: Its First Fifty Years (1905–1955)* (Chicago, IL: Industrial Workers of the World, 1955), augments and amplifies the story of the split: "On the surface the issue was over the degree of centralization, but is causes lay deeper; personal rancors developed in Leavenworth, especially over the issue of accepting conditional pardons…dissatisfaction with the haphazard strike policy…Whatever its explanation, most IWW oldtimers consider this 1924 split the worst thing that ever happened to it…" (Fred Thompson 150–151).
3. To be fair to President Coolidge, he was not speaking of accumulating wealth for its own sake. In the speech that includes the famous quote, he goes on to note that "it calls for additional effort to avoid even the appearance of evil of selfishness." See Calvin Coolidge, "Address to the American Society of Newspaper Editors, Washington, D.C.," 17 January 1925, The American Presidency Project.

4. Howard's earlier play, *Swords*, opened and closed quickly in 1921. According to Brooks Atkinson, the play "told a medieval story in the period of the Guelphs and Ghibellines, it had a gorgeous setting by Robert Edmond Jones, it was written in verse, and it failed—standard practice for the liberal intellectual in the early twenties" (Brooks Atkinson, *Broadway* [New York: Macmillan, 1974], 273). He fared slightly better with a translation of *Casanova*, and cowrote the unsuccessful *Bewitched* with veteran playwright Edward Sheldon.
5. Howard himself credited Dante's Paolo and Francesca legend as his inspiration. See Andrew Longoria, "They Knew What They Wanted," in *The Columbia University Encyclopedia of Modern Drama*, vol. 2 (New York: Columbia University Press, 2007), 1346.
6. The rest of the lyrics, including chorus, are available in *I.W.W. Songs to Fan the Flames of Discontent*, 19th ed. (Chicago, IL: Industrial Workers of the World, 1923), http://www.faubern.ch/_texte/songbook.pdf. Joe, as a recent Wobbly, might well have possessed that particular edition of the songbook, which cost 10 cents. I.W.W. member and later Communist Party of the United States leader Harrison George is credited as lyricist, writing from the Cook County Jail on 18 October 1917.
7. The song would also be used significantly in Sinclair's *Singing Jailbirds*.
8. While Amy uses the term "hobo" as an insult in this case, it was an identity the Wobblies embraced, as is also evident in Sinclair's *Singing Jailbirds*. Wobblies identified themselves as migratory workers (and thinkers), and appropriated the hobo song "Hallelujah, I'm a Bum" as one of their most potent "Little Red Songbook" songs. The creation and spreading of the hobo folk hero myth was an essential part of Wobbly storytelling, as Todd DePastino explains: "One of the most enduring legacies... was a Wobbly frontier myth that venerated the hobo as a manly white pioneer of the industrial West" (Todd DePastino, "An Excerpt from *Citizen Hobo: How a Century of Homelessness Shaped America*" [Chicago: University of Chicago Press, 2003], http://press.uchicago.edu/Misc/Chicago/143783.html).
9. Texting slang acronym for "Shut the Fuck Up."
10. Anders is probably best known to film fans from his role in Orson Welles's *The Lady from Shanghai* from 1948—by then he was a wizened character actor, with little trace of the penetrating gaze he was capable of as evidenced in photographs from the 1920s.

11. In 1928 (a silent version), 1930, and in 1940. Only the 1940 version kept Howard's title.
12. Fred Thompson's account of the fiftieth anniversary caps his overview of the Wobblies' first 50 years: "It was a harmonious gathering, and a remarkable one as a bridge across history.... These delegates had no intention of 'giving up the ghost'" (Thompson 199).

4 JAZZING THE WOBBLIES: JOHN HOWARD LAWSON'S *PROCESSIONAL*

1. While there were definite class divides between the burgeoning motion picture audience and the legitimate drama audience, the 1920s also saw the age of the opulent movie palaces that attracted a more upwardly mobile middle-class clientele with its extravagant show of luxury and enforcement of middle-class rules of audience behavior. See Richard Butsch, *The Making of American Audiences* (New York: Cambridge University Press, 2000), especially the chapter on "Storefronts to Theaters: Seeking the Middle Class."
2. See, for example, the online Encyclopedia of Disney Animated Shorts, "Alice's Egg Plant," http://www.disneyshorts.org/shorts.aspx?shortID=25.
3. See, for example, the Federal Theatre Project poster for *Processional*, on the Library of Congress website, http://www.loc.gov/pictures/resource/cph.3b49553/.
4. As J. Bradford Robinson points out in "The Jazz Essays of Theodor Adorno: Some Thoughts on Jazz Reception in Weimar Germany," *Popular Music* 13.1 (1994): 1–2, http://www.jstor.org/stable/852897, the response to Adorno's jazz essays has been decidedly mixed tending toward the negative: "at best a puzzle, and to many an acute embarrassment." Indeed, Adorno himself later sought to distance himself from essays he felt that he had written without a clear knowledge of its subject. Nevertheless, Robinson sees value in Adorno's writing as "an astute observer of the popular music of his time," which seems germane to how jazz music and jazz "attitude" was used in this particular production (Robinson 1–2). Joseph D. Lewandowski's article "Adorno on Jazz and Society," *Philosophy & Social Criticism* 22 (1996):103, further argues that Adorno "is...both right *and* wrong about jazz and its entwinement with the culture industry of capitalist modernity" (Lewandowski's emphasis).

Lewandowski places this simultaneous "rightness" and "wrongness" squarely in Adorno's fundamental outlook and procedure: "Indeed, Adorno's social interpretation of artworks seeks to discern the ways in which a specific social phenomenon—e.g. jazz—is bound up with the social structure and ensemble of relations in which it emerges and from which it never completely disentangles itself" (Lewandowski 106).

5. Abbott's memory seems faulty on this point. Strasberg is included in the cast list in Stark Young's review; both Strasberg and Meisner are listed as cast members in the Internet Broadway Database. Clurman notes that he met Strasberg and Meisner when they were all young actors at the Guild, but Clurman was not with them in *Processional* (see Clurman, *The Fervent Years*, New York: Hill and Wang, 1957, 9). Abbott's implied joke about Jews playing Klan members is echoed in the play itself, when the Jewish father and the Black loafer are revealed to be part of the Klan.

6. Moeller, previously the director of *They Knew What They Wanted*, continued to have a prominent career directing the premiers of O'Neill plays such as *Mourning Becomes Electra* and *Ah, Wilderness!*, as well as Maxwell Anderson's *Elizabeth the Queen* and S. N. Behrman's *Biography* for the Theatre Guild (Internet Broadway Database).

7. References to the play are from John Howard Lawson, *Processional*, in *Staged Action: Six Plays from the American Workers' Theatre*, ed. Lee Papa (Ithaca, NY: Cornell University Press, 2009), 9–82.

8. For a concise rundown of the West Virginia Mine Wars, see the West Virginia Division of Culture and History website, http://www.wvculture.org/history/minewars.html.

9. See, for example, *The History of the I.W.W.: A Discussion of its Main Features by a Group of Workmen* (Chicago, IL: Industrial Workers of the World, 1923), an overview in dialogue form regarding the major activities of the organization. In this speech, Morrison, "a dock walloper" (that is, a longshoreman) and "a lover of history," discusses I.W.W. solidarity: "Did you notice the way I.W.W. press backed up the striking miners of West Virginia and Kansas during the same period [1921–22]? When it comes to solidarity, that word is written all over I.W.W. history."

10. The conception of "jazz" befuddled many critics of the 1920s who tried to keep up with new musical developments onstage and in clubs. "Jazz" in a review could refer to speed, noise (or conflicting noises), or

newness. See Gerald Bordman's extensive studies of American theatre and particularly American musical theatre.
11. As Ryan Jerving points out, a number of critics read the ending as a happy one, perhaps missing the part when the "Man in the Silk Hat" whispers to the militia to kill all the workers in their beds that night. See Jerving, "An Experiment in Modern Vaudeville: Archiving the Wretched Refuse in John Howard Lawson's *Processional*" (*Modern Drama* 51.4 [Winter 2008]: 528–551).
12. David Savran, in his book *Highbrow/Lowdown: Theater, Jazz, and the Making of the New Middle Class* (Ann Arbor: University of Michigan Press, 2009), notes that Lawson's *Processional* was one of several plays "invariably characterized as prime examples of American expressionism" (140). Ryan Jerving notes that Lawson's collaboration with set designer Mordecai Gorelik conforms to the basic ideas of expressionism as well. See Jerving, "An Experiment in Modern Vaudeville."
13. Lee Papa, in his introduction to his workers' theatre anthology *Staged Action*, refers to *Processional* as "perhaps the most accomplished of all labor dramas" ("The 1920s: Workers In (and Out of) Jail," in *Staged Action: Six Plays from the American Workers' Theatre*, ed. Lee Papa [Ithaca, NY: ILR Press, 2009], 4). While the author might submit that there are more "accomplished" plays under study in this monograph, he must also stipulate that not all of them qualify as "labor plays."

5 DEAD HAND OF THE DEAD: ANDERSON AND HICKERSON'S *GODS OF THE LIGHTNING*

1. The reference materials on the case are numerous, but a fairly recent discovery seems pertinent—a letter in which Upton Sinclair describes a meeting with Sacco and Vanzetti's lawyer: "He...told me that the men were guilty and he told me in every detail how he had framed a set of alibis for them" ("Sacco and Vanzetti: Guilty After All?" in *All Things Considered*, NPR interview with Tony Arthur, 4 March 2006). This discovery, in turn, intensified the ongoing debate regarding the pair's guilt or innocence, and the bearing of their possible guilt on the question as to whether or not they received a fair trial.
2. The Actor's Theatre, a semiprofessional group working out of the Provincetown Theatre, presented an "off-Broadway" revival in early

1931, featuring Sanford Meisner and Robert Lewis. The production gained the attention of Harold Clurman and Lee Strasberg, and Meisner and Lewis went on to contribute prominently to the Group Theatre. See Amnon Kabatchnik, *Blood on the Stage 1925–1950: Milestone Plays of Crime, Mystery, and Detection* (Lanham, MD: Scarecrow Press, 2010), 225 and Robert Lewis, *Slings and Arrows: Theater in My Life* (New York: Applause Books, 1996), 35. Several years later, a 1935 production in Boston partly fanned flames of discontent, as noted by a short piece in the *New York Times* stating that Boston's play censor had ordered the Associated Actors Theatre, Inc. to "delete profanity in the lines before tonight's performance." In what seems to be an inadvertent bit of understatement, the piece goes on to note that the manager felt "the censor's criticism was actuated by a desire to stop the show which some critics have said refers to the Sacco-Vanzetti trial" ("Anderson Play Censored" *New York Times*, 27 November 1935).

3. Alfred S. Shivers, in his biography, *The Life of Maxwell Anderson* (New York: Stein and Day, 1983), refers to the play as "fiery but minor," and feels that "the result was the closest Anderson ever came to pure propaganda" (112 and ftn. 38, p. 311).

4. From the *New York Herald Tribune* of 20 September 1928: "Charles Bickford, who appeared in 'Chicago' and 'Bless You, Sister,' will have the principal role." The blurb also notes that the play was originally titled "Gods of the Night."

5. Leo Bulgakov, Suvorin in *Gods of the Lightning*, would be on hand as well, playing Braham's strongly Yiddish-accented father.

6. See the "Everett Massacre Collection," University of Washington Libraries Digital Collection, https://content.lib.washington.edu/pnwlaborweb/.

7. Arthur Ruhl, writing for the *New York Herald Tribune*, also noted the similarities between the onstage trial and the actual transcripts. The key incidents of the onstage trial that directly use information from the real-life trial are also verified by Felix Frankfurter, writing for the Atlantic in March 1927. In the article, "The Case of Sacco and Vanzetti," Frankfurter, then a Harvard Law School professor (he would be appointed to FDR's Supreme Court in 1939), wrote of the witness using (or misusing) the phrase "dead image," which is picked up in the play, as well as the "woman of doubtful reputation" who bears

similarity to the woman blackmailed in the play by D. A. Salter. See Felix Frankfurter, "The Case of Sacco and Vanzetti," *Atlantic* (March 1927), http://www.theatlantic.com/magazine/archive/1927/03/the-case-of-sacco-and-vanzetti/306625/.

8. Anderson's pity and anger would undergo significant changes by the early 1950s, toward the end of his life (Anderson died in 1959). In a letter to the *New York Times*, he writes regarding the writers who would not be hired by television if they were listed in "Red Channels," a compendium of communists and alleged communists in the United States who worked in radio and television: "Every American Communist is a traitor to his country and to democracy and his forfeited his right to be heard…" ("Maxwell Anderson Writes on 'Red Channels,'" *New York Times*, 18 January 1953). The apparent turnaround in Anderson's outlook was enough to inspire at least one letter in response: "What is particularly shocking is that such a letter could have been written by the same man who immortalized the Sacco-Vanzetti case in 'Gods of the Lightning' and 'Winterset' and as recently as several weeks ago composed an incisive attack on censorship in a television script entitled 'The Trial of Ben Jonson'" (Stark, "Shocking," *New York Times*, 25 January 1953). One might add such a change of mind might only be "shocking" to those who underestimated the power that World War II, the atomic bomb, and the ongoing "cold war" had to veer many a radical from left to right.

9. See *The Sacco and Vanzetti Case*, vol. 5 (New York: Henry Holt, 1929), 4896–4905, http://college.cengage.com/history/ayers_primary_sources/statement_bartolomeo_vanzetti_1929.htm.

10. "Preparedness Day" celebrated the United States' imminent entrance into the Great War, which would take place in April of the following year.

11. In a speech delivered in Chicago in March 1917, the Honorable W. Bourke Cockran declared, "You and I know that when the word anarchist is mentioned, many men—I should say most men—appear to take leave of their senses, and abandon themselves to the most extravagant notions, moved by a belief that anarchy and violence are convertible terms" (Bourke W. Cockran, *A Heinous Plot: An Expose of the Frame-Up System in the San Francisco Bomb Cases against Billings, Mooney, Mrs. Mooney, Weinberg and Nolan* (Chicago, IL: Chicago Federation of Labor, 1917), 2, http://debs.indstate.edu/c666h4_1917.pdf).

12. The final moments of the play also echo accounts of crowds watching for news of the execution. For example, in an account from Paul Avrich's *Sacco and Vanzetti: The Anarchist Background* (Princeton, NJ: Princeton University Press, 1991): "Shortly after midnight in Manhattan's Union Square, a sign was posted in the window of the Daily Worker—SACCO MURDERED. The overflow crowd was stunned into silence. But when another sign proclaimed VANZETTI MURDERED, people gasped, moaned" (347).
13. Vincent Wall, in his article, "Maxwell Anderson: The Last Anarchist," *Sewanee Review* 49.3 (July–September 1941): 339–369, makes a direct accusation: "His [Anderson's] brand of anarchism makes him a defeatist."

6 "WE EVEN SING 'EM IN JAP AND CHINK": UPTON SINCLAIR'S WORKERS' THEATRE CONTRIBUTION

1. In their 1927 manifesto, the New Playwrights specifically referred to themselves as a "workers' Theatre.... a clearing house for ideas and a focus for social protest." John Howard Lawson, "The Crisis in the Theatre," qtd. in George A. Knox and Herbert M. Stahl, *Dos Passos and "The Revolting Playwrights,"* Essays and Studies on American Language and Literature XV (Uppsala, Sweden: A. B. Lundequistska Bokhandeln, 1964), 48.
2. See Martin Zanger, "Politics of Confrontation: Upton Sinclair and the Launching of the ACLU in Southern California," *Pacific Historical Review* 38.4 (November 1969): 383–406. With regard to Sinclair's accounts of his San Pedro arrest, Zanger notes, "Sinclair's evaluation typically exaggerated his role in determining events. His myopic focus obscured the overall picture" (395).
3. Not all histories agree on what Sinclair was reading at the time of his arrest. Fred Thompson, for example, writes that Sinclair was "arrested for reading the Declaration of Independence" (141). With regard to the imprisonment, Sinclair wrote to Los Angeles Chief of Police Louis D. Oaks on 17 May 1923, opening with the following:

    Having escaped from your clutches yesterday afternoon, owing to the fact that one of your men betrayed your plot to my wife, I am now in position to answer your formal statement to the public, that I am "more dangerous than 4,000 IWW." I thank you for this compliment, for to be dangerous to lawbreakers in office such as yourself is the highest duty that a citizen of this community can perform. (Sinclair, *The Land of Orange Groves and Jails: Upton Sinclair's California*, ed. Lauren Coodley [Berkeley, CA: Heyday Books, 2003], 53)

4. Indeed, the play generated a fair share of vitriol even before it was produced, as evidenced by the editorial page of *The Bakersfield Californian* and its caustic review of the printed script that ran 14 November 1925: "It is one of those pseudo-literary effusions in which the hero is spotless, the villain is unbelievably villainous and no single human being, that is no being compounded of both good and evil, is allowed for an instant to intrude upon the proceedings.... Mr. Sinclair, judged upon this work, is not an artist...he is a demagogue..." ("Singing Jailbirds": Editorial Page).

5. See Ahmed A. White, "The Crime of Economic Radicalism: Criminal Syndicalism Laws and the Industrial Workers of the World, 1917–1927," *Oregon Law Review* 85.649 (9 April 2007).

6. The Wobblies were by no means the only ones who questioned the constitutionality of the syndicalism laws. The anonymous H.R.M., writing in the *California Law Review* in September 1922, notes the following: "Criticism of the existing form of government, of government officials, or advocacy of a change in either the statutory or fundamental law by legal methods cannot lawfully be made criminal." While H.R.M. acknowledges the validity of the "clear and present danger" argument, he contends that "the test of guilt should always be the clear and present danger that the agitation will result in violence" (514).

7. Martin Zanger elaborates on Sinclair's affection for the Wobblies and his use of Wobbly and Communist figures and characters in his novels (as well as in *Singing Jailbirds*) in "Politics of Confrontation: Upton Sinclair and the Launching of the ACLU in Southern California," *Pacific Historical Review* 38.4 (November 1969): 386.

8. Socialists helped found the I.W.W., most notably including Socialist Party of the United States presidential candidate Eugene Debs, and both groups agreed that the capitalist system needed to be abolished. While the disagreements were complicated, a key point of contention was the use of direct action, which was favored by the I.W.W., and the use of voting and political action, which the socialists believed in but the Wobblies distrusted. Nevertheless, socialists such as Sinclair as well as Debs often spoke out in favor of the Wobblies and their

legal problems despite their disagreements in ideology and technique. Debs, for example, in his article "The IWW Bogey," originally published in the February 1918 issue of *The International Socialist Review*, comments sardonically regarding ongoing accusations concerning the I.W.W.: "Everything that happens nowadays that the ruling classes do not like and everything that does not happen that they do like is laid at the door of the IWW. Its name is anathema wherever capitalism wields the lash and drains the veins of its exploited victims."

9. A similar instance of the "affectionate" or "inclusive" use of racial and ethnic slurs occurs in Odets's *Waiting for Lefty*, when a union member refers to the titular absent figure, "That Wop's got more guts than a slaughter-house," and in a semi-joking reference to a Jewish comrade, "It's as plain as the nose on Sol Feinberg's face." Since the end of the nineteenth century, there was a concerted effort by union and labor organizers to get workers to overlook prejudices and include new immigrants into the realm or union solidarity. As Robert Asher writes: "Racial and ethnic prejudice were not automatically eliminated by the incorporation of 'despised' groups into the labor movement. But structural assimilation helped facilitate the progress the American labor movement has made in reducing the influence of cultural prejudice" ("Union Nativism and the Immigrant Response," *Labor History*, 1 June 1982, 348).

10. Novelist Wallace Stegner referred to the I.W.W. as a "militant church," a label roundly criticized by Donald E. Winters in *The Soul of the Wobblies: The I.W.W., Religion, and American Culture in the Progressive Era 1905–1917*. Contributions in American Studies, no. 81 (Westport, CT: Greenwood Press, 1985). Winters allows that the I.W.W. and "church" share certain similarities, the label of "church" negates the "revolutionary, largely agnostic quality of the I.W.W." (Winters 7).

11. The relationship between Wobblies and religion was always complicated and fairly often contradictory. While Fred Thompson had fun with the comparison of the I.W.W. and church, pretending to take the idea literally when noting that both meet in buildings, Big Bill Haywood reported that many of the Wobblies who were arrested after the United States entered the Great War would claim the I.W.W. as their religion when asked (Winters 7–8).

12. *Singing Jailbirds*' most recent production was restructured as a musical by the Relevant Stage Company of San Diego, California, in May

2009. The show included many of the Little Red Songbook songs, as well as some period hits and original compositions.
13. The I.W.W. website lists four major "Wobbly origin" theories. The "Eye Wobble Wobble" story has some credence through a letter written by early I.W.W. member Mortimer Downing (Fred Thompson, *The I.W.W.: Its First Fifty Years (1905–1955)* [Chicago, IL: Industrial Workers of the World, 1955], 66–67). The other theories are "the wobble saw," referring to a circular saw mounted in such a way to cut a wide groove; the expression "wobble the works" as a code term for "sabotage" (e.g., wobbling the saw so that it does not cut as efficiently, thus slowing down the work process); and a term originally meant as an insult from the employer class, referring to the I.W.W. as a bunch of drunks who "wobbled" when they walked. Definitive proof for any of these theories is nonexistent. See "What is the Origin of the Term Wobbly?" at http://www.iww.org/history/icons/wobbly.
14. Émile Coué, a French psychotherapist, introduced the familiar affirmation (rendered with some minor variations) "every day, in every way, I'm feeling better and better."
15. Lee Papa, in his introduction to *Singing Jailbirds*, identifies the critic as *New York Times* theatre critic Brooks Atkinson, which is quite likely given the time when the play was produced, and it is certainly true that Atkinson often ventured downtown to weigh in on plays that were outside the commercial mainstream. Nevertheless, Atkinson by then commonly had a byline, and this particular review is unsigned.
16. As Zanger admits, "Atrocities of this kind are difficult to verify." Accounts from Mrs. Sinclair tell of people describing these events personally to her husband, and such stories were also described in I.W.W. pamphlets (Martin Zanger, "Politics of Confrontation: Upton Sinclair and the Launching of the ACLU in Southern California," *Pacific Historical Review* 38.4 [November 1969], 390).

7 YOU I-WON'T-WORK HARP: I.W.W. ELEGY IN *THE ICEMAN COMETH*

1. See Brian A. Oard, "Poetry after Auschwitz: What Adorno Really Said, and Where He Said It" (blog post) 12 March 2011, http://mindfulpleasures.blogspot.com.

2. Eric Bentley, in his 1952 article "Trying to Like O'Neill," dismisses much of the radical element—specifically, the speeches of Larry and Hugo—in the play as "the rotten fruit of unreality." Cutting about an hour from the text when he directed the play, Bentley notes, "One can cut a good many of Larry's speeches since he is forever re-phrasing a pessimism which is by no means hard to understand the first time. One can cut down the speeches of Hugo since they are both too long and too pretentious. It is such a pretentiousness, replete with obvious and unimaginative symbolism, that constitutes the expressionism of the play" (*Kenyon Review* 14.3 [Summer 1952]: 479).
3. The Knights of Labor were, in fact, still in existence, though barely, when the article was written. While not a radical or Socialist group, they sought an eight-hour day for the workers and peaked in membership in the 1880s. Like many similar ambitious groups, perhaps including the I.W.W., the Knights of Labor suffered from lack of organization. See Donald L. Kemmerer and Edward D. Wickersham, "Reasons for the Growth of the Knights of Labor in 1885–1886," *Industrial and Labor Relations Review* 3.2 (January 1950): 213–220.
4. In a 1922 interview with Oliver Sayler, O'Neill articulates what he would be repeating to reporters a generation later: "I suppose that is one reason I have come to feel so indifferent toward political and social movements of all kinds. Time was when I was an active socialist, and, after that, a philosophical anarchist. But today I can't feel that anything like that really matters" (Eugene O'Neill, "What the Theatre Means to Me," in *O'Neill and His Plays: Four Decades of Criticism*, ed. Oscar Cargill, N. Bryllion Fagin, and William J. Fisher [New York: New York University, 1961]).
5. Richard, the young authorial stand-in character of O'Neill's *Ah, Wilderness*, recites the same quote by way of warning his family of impending revolution.
6. Quotation used in Philip Herbst's *Talking Terrorism: A Dictionary of the Loaded Language of Political Violence* (Westport, CT: Greenwood Press, 2003) as well as in Robert J. Goldstein, "The Anarchist Scare of 1908: A Sign of Tensions in the Progressive Era," *American Studies* 15.2 (Fall 1974): 57.
7. See comic strip historian Allan Holtz's *Stripper's Guide* for samples of the "Fitzboomski" strip, later retitled "Fizzboomski the Anarchist." In

a typical strip, Fitzboomski tries to blow up the "Prime Minster-a-vich," but gets blown up himself. 10 November 2009, http://strippersguide.blogspot.com/2009/11/obscurity-of-day-fitzboomski-anarchist.html.
8. For a detailed comparison and proof that O'Neill drew directly from the life and personality (and accent) of Havel, see Doris Alexander, "Hugo of *The Iceman Cometh*: Realism and O'Neill," *American Quarterly* 5.4 (Winter 1953): 357–366. Alexander directly answers Eric Bentley's accusation in "Trying to Like O'Neill" that Hugo as a character had no basis in realism.
9. See Malcolm Cowley, "A Weekend with Eugene O'Neill," in *O'Neill and His Plays*, ed. Oscar Cargill, N. Bryllion Fagin, and William J. Fisher, 1961, as well as Arthur and Barbara Gelb's biography *O'Neill* (New York: Harper & Row, 1973), among many others.
10. As Doris Alexander illustrates in *Eugene O'Neill's Last Plays: Separating Art from Autobiography* (Athens: University of Georgia Press, 2005), O'Neill also fashioned many of Larry's speeches on his friend Terry Carlin's musings, as evidenced from this quote: "I once thought that I could help the mob to organize its own freedom. But now I see that we are all mob, that all human beings are alike, and that all I or anyone can do is to save his own soul, to win his own freedom, and perhaps to teach others to do the same..." (qtd. in Alexander 43).
11. See Frazer, "'Revolution' in *The Iceman Cometh*," *Modern Drama* 22.1 (Spring 1979), as well as Arthur and Barbara Gelb, *O'Neill* (245). Apparently, O'Neill's memory of the translation is inexact, as a better translation of the final lines would be singular: "The day grows hot, O Babylon" (Frazer 5).
12. Lumping the I.W.W. with the "Bolsheviki" was a common editorial practice at the time Iceman was set. In a *Life* article from 1918, the writer E. S. M. makes the somewhat unflattering comparison of the movement(s) to a purgative:
>The Bolsheviki are intent mainly on making revolution, not only in Russia, but all over Europe. They are primarily a purgae. They want to sweep the existing order—capitalism, they call it—off the earth and substitute a rule that they and their like shall dominate. They are to politics what calomel is to medicine.... The I.W.W.... and all that company in these States are political calomel. They are mighty trying. They taste bad. There is no substance in calomel. You

can't live on it. (E. S. M. "The Bolsheviki," in *Life (1883–1936)*, 71.1844 [28 February 1918]).
13. As Sam Dolgoff writes in "Revolutionary Tendencies in American Labor," *The American Labor Movement: A New Beginning* (Chicago, IL: Industrial Workers of the World, 1980), the I.W.W. acknowledged the general philosophy of the Knights of Labor as a forerunner to the Wobblies. The most significant difference in platforms was that the Knights did not believe in strikes or other forms of direct action, but rather through respectful cooperation with the capitalist class: "Strikes and other forms of direct economic action for more wages, shorter hours, better working conditions should, according to the policy of the Knights, 'be avoided wherever possible.' Conflicts should be amicably settled by employers and employees, and failing that, by arbitration. Social changes should be made by enacting favorable legislation, via the ballot" (Dolgoff "Revolutionary Tendencies").
14. The I.W.W. made total inclusion part of their agenda as a response to such practices by the major unions.
15. Dennehy also more recently played Larry to Nathan Lane's Hickey in Chicago.

8 POSTSCRIPT: NOT TIME YET

1. The *New York Times* also covered a 1994 revival of the play by the Rainbow Theater in Stamford, Connecticut, calling the production "a most hapless non-event." The reviewer, Alvin Klein, laments the missing songs of Frank Loesser's *The Most Happy Fella*, and dismisses Joe's "restlessness and political activism" as "heavy-duty issues the musical happily avoided" (Alvin Klein, "A Pulitzer Winner in Revival," *New York Times*, 22 May 1994). Nevertheless, on a happier note, the Westport Country Playhouse (Westport, CT) included *They Knew What They Wanted* in their "Script in Hand" series in 2008 under the direction of Joanne Woodward. In a statement from artistic advisor Annie Keefe, Howard's work was validated in a way that probably would have pleased him a great deal: "Having seen what may seem like dated plays, such as… *They Knew What They Wanted*, move an audience to tears, I have learned to trust that good writing will carry

the day" (David Kennedy, "Spotlight on the Script in Hand Series," Westport Country Playhouse, February 2011).
2. Perhaps significantly, neither the term "I.W.W." nor "Wobblies" appears in Hyman's study (Colette A. Hyman, *Staging Strikes: Workers' Theatre and the American Labor Movement* [Philadelphia, PA: Temple University Press, 1997])
3. Bird codirected the documentary *The Wobblies* (1979); his documentary play on the Haywood trial was published the next year. Barrie Stavis, who remained an active playwright until his death at age 100 in 2007, wrote extensively on Joe Hill, and his play premiered at the Jan Hus Theatre on New York's Upper East Side in 1958. The *Village Voice* referred to *The Man Who Never Died* as "an uninteresting play," noting that "the Wobblies are here represented as an age-dimmed textbook labor group" and that "the production is uniformly inept" (Smith, "Theatre: The Man Who Never Died," *Village Voice*, 26 November 1958).
4. Fred Thompson closes his 50-year study on a considerably more hopeful note: "The IWW had been near to extinction and pronounced dead many times before, but had always come to life again. Why give up in a world that plainly needed the sort of unionism the IWW had been championing these fifty years?" (Fred Thompson, *The I.W.W.: Its First Fifty Years (1905–1955)* [Chicago, IL: Industrial Workers of the World, 1955], 200).
5. *Beauty and the Beast*, also known as *Disney's Beauty and the Beast*, ran some 5,461 performances from April 1994 to June 2007. *The Lion King* opened in November of 1997 and is still running as of December 2013.
6. Kushner would win the Pulitzer Prize for drama the following year.
7. Such an event would not happen again until Quiara Alegria Hudes won the 2012 Pulitzer for *Water by the Spoonful*; the play made its New York debut in January of 2013, running just over a month.
8. Of O'Neill's planned epic cycle, only *A Touch of the Poet* and a draft of *More Stately Mansions* were completed.
9. See the chapter on *Processional* for the background of I.W.W. strike activity in West Virginia.
10. The songs used in the play were not, in fact, Wobbly songs from The Little Red Songbook, but older folk songs as well as the song "Step by Step," generally associated with the C.I.O. This information is available in the acting edition of the play (published through Dramatists

Play Service); in the Plume Book/Penguin edition, the stage directions merely call for singing without mentioning specific titles. For a more extensive examination of union songs and their context, see Robert Weir, *Beyond Labor's Veil: The Culture of the Knights of Labor* (University Park: Pennsylvania State University Press, 1996).

11. "Sewer rat" was a favorite expression of Mother Jones. For one of fairly numerous examples, see her autobiography: "My guards were nice young men, respectful and courteous with the exception of a fellow called Lafferty, and another sewer rat whose name I have not taxed my mind with" (Mary Harris Jones, *Autobiography of Mother Jones* 1925 [Mineola, NY: Dover, 2004], 98).

12. The adult Joshua, as a labor leader, repeats Abe's words in the beginning of the next play in the cycle, "Which Side are You On?" (Robert Schenkkan, *The Kentucky Cycle* [New York: Dramatists Play Service, 1994], 270).

13. With regard to the specific case of "Fire in the Hole," Rich sardonically notes, "Typically, the moment a new character gives his name as Abe Steinman at the mining camp in the 1920s, we know he is the Jewish Labor Organizer, and we know exactly what will happen to him." See Frank Rich, "200 Years of a Nation's Sorrows, in 9 Chapters," *New York Times* 15 November 1993: C13.

14. Schenkkan also received some stinging criticism from Kentucky native historians and professors, who recognized the playwright's fictional "Howsen County" as Harlan County, the site of many well-documented labor battles involving the miners. As associate professor of English at the University of Kentucky, Gurney Norman complained, "If this play were about another culture, there would have been a national uproar. The play would have never been funded. But it's about hillbillies and mountain people who, despite the era of political correctness, can still be discriminated against. It's still safe to poke fun at hillbillies" (Jeffrey Fleishman, "Play About Appalachia Wins No Praise in Region," *Philadelphia Inquirer* 15 November 1993). See also Alessandro Portelli, *They Say in Harlan County: An Oral History* (New York: Oxford University Press, 2011): "Schenkkan meant to make Appalachia a metaphor for America, based on the myth of the frontier; however, these 'good intentions' are defeated by the play's historical inaccuracies and primitivistic stereotypes" (244).

15. While beating and driving union organizers out of town were not uncommon occurrences in the Kentucky coal mining towns, the bloodier mine wars of Kentucky were to come during the Depression. As Harry M. Caudill writes in *Night Comes to the Cumberlands: A Biography of a Depressed Area* (Boston, MA: Little, Brown, 1963), acknowledged as Schenkkan's principal research source, the miners of the early 1920s were "almost as conservative as the operators themselves.... In the union membership drives of the early 1920s, most miners had spurned the entreaties of the 'field workers'" (192).
16. See note 6, as well as the acting edition of Schenkkan's *The Kentucky Cycle* (New York: Dramatists Play Service, 1994).
17. For the attribution to Mother Jones, see "Proceedings Held at Front Steps of the Capitol in Charleston, August 15, 1912: A Speech by Mother Jones," in *Gun Thugs, Rednecks, and Radicals: A Documentary History of the West Virginia Mine Wars*, ed. David Alan Corbin (Oakland, CA: PM Press, 2011), 78, as well as Chris Hedges, "The Battle of Blair Mountain," 16 July 2012, http://www.truthdig.com/report/item/the_battle_of_blair_mountain_20120716. Schenkkan uses excerpts from the same speech for Mother Jones's dialogue throughout "Fire in the Hole."
18. As Rich noted in his review, audiences would also have been familiar with the more specific figure of the "Jewish Labor Organizer" from such union-minded entertainments as *Norma Rae*, a popular and well-received film from 1979. Interestingly, the Jewish-identified Steinman was not played by a particularly ethnic-looking actor, which was not an uncommon practice on Broadway. The casting in this case is at least partially explained by the fact that actor Tuck Milligan, along with the other actors in the cast, had to take on several different roles throughout the 9-play, 2-part epic production.
19. According to an interview with Schenkkan in October 2012, universities, colleges, and smaller professional theatres were the ones most willing to produce the play: "I think in certain ways, perhaps large institutions are a little intimidated by the size and they get a little too wrapped up in how we can make this work for subscribers." See Robert Trussel, "Small Theater Company Takes on a Big 'Kentucky Cycle,'" *Kansas City Star*, 24 October 2012, http://www.kansascity.com/2012/10/24/3881405/small-theater-takes-on-a-big-kentucky.html.

20. See, for example, "Anarchy, Precarity, and the Revenge of the IWW: An Interview with Starbucks Union Organizer Daniel Gross," 30 April 2007, http://libcom.org/library/anarchy-precarity-and-revenge-iww-interview-starbucks-union-organizer-daniel-gross.
21. The reference is to defeated 2012 presidential candidate Mitt Romney.

Works Cited

"36 Play Jurors Clear 3 shows on First Ballot." *New York Herald, New York Tribune*, 14 March 1925: 8. ProQuest ID: 1113060310.

Abbott, George. *Mister Abbott*. New York: Random House, 1963.

Adorno, Theodor. *Aesthetic Theory*. London: Routledge and Kegan Paul, 1984.

———. *Minima Moralia: Reflections from Damaged Life*. 1951. Translated by E. F. N. Jephcott. London: Verso, 1984.

———. *Negative Dialectics*. Translated by E. B. Ashton. New York: Continuum, 1973. London: Seagull Books, 2009.

———. *Night Music: Essays on Music 1928–1962*. Edited by Rolf Tiedemann. Translated by Wieland Hoban. London: Seagull Books, 2009.

———. *Prisms*. Translated by Shierry Weber Nicholsen and Samuel Weber. Cambridge, MA: MIT Press, 1983.

Alexander, Doris. *Eugene O'Neill's Last Plays: Separating Art from Autobiography*. Athens: University of Georgia Press, 2005.

———. "Hugo of *The Iceman Cometh*: Realism and O'Neill." *American Quarterly* 5.4 (Winter 1953): 357–366. http://www.jstor.org/stable/3031329.

"Anarchy, Precarity, and the Revenge of the IWW: An Interview with Starbucks Organiser Daniel Gross." 30 April 2007. http://libcom.org/library/anarchy-precarity-and-revenge-iww-interview-starbucks-union-organizer-daniel-gross.

Anderson, Maxwell, and Harold Hickerson. *Gods of the Lightning. Twenty-Five Best Plays of the Modern American Theatre, Early Series*. Edited by John Gassner. New York: Crown, 1949.

Anderson, Maxwell. *Winterset*. 1935. New York: Dramatists Play Service, 1973.

"Anderson Play Censored." *New York Times*, 27 November 1935: 17. ProQuest ID: 101309750.

Asher, Robert. "Union Nativism and the Immigrant Response." *Labor History*, 1 June 1982: 348.

Atkinson, Brooks. *Broadway*. New York: Macmillan, 1974.

———."Four-Hour O'Neill." *New York Times*, 20 October 1946, X1. ProQuest ID: 107491108.

———. *The Lively Years 1920–1973*. New York: Association Press, 1973.

———. "The Play: Based on the Sacco-Vanzetti Case." *New York Times*, 25 October 1928: 27. ProQuest ID: 104430120.

Avrich, Paul. *Sacco and Vanzetti: The Anarchist Background*. Princeton, NJ: Princeton University Press, 1991.

Bakunin, Mikhail. "Recollections on Marx and Engels." From *Bakunin on Anarchy*. Marxists Internet Archive. http://www.marxists.org/reference/archive/bakunin/works/various/mebio.htm.

———. "Where I Stand." *Bakunin's Writings*. 1947. Anarchy Archives. http://dwardmac.pitzer.edu/Anarchist_Archives/bakunin/writings/whereistand.html.

Benchley, Robert. "The Theatre: Harpo, Groucho, Chico, Zeppo, and Karl." *Life* 92, 16 November 1928: 14. ProQuest ID: 90877415.

Bentley, Eric. "The Return of Eugene O'Neill." *Atlantic Monthly* (November 1946): 65. http://www.eoneill.com/artifacts/reviews/ic1_atlantic.htm.

———. "Trying to Like O'Neill." *Kenyon Review* 14.3 (Summer 1952): 476–492. http://www.jstor.org/stable/4333352.

Bickford, Charles. *Bulls, Balls, Bicycles & Actors*. New York: Paul S. Eriksson, 1965.

Black, Bob. "Beautiful Losers: The Historiography of the Industrial Workers of the World." *Bob Black: The Abolition of Work and Other Essays*. http://inspiracy.com/black/.

Blake, Casey Nelson. "A New Social Art: The Paterson Strike Pageant." *The Armory Show at 100*. New York: New York Historical Society Museum & Library, 2013. http://armory.nyhistory.org/a-new-social-art-the-paterson-strike-pageant/.

Block, Anita. *The Changing World in Plays and Theatre*. Boston, MA: Little, Brown, 1939.

Bourdieu, Pierre. "Habitus." *Habitus: A Sense of Place*. Edited by Jean Hillier and Emma Rooksby. Burlington, VT: Ashgate, 2002.

Bowen, Croswell. *Eugene O'Neill: Curse of the Misbegotten*. New York: Ballentine Books, 1965.

Brissenden, Paul Frederick. *The I.W.W.: A Study in American Syndicalism.* PhD diss, Columbia University, 1919. http://archive.org/details/iwwstudyofameric00brisuoft.

Brooks, John Graham. *American Syndicalism: The I.W.W.* New York: Macmillan, 1913.

Broun, Heywood. "Seeing Things at Night." *Boston Daily Globe,* 30 November 1924: 57. ProQuest ID: 498024737.

———. "Seeing Things at Night." *Boston Daily Globe,* 18 January 1925, A48. ProQuest ID: 860753725.

Brustein, Robert. "Robert Brustein on Theater: Hillbilly Blues." *New Republic* 209.18 (November 1993): 28–30. Academic Search Complete, EBSCOhost.

Burgmann, Verity. *Revolutionary Industrial Unionism: The Industrial Workers of the World in Australia.* New York: Cambridge University Press, 1995.

Butsch, Richard. *The Making of American Audiences: From Stage to Television, 1750–1990.* New York: Cambridge University Press, 2000.

Cadigan, Robert J. "The Drama and Social Problems." *English Journal* 28.7 (1939). National Council of Teachers of English.

Cannon, James B. "The I.W.W." *Fourth International* (Summer 1955), http://www.marxists.org/archive/cannon/works/1955/iww.htm.

Carlson, Marvin. "Theatre Audiences and the Reading of Performance." *Interpreting the Theatrical Past: Essays in the Historiography of Performance.* Edited by Thomas Postlewait and Bruce A. McConachie. Iowa City: University of Iowa Press, 1989.

Caudill, Harry M. *Night Comes to the Cumberlands: A Biography of a Depressed Area.* Boston, MA: Little, Brown, 1963.

Chambers, Jonathan L. *Messiah of the New Technique: John Howard Lawson, Communism, and American Theatre, 1923–1937.* Carbondale: Southern Illinois University Press, 2006.

Chandler, Alfred D., Jr. *The Visible Hand: The Managerial Revolution in American Business.* Cambridge, MA: Belknap Press of Harvard University Press, 1977.

"Chronology of IWW History." Industrial Workers of the World. http://www.iww.org/history/chronology.

Chura, Patrick J. "'Vital Contact': Eugene O'Neill and the Working Class." *Twentieth Century Literature* 49.4 (Winter 2003): 520–546. http://www.jstor.org/stable/3176038.

Clurman, Harold. *The Fervent Years*. New York: Hill and Wang, 1957.

Cockran. W. Bourke. *A Heinous Plot: An Expose of the Frame-Up System in the San Francisco Bomb Cases against Billings, Mooney, Mrs. Mooney, Weinberg and Nolan*. Chicago, IL: Chicago Federation of Labor, 1917. http://debs.indstate.edu/c666h4_1917.pdf.

Collins, Glenn. "On Stage, and Off." *New York Times*, 30 July 1993: C2. ProQuest ID: 109096687.

Conlin, Joseph R. "The I.W.W. and the Question of Violence." *The Wisconsin Magazine of History*, 51. 4 (Summer 1968): 316–326. http://www.jstor.org/stable/4634357.

Coolidge, Calvin. "Address to the American Society of Newspaper Editors, Washington, D.C." 17 January 1925. The American Presidency Project. http://www.presidency.ucsb.edu/ws/?pid=24180.

Cowley, Malcolm. "A Weekend with Eugene O'Neill." *O'Neill and His Plays: Four Decades of Criticism*. Edited by Oscar Cargill, N. Bryllion Fagin, and William J. Fisher. New York: New York University Press, 1961.

"Court Asked to Suppress 'Hairy Ape' as Indecent." *New York Tribune*, 19 May 1922: 1.

Crabtree, Brian. "The History of Anarchism." 1992. Spunk Library. http://www.spunk.org/library/intro/sp000282.txt.

"The Death of Carlo Tresca." *New York Times*, 13 January 1943: 22.

Debs, Eugene V. "The IWW Bogey." Originally published in *International Socialist Review*, 18. 8 (February 1918): 395–396. Marxists Internet Archive Library. http://www.marxists.org/archive/debs/index.htm

"Deficit of $1,996 from Strike Show." *New York Times*, 25 June 1913: 18. ProQuest ID: 97541020.

De Marinis, Marco. "Dramaturgy of the Spectator." *The Drama Review: TDR* 31. 2 (Summer 1987). http://ww.jstor.org/stable/1145819.

DePastino, Todd. "An Excerpt from *Citizen Hobo: How a Century of Homelessness Shaped America*." Chicago: University of Chicago Press, 2003. http://press.uchicago.edu/Misc/Chicago/143783.html.

Diggins, John Patrick. *Eugene O'Neill's America: Desire under Democracy*. Chicago, IL: University of Chicago Press, 2007.

"Direct Action and Sabotage." Industrial Workers of the World. http://www.iww.org/history/icons/sabotage.

Dolgoff, Sam. *The American Labor Movement: A New Beginning.* Champaign, IL: Resurgence, 1980. http://www.iww.org/history/library/Dolgoff/newbeginning.

Dubofsky, Melvyn. *We Shall Be All: A History of the Industrial Workers of the World.* Urbana: University of Illinois Press, 2000.

Duffy, Susan. *American Labor on Stage: Dramatic Interpretations of the Steel and Textile Industries in the 1930s.* Westport, CT: Greenwood Press, 1996.

Eaton, Walter Prichard. "The Hairy Ape." *Freeman*, 26 April 1922. http://www.eoneill.com/index.htm.

Ehrenreich, Barbara, and John Ehrenreich. "The Professional-Managerial Class." *Between Labor and Capital.* Edited by Pat Walker. South End Press Controversies Series, vol. 1. Boston, MA: South End Press, 1979.

Encyclopedia of Disney Animated Shorts. "Alice's Egg Plant." http://www.disneyshorts.org/shorts.aspx?shortID=25.

"Errico Malatesta: Italian Anarchist, Agitator & Theorist." *The Anarchist Encyclopedia: A Gallery of Saints and Sinners.* Recollection Used Books. http://recollectionbooks.com/bleed/Encyclopedia/MalatestaErrico.htm.

E. S. M. "The Bolsheviki." *Life (1883–1936)*, 71.1844 (28 February 1918): 329. ProQuest ID: 90819530.

"Everett Massacre Collection." University of Washington Libraries Digital Collection. https://content.lib.washington.edu/pnwlaborweb/.

"'The Fatal Mallet' or Was Charlie Chaplain's Tramp in the IWW?" *Cinema, Movies, and Motion Pictures.* 28 September 2013. http://picturesmove211.wordpress.com/2013/09/28/the-fatal-mallet-or-was-charlie-chaplins-tramp-in-the-iww/.

"Federal Theatre presents 'Processional' by John Howard Lawson: The First Modern American Play." *Library of Congress.* Washington, DC: Library of Congress. http://www.loc.gov/pictures/ resource/cph.3b49553/.

"Fifth Avenue Gay with Easter Host." *New York Times*, 13 April 1914: 5. ProQuest ID: 97546889.

Fisher, Richard B. *The Last Muckraker: The Social Orientation of the Thought of Upton Sinclair.* New Haven, CT: Yale University, 1953.

Fleishman, Jeffrey. "Play About Appalachia Wins No Praise in Region." *Philadelphia Inquirer*, 15 November 1993. http://articles

.philly.com/1993-11-15/entertainment/25946669_1_strip-mining-appalachians-coal-mining.

Flexner, Eleanor. *American Playwrights, 1918–1938: The Theatre Retreats from Reality.* New York: Simon and Schuster, 1938.

Frankfurter, Felix. "The Case of Sacco and Vanzetti." *Atlantic* (March 1927). http://www.theatlantic.com/magazine/archive/1927/03/the-case-of-sacco-and-vanzetti/306625/.

Foner, Philip S. *History of the Labor Movement in the United States: Postwar Struggles 1918–1920.* New York: International Publishers, 1988.

Frazer, Winifred L. "Revolution in *The Iceman Cometh*." *Modern Drama* 22.1 (Spring 1979): 1–8.

Gartman, David. "Bourdieu and Adorno: Converging Theories of Culture and Inequality." *Theory & Society* 41 (2012): 41–72. DOI: 10.1007/s11186-011-9159-z.

Gassner, John. "Introduction: *Gods of the Lightning.*" *Twenty-Five Best Plays of the Modern American Theatre, Early Series.* Edited by John Gassner. New York: Crown, 1949.

———. "The Happy Years, the Advancing Theatre." *Twenty-Five Best Plays of the Modern American Theatre, Early Series.* Edited by John Gassner. New York: Crown, 1949.

———. "Introduction: *They Knew What They Wanted.*" *Twenty-Five Best Plays of the Modern American Theatre, Early Series.* Edited by John Gassner. New York: Crown, 1949.

———, ed. *Twenty-Five Best Plays of the Modern American Theatre, Early Series.* New York: Crown, 1949.

Gelb, Arthur, and Barbara Gelb. *O'Neill.* New York: Harper & Row, 1973.

Gelb, Arthur, Barbara Gelb, and Rick Burns. *Eugene O'Neill: A Documentary Film.* Directed by Rick Burns. WGBH Educational Foundation and Steeplechase Films, 2006.

George, Harrison. *The I.W.W. Trial. (Mass Violence in America).* Edited by Robert M. Fogelson and Richard E. Rubenstein. New York: Arno Press and *New York Times*, 1969.

Gilbert, James. *Writers and Partisans: A History of Literary Radicalism in America.* New York: Columbia University Press, 1992.

Goldman, Emma. *Syndicalism: The Modern Menace to Capitalism.* New York: Mother Earth Publishing Association, 1913. *Anarchy Archives.* http://dwardmac.pitzer.edu/Anarchist_Archives/goldman/syndicalism.html.

Goldstein, Robert J. "The Anarchist Scare of 1908: A Sign of Tensions in the Progressive Era." *American Studies* 15.2 (Fall 1974): 57.

Grainger, Boine. "In the Dramatic Mail Bag: That Play 'Processional.'" *New York Times*, 8 March 1925: X2. ProQuest ID: 103564898.

Gross, Ernest W. "News and Comment of the Theater, Here and Abroad: Germans Adapt Upton Sinclair's Prison Drama." *New York Herald Tribune*, 6 November 1927: E2. ProQuest ID: 1133501957.

G. S. "The Theatre." *The Dial* (May 1922): 548. ProQuest ID: 89685699.

"The Hairy Ape: A Serio-Comedy of Ancient and Modern Life." *The Current Opinion* 72 (June 1922): 768–776.

Hammond, Percy. "The New Play: 'The Hairy Ape' Shows Eugene O'Neill in a Bitter and Interesting Humor." *New York Tribune*, 10 March 1922: 8. ProQuest ID: 576577720.

———. "The Theaters: Some Mysterious Proceedings at the Garrick Theater." *New York Herald, New York Tribune*, 13 January 1925: 12. ProQuest ID: 1112892031.

———. "The Theaters: 'They Knew What They Wanted' is Not Only a Good Play, but a Good Show." *New York Herald, New York Tribune*, 25 November 1924: 16. ProQuest ID: 1113052758.

Hedges, Chris. "The Battle of Blair Mountain," 16 July 2012. http://www.truthdig.com/report/item/the_battle_of_blair_mountain_20120716.

Helmling, Steven. "A Martyr to Happiness: Why Adorno Matters." *Kenyon Review*, New Series, 28.4 (Autumn, 2006): 156–172, Article Stable URL: http://www.jstor.org/stable/4338968.

Herbst, Philip. *Talking Terrorism: A Dictionary of the Loaded Language of Political Violence*. Westport, CT: Greenwood Press, 2003.

"Hillstrom is Cremated: Attacks on Utah Officials Feature of Funeral of I.W.W. Poet." *New York Times*, 26 November 1915: 7.

Hischak, Thomas S. *The Theatregoer's Almanac: A Collection of Lists, People, History, and Commentary on the American Theatre*. Westport, CT: Greenwood Press, 1997.

The History of the I.W.W.: A Discussion of its Main Features by a Group of Workmen. Chicago, IL: Industrial Workers of the World, 1923.

Holtz, Allan. "Obscurity of the Day: Fitzboomski the Anarchist." *Stripper's Guide*. 10 November 2009. http://strippersguide.blogspot.com/2009/11/obscurity-of-day-fitzboomski-anarchist.html.

Horkheimer, Max, and Theodor Adorno. *Dialectic of Enlightenment*. New York: Herder and Herder, 1972.

Houseman, Arthur L. "Sidney Howard and Production." *Educational Theatre Journal* 11.1 (March 1959):13.

Howard, Sidney. "Our Professional Patriots VIII: The Constitution Worshippers." *The New Republic* 40.513 (15 October 1924): 171–173.

———. "The Labor Spy: A Survey of Industrial Espionage." Originally published in *The New Republic*, 1921. http://www.rebelgraphics.org/wfmhall/sidneyhowardsthelaborspy01.html.

———. *They Knew What They Wanted. Twenty-Five Best Plays of the Modern American Theatre, Early Series*. Edited by John Gassner. New York: Crown, 1949.

Hoxie, R. F. "The Truth about the I.W.W." *Journal of Political Economy* 21.9 (November 1913): 785–797.

H. R. M. "Criminal Law: Criminal Syndicalist Act: Constitutional Law: Validity of the Act under the Free Speech Clause." *California Law Review* 10.6 (September 1922): 512–518. http://www.jstor.org/stable/3474218.

Hyman, Colette A. *Staging Strikes: Workers' Theatre and the American Labor Movement*. Philadelphia, PA: Temple University Press, 1997.

The Immediate Demands of the I.W.W. Jim Crutchfield's I.W.W. Page. http://www.workerseducation.org/crutch/pamphlets/immediate.html.

"Industrial Workers of the World Photograph Collection: IWW Song Book." Seattle: University of Washington Libraries, 2013. http://guides.lib.washington.edu/content.php?pid=318431&sid=2643533.

Isaacs, Edith J. R. "Maxwell Anderson." *English Journal* 25.10 (December 1936): 795–804.

"IWW Chronology (1932–1944)." Industrial Workers of the World: A Union for All Workers. http://www.iww.org/about/chronology/5.

"IWW Chronology (1946–1971)." Industrial Workers of the World: A Union for All Workers. http://www.iww.org/about/chronology/6.

"IWW Chronology (1990–1995)." Industrial Workers of the World: A Union for All Workers. http://www.iww.org/about/chronology/10.

"IWW Cultural Icons." Industrial Workers of the World: A Union for All Workers. http://www.iww.org/.

"The I.W.W." *New York Times*, 4 August 1917: 6. ProQuest ID: 99893732.

"I.W.W. is 50 Years Old." *New York Times*, 26 February 1955: 32. ProQuest ID: 113202232.

I.W.W. Songs to Fan the Flames of Discontent, 19th ed. Chicago, IL: Industrial Workers of the World, 1923. http://www.faubern.ch/_texte/songbook.pdf.

"The I.W.W. Strike." *New York Times*, 16 April 1920: 12. ProQuest ID: 98240876.

"I.W.W. Trial Starts Today." *New York Times*, 1 April 1918: 20. ProQuest ID: 100020405.

"The I.W.W.: What it Is and What it Is Not." "I.W.W. Pamphlets and Other Literature," Jim Crutchfield's I.W.W. Page.http://www.workerseducation.org/crutch/pamphlets/what/whatitis.html.

Jerving, Ryan. "An Experiment in Modern Vaudeville: Archiving the Wretched Refuse in John Howard Lawson's *Processional*." *Modern Drama* 51.4 (Winter 2008): 528–551.

Jones, James. *From Here to Eternity*. New York: Scribner's, 1951.

Jones, Mary Harris. *Autobiography of Mother Jones*. 1925. Mineola, NY: Dover, 2004.

Kabatchnik, Amnon. *Blood on the Stage 1925–1950: Milestone Plays of Crime, Mystery, and Detection*. Lanham, MD: Scarecrow Press, Inc., 2010.

Kalem, T. E. "Theater: Monopod." *Time Magazine*, 22 October 1979.

Kantor, Louis. "O'Neill Defends His Play of Negro." *New York Times*, 11 May 1924: 5.

———. "O'Neill Defends His Play of Negro." *Conversations with Eugene O'Neill*. Edited by Mark Estrin. Jackson: University Press of Mississippi, 1990.

Kemmerer, Donald L., and Edward D. Wickersham. "Reasons for the Growth of the Knights of Labor in 1885–1886." *Industrial and Labor Relations Review* 3.2 (January 1950): 213–220.

Kennedy, David. "Spotlight on the Script in Hand Series." Westport Country Playhouse, February 2011. http://www.westportplayhouse.org/enewsletter/february2011.aspx.

Kennedy, Jeffrey. Provincetown Playhouse. http://www.provincetownplayhouse.com/home.html.

Kerr, Walter. "Stage View: Melodrama Isn't Always a Dirty Word." *New York Times*, 8 February 1976: D5. ProQuest ID: 122769222.

Klein, Alvin. "A Pulitzer Winner in Revival." *New York Times*, 22 May 1994: CN13. ProQuest ID: 109327311.

Knox, George A., and Herbert M. Stahl. *Dos Passos and "The Revolting Playwrights."* Essays and Studies on American Language and Literature XV. Uppsala, Sweden: A. B. Lundequistska Bokhandeln, 1964.

Kornbluh, Joyce, editor. *Rebel Voices: An I.W.W. Anthology.* Ann Arbor: University of Michigan Press, 1968.

Kornbluh, Joyce. "The Industrial Workers of the World (IWW)—A Short History." faculty.ccbcmd.edu/~wbarry/labhisII/kornbluh.doc.

Kramm, Joseph. "A Personal History." *New York Times*, 24 February 1952: X1. ProQuest ID: 112524100.

Kropotkin, Peter. "Anarchism: Its Philosophy and Ideal." 1898. Anarchy Archives. http://dwardmac.pitzer.edu/Anarchist_Archives/kropotkin/philandideal.html.

Krutch, Joseph Wood. *The American Drama Since 1918: An Informal History.* New York: George Braziller, 1957.

Lacher, Irene. "Go West, Young Playwright." *New York Times.* 8 January 2006: A8. ProQuest ID: 93160964.

Larabee, Ann. "'The Drama of Transformation': Settlement House Idealism and the Neighborhood Playhouse." *Performing America: Cultural Nationalism in American Theater.* Edited by Jeffery D. Mason and J. Ellen Gainor. Ann Arbor: University of Michigan Press, 1999.

Lawson, John Howard. "On Processional." *New York Times*, 1 February 1925: X2.

———. *Processional. Staged Action: Six Plays from the American Workers' Theatre.* Edited by Lee Papa. Ithaca, NY: ILR Press, 2009.

Leier, Mark. *Bakunin: The Creative Passion—A Biography.* New York: Seven Stories Press, 2011.

Lewandowski, Joseph D. "Adorno on Jazz and Society." *Philosophy & Social Criticism* 22 (1996):103–121. DOI: 10.1177/019145379602200506.

Lewis, Robert. *Slings and Arrows: Theater in My Life.* New York: Applause Books, 1996.

"Listing the Attractions for the Holiday Trade." *New York Times*, 23 December 1928: 84. ProQuest ID: 104374752.

Longoria, Andrew. "*They Knew What They Wanted.*" *The Columbia University Encyclopedia of Modern Drama.* Edited by Gabrielle H. Cody and Evert Sprinchorn, vol. 2. New York: Columbia University Press, 2007.

Lowry, Helen Bullitt. "They Like Unsuccessful Strikes." *New York Times*, 25 April 1920: XX1. ProQuest ID: 97885577.

Mantle, Burns. "'Gods of Lightning' Strikes Fire." *New York Daily News*, 25 October 1925: 39.

———. "'Processional' is a Discordant Jumble." *New York Daily News*, 13 January 1925: 24.

———. "'What They Wanted' is Life in the Raw." *New York Daily News*, 25 November 1924: 24.

"Maxwell Anderson Writes on 'Red Channels.'" *New York Times*, 18 January 1953: X13. ProQuest ID: 112647364.

McPherson, William L. "News and Comment of the Theater, Here and Abroad: Oil and Drama Make a Good Berlin Mixture." *New York Herald Tribune*, 6 January 1929: F2. ProQuest ID: 1111940569.

———. "The Germans Discover America; Incidentally, Mr. Upton Sinclair." *New York Herald Tribune*, 22 April 1928: F2. ProQuest ID 1113369527.

"Mother Jones is Defiant: Says She'll Unionize West Virginia if It Costs Her Life." *New York Times*, 19 May 1913: 2.

Murphy, Brenda. *The Provincetown Players and the Culture of Modernity*. New York: Cambridge University Press, 2005.

"Myth #1: I.W.W. Stands for International Workers of the World." Industrial Workers of the World. http://www.iww.org/history/ myths/1.

Norton, Elliot. "Puffers, Pundits and Other Play Reviewers: A Short History of American Dramatic Criticism." *The American Theatre: A Sum of Its Parts*. Edited by Henry B. Williams. New York: Samuel French, 1971.

Oard, Brian A. "Poetry after Auschwitz: What Adorno Really Said, and Where He Said It." Blog post, 12 March 2011. http://mindfulpleasures.blogspot.com.

Odets, Clifford. *Waiting for Lefty*. 1935. New York: Dramatists Play Service, 1998.

O'Neill, Eugene. *The Hairy Ape. Twenty-Five Best Plays of the Modern American Theatre, Early Series*. Edited by John Gassner. New York: Crown, 1949.

———. *The Iceman Cometh*. New York: Vintage Books, 1967.

———. *Selected Letters of Eugene O'Neill*. Edited by Travis Bogard and Jackson N. Bryer. New Haven, CT: Yale University Press, 1988.

———. "What the Theatre Means to Me." *O'Neill and His Plays: Four Decades of Criticism*. Edited by Oscar Cargill, N. Bryllion Fagin, and William J. Fisher. New York: New York University, 1961.

"O'Neill's 'Hairy Ape' Escapes Charge of Talking 'Indecently.'" *New York Tribune*, 20 May 1922: 18.

Palmer, A. Mitchell. "Case Against the Reds." *Forum* 63 (February 1920):173–180. http://www.marxists.org/history/usa/government/fbi/1920/0200-palmer-redscase.pdf.

Papa, Lee. "The 1920s: Workers In (and Out of) Jail." *Staged Action: Six Plays from the American Workers' Theatre.* Edited by Lee Papa. Ithaca, NY: ILR Press, 2009.

"Paterson Strikers Anxious for $6,000." *New York Times*, 24 June 1913: 1. ProQuest ID: 97374450.

"Paterson Strikers Now Become Actors." *New York Times*, 8 June 1913: 7.

Patterson, James. "Off the Record." *Billboard*, 15 April 1922: 18. ProQuest ID: 1031697390.

———. "The Hairy Ape." *The Billboard* (15 April 1922) 34, 15:19. ProQuest ID 1031697453.

Pietaro, John. "Solidarity Forever: The IWW and the Protest Song." The Cultural Worker (10 December 2010). http://theculturalworker.blogspot.com/2010/12/solidarity-forever-iww-and-protest-song.html.

"Pointed Paragraphs." *The Newark Daily Advocate*, 10 August 1917: 4. http://access.newspaperarchive.com.

Portelli, Alessandro. *They Say in Harlan County: An Oral History.* New York: Oxford University Press, 2011.

Preston, William. *Aliens and Dissenters: Federal Suppression of Radicals 1903–1933.* Champaign: University of Illinois Press, 1994.

"Proceedings Held at Front Steps of the Capitol in Charleston, August 15, 1912: A Speech by Mother Jones." *Gun Thugs, Rednecks, and Radicals: A Documentary History of the West Virginia Mine Wars.* Edited by David Alan Corbin. Oakland, CA: PM Press, 2011.

"Radical Play Goes Well on Great White Way." *The Industrial Worker*, 22 December 1928: 3.

"Radio: Drama for an Hour." *Time Magazine*, 5 May 1952.

"A Reality Check from a Century Past." ABC News, 16 October 2007. http://abcnews.go.com/Politics/Vote2008/story?id=3733457.

Reed, John. "The Social Revolution in Court." *Liberator* 1.7 (September 1918): 22–24.

———. "War in Paterson." *The Masses* (June 1913). Marxist Internet Archive Library. http://www.marxists.org/archive/reed/1913/masses06.htm.

Rich, Frank. "200 Years of a Nation's Sorrows, in 9 Chapters," *New York Times*, 15 November 1993: C13. ProQuest ID: 109144468.

Richards, David. "Smashing America's Favorite Myths." *New York Times*, 21 November 1993: H5. ProQuest ID: 109095862.

Ridley, F. F. *Revolutionary Syndicalism in France: The Direct Action of its Time.* New York: Cambridge University Press, 1970.

"Ritual of Industrial Workers of the World." 7 July 1905. Jim Crutchfield's I.W.W. Page. http://www.workerseducation.org/crutch/constitution/ritual.html.

Robinson, J. Bradford. "The Jazz Essays of Theodor Adorno: Some Thoughts on Jazz Reception in Weimar Germany." *Popular Music* 13.1 (1994): 1–2. http://www.jstor.org/stable/852897.

Ruhl, Arthur. "I.W.W. 'Wobbly' Glorified in New Sinclair Play." *New York Herald Tribune*, 5 December 1928: 33. ProQuest ID: 113407261.

———. "Off Stage and On." *New York Herald Tribune*, 29 October 1928: 14. ProQuest ID: 1113622688.

———. "Second Nights." *New York Herald Tribune*, 9 December 1928: F1. ProQuest ID: 1113411514.

The Sacco and Vanzetti Case, vol. 5. New York: Henry Holt, 1929, 4896–4905. http://college.cengage.com/history/ayers_primary_sources/statement_bartolomeo_vanzetti_1929.htm.

"Sacco and Vanzetti: Guilty After All?" *All Things Considered*, NPR interview with Tony Arthur, 4 March 2006. http://www.npr.org/templates/story/story.php?storyId=5245754.

Sarlos, Robert Karoly. *Jig Cook and the Provincetown Players: Theatre in Ferment.* Amherst: University of Massachusetts Press, 1982.

Savran, David. *Highbrow/Lowdown: Theater, Jazz, and the Making of the New Middle Class.* Ann Arbor: University of Michigan Press, 2009.

S. B. "The Theatre: Upton Sinclair's Play." *Wall Street Journal*, 6 December 1928: 4. ProQuest ID: 1350511631.

Schenkkan, Robert. *The Kentucky Cycle.* New York: Dramatists Play Service, 1994.

———. *The Kentucky Cycle.* New York: Plume, 1993.

Schriftgiesser, Karl. "The Iceman Cometh." *New York Times*, 6 October 1946: X1. ProQuest ID: 107510896.

Schwartz, Michael. *Broadway and Corporate Capitalism: The Rise of the Professional-Managerial Class, 1900–1920.* New York: Palgrave Macmillan, 2009.

Seaver, Edwin. "In the Dramatic Mail Bag: A Blast for 'Processional.'" *New York Times*, 1 February 1925: X2. ProQuest ID: 103702793.

"Second Balcony: Gods of the Lightning." *Barnard Bulletin*, 16 November 1928: 2.

Shivers, Alfred S. *The Life of Maxwell Anderson*. New York: Stein and Day, 1983.

Sinclair, Upton. "From Upton Sinclair." *New York Times*, 23 December 1928: 86.

———. *Singing Jailbirds*. Pasadena, CA: Author, 1924.

———. *The Land of Orange Groves and Jails: Upton Sinclair's California*. Edited by Lauren Coodley. Berkeley, CA: Heyday Books, 2003.

"Singing Jailbirds." *The Bakersfield Californian*, 14 November 1925: Editorial Page.

"'Singing Jailbirds' Called Propaganda: Company Makes Good Showing with an Absurd Situation." *New York Times*, 5 December 1928: 40.

Sisk, Robert F. "Play with 'Moral' Hits Mark Well." *Baltimore Sun*, 28 October 1928: LT1. ProQuest ID: 543571801.

Smith, Frederick James. "Hopkins Skids in Voltaire." *Los Angeles Times*, 26 March 1922: III35. ProQuest ID: 160980879.

Smith, Michael. "Theatre: The Man Who Never Died." *Village Voice*, 26 November 1958: 8. http://news.google.com/newspapers?nid=1299& dat=19581126&id=sdpHAAAAIBAJ&sjid=NYwDAAAAIBAJ&pg =6240,3849608.

Smith, Walker C. "Their Court and Our Class: A One Act Sketch." *Rebel Voices: An I.W.W. Anthology*. Edited by Joyce L. Kornbluh. Ann Arbor: University of Michigan Press, 1968.Stark, Irwin. "Shocking." *New York Times*, 25 January 1953: X13. ProQuest ID: 112539954.

St. John, Vincent. "The I.W.W. and Political Parties." Industrial Workers of the World http://www.iww.org/history/library/SaintJohn/parties.

Stone, Percy N. "Broadway Offers an Even Half Dozen New Plays." *New York Herald, New York Tribune*, 25 January 1925: C14. ProQuest ID: 1113156921.

"Straining 'Free Speech.'" *Mansfield News*, 30 November 1920: 6. http:// access.newspaperarchive.com.mansfield-news.

Susman, Warren I. *Culture as History: The Transformation of American Society in the Twentieth Century*. New York: Pantheon Books, 1984.

Swan, Gilbert. "Sacco and Vanzetti Return in Guises to Give Broadway a Thrill." Syndicated column, 4 November 1928.

"Taft Blames I.W.W. on Smug Cynicism." *New York Times*, 8 March 1914: 4. ProQuest ID: 97569035.

Taylor, Frederick Winslow. *Principles of Scientific Management*. 1911. Marxists Internet Archive. http://www.marxists.org/reference/subject/economics/taylor/principles/introduction.htm.

"Theater News: 'Gods of the Lightning' to be on Broadway Oct. 24." *New York Herald Tribune*, 13 October 1928: 10. ProQuest ID: 1113449433.

Thompson, Charles Willis. "The New Socialism that Threatens the Social System: The New Socialism that Threatens Society." *New York Times*, 17 March 1912, SM1. ProQuest ID: 97317485.

Thompson, Fred. *The I.W.W.: Its First Fifty Years (1905–1955)*. Chicago, IL: Industrial Workers of the World, 1955.

"Three New Anderson Plays." *New York Herald, New York Tribune*, 20 September 1928: 22. ProQuest ID: 1113494621.

Townsend, Kerry. "Frank Tannenbaum: 'Dramatization of Evil.'" *Criminological Theory*. Dr. Cecil E. Greek, http://www.criminology.fsu.edu/crimtheory/tannenbaum.htm.

Tripp, Anne Huber. *The I.W.W. and the Paterson Silk Strike of 1913*. Urbana, IL: University of Chicago Press, 1987.

Trussell, Robert. "Small Theater Company Takes on a Big 'Kentucky Cycle.'" *Kansas City Star*, 24 October 2012. http://www.kansascity.com/2012/10/24/3881405/small-theater-takes-on-a-big-kentucky.html.

"Two Pageants—A Contrast." *New York Times*, 9 June 1913: 8. ProQuest ID: 97508842.

"Upton Sinclair Abroad." *New York Times*, 20 May 1928: 102.

"Village Views Upton Sinclair I.W.W. Drama." *New York Daily News*, 5 December 1925: 35.

Wall, Vincent. "Maxwell Anderson: The Last Anarchist." *Sewanee Review* 49.3 (July–September 1941): 339–369.

Watts, Richard, Jr. "News and Comment of the Theater, Here and Abroad: 'Gods' on the New York Stage, and a Year Ago in the Courts." *New York Herald Tribune*, 4 November 1928: F2. ProQuest ID: 1113652360.

Weir, Robert. *Beyond Labor's Veil: The Culture of the Knights of Labor.* University Park: Pennsylvania State University Press, 1996.

Weisbord, Albert. *The Conquest of Power.* 1937. The Albert & Vera Weisbord Archives. www.marxists.org/archive/weisbord.

"West Virginia's Mine Wars." West Virginia Archives and History. West Virginia Division of Culture and History, 2013. http://www.wvculture.org/history/minewars.html.

Wetzsteon, Ross. *Republic of Dreams, Greenwich Village: The American Bohemia, 1910–1960.* New York: Simon & Schuster, 2002.

"What is the Origin of the Term Wobbly?" Industrial Workers of the World http://www.iww.org/history/icons/wobbly.

"What's Wrong with Labor?" *New York Times*, 26 October 1919: SM1. ProQuest ID: 100339728.

White, Ahmed A. "The Crime of Economic Radicalism: Criminal Syndicalism Laws and the Industrial Workers of the World, 1917–1927." *Oregon Law Review* 85 (9 April 2007): 649.

Wilk, Max. *They're Playing Our Song: Conversations with Classic Songwriters.* Westport, CT: Easton Studio Press, 2008.

Williams, Raymond. *Modern Tragedy.* London: Chatto and Windus, 1969.

Wilmer, S. E. "Censorship and Ideology: Eugene O'Neill (*The Hairy Ape*)." *Cycnos* 9 (12 June 2008). http://revel.unice.fr/cycnos/?id=1250.

Winchell, Walter. "Your Broadway and Mine." Syndicated column, *Harrisburg Telegraph*, 3 November 1928.

Winters, Donald E. *The Soul of the Wobblies: The I.W.W., Religion, and American Culture in the Progressive Era 1905–1917.* Contributions in American Studies, no. 81. Westport, CT: Greenwood Press, 1985.

Witchel, Alex. "On Stage, and Off." *New York Times*, 10 April 1992: C2. ProQuest ID: 108942407.

Woollcott, Alexander. "The Play: Eugene O'Neill at Full Tilt." *New York Times*, 10 March 1922: 22. ProQuest ID: 98680259.

"Young Boswell Interviews O'Neill." *New York Tribune*, 24 May 1923: 13. ProQuest ID: 1237358423.

Young, Stark. "The Play: Jazzing Folly and Beauty." *New York Times*, 13 January 1925: 17.

———. "The Play: Love in the Valley." *New York Times*, 25 November 1924: 27. ProQuest ID: 103286600.

Zanger, Martin. "Politics of Confrontation: Upton Sinclair and the Launching of the ACLU in Southern California." *Pacific Historical Review* 38.4 (November 1969): 383–406.

Zinn, Howard. *A People's History of the United States 1492–Present.* New York: Perennial Classics, 2001.

Zinn, Howard, and Anthony Arnove. *Voices of a People's History of the United States.* New York: Seven Stories Press, 2004.

Zolotow, Sam. "'Iceman Cometh' to Start at 5:30." *New York Times*, 6 September 1946: 17. ProQuest ID: 107643903.

Index

Abbott, George, 13, 62–4, 68, 71, 72, 73, 97, 152n5
Adorno, Theodor, 13, 23, 91
  on art and mass culture, 57–8
  on art and the marketplace, 13
  on jazz, 61, 67, 74, 151–2n4
  on poetry, 109, 159n1
  on "underdogs," 106, 147n1
Alexander, Doris, 110, 161n8
"Alice's Egg Plant" (cartoon), 60
American Civil Liberties Union (Southern California), 95, 107
American Federation of Labor (AFL), 14, 17, 122
anarchists, 6, 87, 145n10, 155n11
  anti-anarchist values, 31
  and distinctions among radicals, 18, 112, 119
  fear of in U.S., 116
  and Haymarket Affair, 116
  and I.W.W. (wobblies), 12, 16, 76, 140
  "philosophical anarchist," 114, 117, 160n4
  Sacco and Vanzetti and, 76
  violence against, 82
  in *Winterset*, 91
anarcho-syndicalism, 17, 111–12
Ancient Order of Hibernians, 121
Anders, Glenn, 50–2, 97, 150n10
Anderson, Maxwell, 6, 10, 12, 33, 74, 75, 77–82, 87–9, 91, 95, 139, 152n6, 154n3, 155n8, 156n13
Anne of the Thousand Days, 33

Gods of the Lightning, 10, 12, 74, 75, 77–8, 87, 90, 92, 95, 105, 128, 129, 139, 154n5, 155n8
  anarchists and anarchism in, 77, 79–82, 85, 86
  Sacco and Vanzetti and, 74, 75, 76, 77, 78, 80, 83–9, 91, 95
Winterset, 74, 91, 92, 155n8
  see also Hickerson, Harold; Sacco and Vanzetti
Angels in America (play), 132
Atkinson, Brooks, 63, 64, 84, 115, 150n4, 159n15
Atlantic Monthly, 120
Auschwitz, 109
Awake and Sing (play), 80

Bakunin, Michael (Mikhail), 110, 123–5
  see also nihilism
Barnard Bulletin, The (newspaper), 83
"Battle Hymn of the Republic, The" (song), 103
Beauty and the Beast (play), 132, 163n5
Benchley, Robert, 83
Bennett, Richard, 45
Bentley, Eric, 120, 160n2, 161n8
Berlyne, Daniel, 31
Bickford, Charles, 79–81, 84, 85, 89, 154n4
Billboard (magazine), 33
Bird, Stewart, 130, 163n3
Bisbee deportations, 81–2
Black, Bob, 27

Blair Creek, 64
Blake, William Dorsey, 2
Block, Anita, 35, 36, 79, 91, 92
Bohemians, 30
Bourdieu, Pierre, 23
Bourne, Randolph, 8
Bradfort, Walter, 116
Braham, Horace, 79–80, 154n5
Brissenden, Paul, 3, 4, 17, 25, 146n17
Broadway, 4, 9, 15, 16, 18, 24, 36, 45, 60, 69, 75, 77, 79, 83, 84, 88, 91, 93, 109, 113, 129
    "cleaning up" of, 53–4
    see also Industrial Workers of the World ("Wobblies on Broadway" and "audiences and Wobblies")
Brooks, John Graham, 14–15
Brookwood Labor Players, 106
Broun, Heywood, 33, 53, 66
Brustein, Robert, 134
Bulgakov, Leo, 154n5
Burgess, Grover, 96–7

Cadigan, Robert J., 98
Cagney, James, 79
Carlin, Terry, 117, 161n10
"Carmagnole" (song), 111
Casey, John M., 77
Chura, Patrick J., 128
Clurman, Harold, 62, 152n5, 154n2
Cohan, George M., 68–9
Commins, Saxe, 110
Communism (Communists), 19, 26, 36, 113, 123, 138, 155n8, 157n7
    Communist Party (CP), 43, 60, 150n6
Confederation General du Travail (C.G.T.), 111
"Contemporaries" (play), 9
Cook, George "Cram," 9
Coolidge, Calvin, 44, 149n3
Cooper Institute, 121

corporate capitalism (American), 5, 18, 21, 80, 122, 144n6
Coué, Émile, 102, 159n14
Cowley, Malcolm, 117, 161n9
Czolgosz, Leon, 116

Daily Masses, The (newspaper), 138
De Marinis, Marco, 12, 94
Debs, Eugene, 157–8n8
Dennehy, Brian, 126, 162n15
Department of Justice, 77, 84
Dial, The (magazine), 33
"*Die Revolution*" (poem), 115
direct action, 4, 17, 18, 19, 34, 70, 117, 120, 157n8, 162n13
    see also direct action; Industrial Workers of the World
Disney, Walt, 60
"Disneyfication," 132
Dodge, Mabel, 7
Dos Passos and "The Revolting Playwrights" (book), 93, 156n1
Dubofsky, Melvyn, 20
Duffy, Susan, 1, 127, 143n1

Easter Parade (New York City), 23
Eastman, Max, 89
Ehrenreich, Barbara and John, 21
Equity Library Theatre, 77
Espionage Act of 1917, 97, 118
Ethical Culture Society, 54
Ettor, Joseph, 4
Everett massacre, 81–2, 144n4, 154n6, 171
expressionism, 61, 73, 153n12, 160n2

Federal Theater Project, 128
"Fire in the Hole," 133–6, 164n13, 165n17
    see also Schenkkan, Robert
First International, 121
Fisher, Richard B., 97
"Fitzboomski the Anarchist" (comic strip), 116, 160–1n7

Flexner, Eleanor, 35
Flynn, Elizabeth Gurley, 7, 43, 113
Foner, Philip, 25
Ford, John, 11
Frazer, Winifred, 115, 121
Freilgrath, Ferdinand, 115
French syndicalism, 17, 110, 112
   see also syndicalism
Frick, Henry, 116
Fried, Manny, 130
From Here to Eternity (novel), 1, 138
   see also Jones, James

Gabriel, Gilbert, 61
Garland, Robert, 84–5
Gartman, David, 57
Gassner, John, 45, 57, 62, 75, 77, 86, 88, 90
Gelb, Barbara and Arthur, 30
George, Harrison, 25
Glaspell, Susan, 9
Gods of the Lightning (play)
   see Anderson, Maxwell; Hickerson, Harold
Golden, John, 62
Goldman, Emma, 119
Gompers, Samuel, 14
Gone with the Wind (film), 45
Great War (World War I), 8, 19, 24, 26, 31, 38, 43, 75, 80, 82, 97, 104, 116, 118, 125, 147n2, 155n10, 158n11
Greenwich Village, 30
Grove Street Theatre, 99

Hairy Ape, The (play)
   see O'Neill, Eugene
Halton, Charles, 71–2
Hammond, Percy, 33, 51, 66
Havel, Hippolyte, 115, 116, 161n8
Haymarket Affair, 116
Haywood, William ("Big Bill"), 21, 24, 25, 43, 113, 130, 158n11, 163n3

Hickerson, Harold, 6, 10, 74, 75, 77, 78, 79, 80, 82, 87, 95, 105
   see also Anderson, Maxwell
Hill, Joe, 6, 99, 113, 130, 135, 144n7, 144n8, 145n9, 163n3
Holmes, Oliver Wendell Jr., 97
Homestead Strike, 116
Howard, Bronson, 53
Howard, Sidney, 10, 43–50, 52–7, 90, 95, 129, 131, 150n4, 150n5, 151n11, 162n1
   They Knew What They Wanted, 10, 43, 44, 58, 94, 110, 128, 129, 131, 152n6, 162n1
   scandal of, 52–4
   use of I.W.W. (Wobblies) in, 45–9, 52, 54–7, 139
Hoxie, R. F., 16
Hyman, Colette, 106, 129, 163n2

I.W.W.: A Study in American Syndicalism, 3, 146n17
Iceman Cometh, The (play)
   see O'Neill, Eugene
Industrial Union Bulletin, 21
Industrial Union Congress, 14
Industrial Workers of the World (I.W.W. or IWW), or "Wobblies"
   agenda of, 2, 4, 8, 11, 12, 13, 14, 20, 38, 39, 40, 68, 69, 74, 94, 95, 97, 98, 124, 139, 140, 162n14
   audiences and, 3–5, 11–12, 15, 19–22, 27, 28, 32, 34, 39, 41, 43–4, 46–52, 55–7, 59, 72, 73–4, 78–9, 85, 90, 91, 93–4, 104, 106, 112, 130, 131, 132, 133, 134, 137
   belonging or fitting on Broadway, 2, 13, 14, 29, 31, 40–1, 57–8, 69, 85, 90, 93, 127–8, 130, 133, 136, 138
   changing technology and, 43

Industrial Workers—*Continued*
   communism and, 19, 26, 43, 60, 113, 147n3, 161–2n12
   criminal conspiracy trial (1917) and, 24–5, 49
   direct action and, 4, 19, 70, 157n8
   ending of I.W.W. histories, 55, 59, 146–7n20
   environmental issues and, 131
   folk heroes and folklore, 3–6, 11, 58, 63–4, 73, 74, 95, 99, 136, 137, 150n8
   folk songs (music) and, 5–6, 11, 12, 25, 46, 51, 56, 64, 70, 99, 101–3, 110, 117, 129, 137, 141, 143–4n3, 150n6, 150n8, 163–4n10
   forgetting and nostalgia, 1–2, 56, 113
   free speech and, 4, 20, 79, 97
   Great War and, 19, 24–6, 97, 116, 118
   history of, 2, 4, 13–20, 110, 111, 113–14, 121, 123, 131, 136, 140, 146–7n, 148n, 152n9, 162n13
   "I-Won't-Work," 109, 119, 126, 148n5
   internet presence of, 132
   Iraq War and, 132
   launching of, 14
   loss of leadership and, 25–6
   media perceptions of, 4, 6–9, 10, 15–16, 19, 27–8, 36–8, 104, 112–13, 161n12
   "One Big Union," 5, 81, 100, 112
   onstage physicality of (character types), 3, 11–13, 31–4, 38–9, 46, 50–1, 71–3, 78, 79–81, 95, 97, 115–18, 133–4, 138–40
   origin of nickname "wobbly," 101, 159n13
   Paterson Silk Strike Pageant and, 7–9, 90, 118, 131, 145n11
   playwrights' perceptions of, 3, 12, 22, 41, 114–15, 118, 125
   preamble of, 14, 19, 99, 146n16
   Provincetown Players and, 9
   public perception of, 2, 8, 10, 11, 12, 14, 15, 16, 20, 24, 26, 36, 44, 46, 47, 56, 60, 76, 112, 113, 119, 143n2
   red identification cards, 8, 49, 138
   Red Scare and, 26
   religion and, 6, 40, 100, 103, 134, 137, 138, 158n10–11
   socialism and, 18–19, 29, 98, 120, 140, 157–8n8
   split in organization, 43, 60, 75, 114, 149n2
   strikes led by, 11, 19, 44, 49, 59, 60, 64, 76, 94–5, 105, 112, 132, 163n9
   support for Sacco and Vanzetti and, 75–6, 78
   syndicalism and, 15, 17–18, 25, 52, 97, 110–13, 119, 157n6
   "theatricals" and, 5–6, 70, 144n4
   violence and, 5, 14, 20–1, 37–8, 76, 81, 82, 88, 105, 107, 116
   "Wobblies on Broadway" (staging of Wobblies), 2–3, 7, 10, 12–13, 22, 29, 32, 40, 44, 47, 57, 58, 62, 64, 70, 74, 80, 90, 92, 94, 95, 106, 111, 118, 126, 127, 128, 130, 131, 135, 138, 139, 140, 141
   see also Broadway; direct action
International Longshoreman's Association, 59
Isaacs, Edith J. R., 78, 80, 82
It's a Wonderful Life (film), 71

jazz, 58, 95, 153n12
   critics on, 67, 152n10
   see also "jazz" in *Processional*; "jazz" in *Singing Jailbirds*
Jerving, Ryan, 71, 153n11
"John Brown's Body" (song), 103

Jones, James, 1, 40, 138
   see also *From Here to Eternity*
Jones, Robert Edmond, 150n4

Kaufman, Moises, 130
Kentucky Cycle, The (play)
   see Schenkkan, Robert
Kerr, Alfred, 96
Kerr, Walter, 128
Knights of Labor, 112, 121, 160n3, 162n13, 164n10
Knox, George, 93, 96
Kornbluh, Joyce, 7, 16, 19, 24, 43, 76, 82, 144n4, 149n1
Kramm, Joseph, 72
Kropotkin, Peter, 110, 123–5
Krutch, Joseph Wood, 52, 53
Ku Klux Klan, 62, 152n5
Kushner, Tony, 132, 163n6

Lane, Nathan, 126, 162n15
Lawrence textile strike, 19
Lawson, John Howard, 10, 58, 59, 61–70, 72–4, 90, 95, 103, 134, 152n7, 153n11, 156n1
   Processional, 10, 52, 58, 59, 60, 68, 128, 129, 130, 134, 151n3, 152n5, 153n12–13, 163n9
      anarchism in, 66, 71
      critical response to, 61, 67
      expressionism and, 73
      I.W.W. (Wobbly) presence in, 13, 62–5, 69–72, 74, 139
      "jazz" in, 61–2, 67, 95, 103
   Roger Bloomer, 67
   see also jazz
Lenin (Vladimir), 123
Liberator, The, 89, 143–4n3
Life and Adventures of Nicholas Nickleby, The (play), 132
Lion King, The (play), 132, 163n5
Little, Frank, 38
Little Red Songbook, 5, 101, 143n2, 150n8, 159n12, 163n10

Little Theatre, The, 77, 84, 85
Loesser, Frank, 45, 46, 56, 129, 162n1
London, Jack, 29
Lonner, Ernst, 104
Los Angeles Times (newspaper), 30
Lowry, Helen Bullitt, 27, 28

MacDonald, Donald, 69
Madeiros, Celestino, 86
Madison Square Garden, 7, 8
Malatesta, Errico, 123, 125
Mamet, David, 130
Man Who Never Died, The (play), 130, 163n3
Man Who Shot Liberty Valence, The (film), 11
Mansfield News (newspaper), 36
Mantle, Burns, 51, 52, 67, 68
Marine Transit Workers Strike (or "Maritime Workers Union strike"), 49, 94, 98
Marine Transport Workers, 59
Marx, Karl, 115, 121, 124
Marxist (Marxism), 16, 120
Matewan, 64
Matthews, George, 72
McGee, Harold, 33, 34
Meisner, Sanford, 62, 152n5, 154n2
Miller, Arthur, 130
Milligan, Tuck, 133, 165n18
Modestino, Valentino, 8
Moeller, Philip, 62, 68, 72, 152n6
Molly Maguires, 121
Mooney, Tom, 88, 155n11
Most Happy Fella, The (play), 45, 56, 128, 162n1
Mother Jones, 5, 123, 134, 136, 137, 140, 164n11, 165n17
"Mr. Block," 5

New Playwrights Theatre, 9, 74, 93, 94, 96, 103, 104, 105, 106, 156n1
New Republic, The, 44, 50

New York Herald Tribune, 89, 96, 154n4
New York Telegram-Mail, 61
New York Times, 6, 8, 9, 22, 23, 25, 27, 28, 32, 34, 36, 37, 38, 44, 51, 56, 61, 65, 66, 67, 84, 100, 104, 105, 110, 112, 113, 115, 128, 132, 133, 136, 145n12, 154n2, 155n8, 159n15, 162n1
New York World, 33
New York World-Telegram, 84
Newark Daily Advocate, 37
nihilism (nihilists), 6, 124, 140
  see also Bakunin, Michael (Mikhail)

Odets, Clifford, 80, 86, 158n
off-Broadway, 77, 133
O'Neill, Eugene, 9, 10, 12, 20, 24, 26, 29–36, 38–40, 50, 52, 54, 80, 90, 107, 109–26, 127, 128, 129, 132, 134, 140, 141, 148n6, 152n6, 160n4, 161n8, 161n10, 163n8
  Ah, Wilderness!, 152n6, 160n5
  Anna Christie, 30
  Beyond the Horizon, 30, 40
  Desire Under the Elms, 54
  Hairy Ape, The, 10, 24, 26, 29
    critical response to, 33
    humanism and, 35–6, 50
    I.W.W. (Wobblies) and, 29–40, 52, 109, 148n6
    modernity and, 40
  Iceman Cometh, The, 10, 80, 109, 120, 127, 132
    anarchists and anarchism in, 12, 110, 111, 112, 115, 116, 121, 123–4, 125
    attitude toward I.W.W. in, 118
    decline of I.W.W. and, 113–14, 118
    I.W.W. postmortem, 80, 107, 109, 115, 126
    "the Movement" and, 111, 117, 119, 122
    nihilism in, 124
  More Stately Mansions, 163n8
  Mourning Becomes Electra, 152n6
  Touch of the Poet, A, 163n8
  Outside Looking In (play), 79

Paint Creek-Cabin Creek Strike, 64, 134
Palmer, A. Mitchell, 26, 36
Palmer Raids, 26
Papa, Lee, 105, 130, 153n13, 159n15
Paterson silk strike pageant, 7–9, 90, 118
  silk strike, 7, 19, 112, 118, 145n11
Patterson, James, 33
"pie in the sky," 6, 117, 135, 144n8
Pins and Needles (play), 129
Piscator (Erwin), 104
Plymouth Theater, 24
"Preacher and the Slave, The" (song), 6
Preston, William, 116
Processional (play)
  see Lawson, John Howard
Professional-Managerial class, 21, 34
Provincetown Players, 9, 39, 92, 115, 117, 145n14
Provincetown Playhouse, 1, 24, 30, 93, 96, 99, 106

"Rebel Girl, The" (song), 113
Red Scare, 19, 26
Redwood Summer, 131
Reed, John, 7, 113, 143n3, 144n4, 145n10
Relevant Stage Company, 158n12
"Remember" (song), 46, 56, 110
"Revolting Playwrights," 93, 105, 106, 156n1
Rice, Elmer, 69, 80
Rich, Frank, 136, 164n13, 165n18
Ridley, F. F., 111
Robards, Jason, 126
Roger Bloomer (play), 67

Romney, Mitt, 166n21
Royal Shakespeare Company, 132
Ruhl, Arthur, 89, 96, 154n7

Sablich, Milka, 76
sabotage, 18, 20, 22, 37, 58, 68, 97, 126, 141, 159n13
Sacco and Vanzetti, 59, 153n1, 155n8, 156n12
  see also Anderson, Maxwell (*Gods of the Lightning*)
Salsedo, Andrea, 82
Salt Lake Telegram (newspaper), 37
Savran, David, 50, 148n7, 153n12
Sayler, Oliver, 31, 160n4
Schenkkan, Robert, 131–7, 141, 164n14, 165n15–16, 165n19
  The Kentucky Cycle, 10, 131–3, 164n12, 165n16
    critical response to, 136
    I.W.W. (Wobbly) elements of, 133, 136–7, 139
    see also "Fire in the Hole"
Schriftgiesser, Karl, 112
"scissor bill," 5
Sheldon, Edward, 150n4
Shrike, The (play), 72
Sinclair, Mary Craig, 95, 159n16
Sinclair, Upton, 6, 10, 12, 25, 49, 74, 77, 92–107, 114, 117, 129, 140, 145n8, 150n7–8, 153n1, 156–7n3
  Boston (novel), 77
  critical response to, 90, 96, 104–5
  I.W.W. (Wobbly) activism in, 24–5, 49, 95, 97–103, 107
  "jazz" in, 95, 102–3
  New Playwrights Theatre and, 74, 93, 96, 105, 106
  Singing Jailbirds, 9, 10, 12, 92, 94, 114, 128, 129, 130, 134, 139, 145n8, 150n7–8, 157n7, 158n12
    see also jazz

Singing Jailbirds
  see Sinclair, Upton
Sinnott, James, 84
Smith, Anna Devere, 130
Smith, Frederick James, 30
socialism (socialists), 6, 15, 16, 18, 29, 36, 98, 113, 120, 121, 123, 140, 157n8
Socialist Party, 18, 157n8
Solidarity (newspaper), 31
"Solidarity Forever" (song), 102, 104
Spacey, Kevin, 126
St. John, Vincent, 17, 18
Stahl, Herbert, 93, 96
Stalin, Joseph, 123
Stavis, Barrie, 130, 163n3
Steele, Wilbur Daniel, 9–10
Strasberg, Lee, 62, 152n5, 154n2
Strike! (play), 2
Susman, Warren, 29
Swan, Gilbert, 83, 84
syndicalism (syndicalists), 3, 15, 17–18, 25, 52, 73, 97, 98, 110–13, 117, 119, 123, 157n6
  see also French Syndicalism
Syndicalism: The Modern Menace to Capitalism, 119

Taft, William Howard, 16
Tannenbaum, Frank, 9–10
Tectonic Theatre, 130
Thayer, Judge Webster, 87
Theatre Guild, 44, 60, 62, 65, 67, 152n6
They Knew What They Wanted (play)
  see Howard, Sidney
Thompson, Charles Willis, 15
Thompson, Fred, 14, 15, 37, 55, 59, 113, 114, 149n2, 151n12, 156n3, 158n11, 163n4
Times Square, 90, 91, 132
Tresca, Carlo, 7, 112, 113
Tripp, Anne Huber, 9, 145n11
Twenty-five Best Plays of the Modern American Theatre, 45, 77

U.S. Steel Company, 20

Vorse, Mary Heaton, 2

Waiting for Lefty (play), 80, 86, 91, 129, 158n9
Walker, James (mayor), 84
West, Harold, 33
Western Federation of Miners, 15, 121, 146n17
Williams, Raymond, 35
Wilson, August, 130
Winchell, Walter, 83–4
Witchel, Alex, 133

Wobblies: The U.S. vs. Wm. D. Haywood, et al.: [A Play], 130
Wolheim, Louis, 39, 52
Woollcott, Alexander, 32, 33, 93
workers' theatre, 90, 91, 93, 94, 105, 106, 107, 128, 129, 130, 136, 138, 153n13, 156n1
Workingmen's party, 121
World War II, 10, 11, 91, 109, 155n8

Young, Stark, 51, 66, 67, 152n5

Zinn, Howard, 4, 16, 20, 26, 76, 122, 144n5, 147n2

GPSR Compliance

The European Union's (EU) General Product Safety Regulation (GPSR) is a set of rules that requires consumer products to be safe and our obligations to ensure this.

If you have any concerns about our products, you can contact us on

ProductSafety@springernature.com

In case Publisher is established outside the EU, the EU authorized representative is:

Springer Nature Customer Service Center GmbH
Europaplatz 3
69115 Heidelberg, Germany

www.ingramcontent.com/pod-product-compliance
Lightning Source LLC
LaVergne TN
LVHW011823060526
838200LV00053B/3887